PERFECT TIME-BASED PRODUCTIVITY

A UNIQUE WAY TO PROTECT YOUR PEACE OF MIND
AS TIME DEMANDS INCREASE

FRANCIS WADE

2Time
Labs

Perfect Time-Based Productivity

A unique way to protect your peace of mind as time demands increase.

Francis Wade

For consent, contact the author at http://ReplytoFrancis.info

First edition: November 2014

Published in the United States by 2Time Labs Press

ISBN-13: 978-1505408096

ISBN-10: 1505408091

This book is available for bulk purchases, at a special discount.

All characters appearing in this work are fictitious. Any resemblance to real persons, living or dead, is purely coincidental. The sole exceptions are authors and researchers whose ownership of their work is clearly cited.

To improve is to change; to be perfect is to change often.

Winston Churchill

Dedication

The professional athlete doesn't get distracted by top ten tips on blogs or bits of advice floating around in tweets or pics. Instead, he relies on a nuanced analysis of his strengths and weaknesses in order to improve his performance. He knows that with new understanding, improvements become easier.

As a productive professional, you are no different.

This book is for you.

Table of Contents

Frequently Asked Questions: Start Here

This book is about bringing peace of mind to your life. But first, you need to be at peace with this book. Let's take a look at some of the questions you might be asking.

Why do I need this?

Not everyone needs the principles in this book. However, if you wish you had more time to complete your commitments, you'll benefit from the steps I lay out in the chapters that follow.

You're about to find the gaps in your current habits. You'll be able to compare what you're doing now with the best-in-class practices uncovered in the latest research. Plus, in the workplace of the future, it's safe to expect increased demands on your time and even higher expectations. I will show you how to expand your capacity to meet these challenges and prepare yourself for a continued information explosion being driven by ever-changing technology.

Where do these ideas come from? Can I trust you?

While I have been working on these ideas for the better part of a decade, you'll be able to separate my opinions from the findings of experts who have gathered empirical evidence from studies involving thousands of participants. While you read, spend time in the Lab Notes at the end to see how I arrived at key conclusions. You may even want to read articles, posts and studies from the references as you make up your own mind based on the evidence.

Can I benefit if I'm a novice (or an expert)?

The reason everyone can follow the steps I'm about to share is that I will start with an assumption: you already know a lot about "time management," and your knowledge is embedded in the methods you employ today. Perfect Time-

Based Productivity will uncover this knowledge, giving you a unique, in-depth understanding of the "system" you use right now. You'll measure your skills against world-class standards and develop a new improved approach that works to meet your needs, regardless of your current performance. Plus, near the end of the book, you will have the unique opportunity to compare your skills with participants from my live programs, providing you with a fact-based reality check

Do I have to be a professional?

Not necessarily. This book is written for the knowledge worker who wants to use a "professional approach," which I define as the use of research and science as a starting point, rather than individual stories, examples or anecdotes. Many of these findings are recent, so you'll be exposed to the latest thinking from hundreds of studies. So, before you make any changes, I will show you the foundational reasoning behind them, giving you some confidence based on your knowledge of the facts.

Is this time management?

You may already know or suspect that time itself cannot be managed. The solution isn't "self-management," either, because managing yourself is an activity that's inherent in all forms of management. Instead, it's about managing tasks, commitments and priorities through the lens of a new construct we'll study: a "time demand." Using this idea will remove the frustration of trying to do the impossible – manage time – and the feeling of failure many have experienced.

How is this book different from other books?

This is one of the few books in the genre to rely heavily on recent academic research in multiple fields. Prepare to be informed by the collective wisdom of brain scientists, psychologists, industrial engineers, management theorists and adult learning experts. I also include a wide variety of stories that illustrate their findings. This diverse body of work has never been brought together into a single tapestry of knowledge, making the message of this book unique.

Prepare, therefore, to challenge the conventional wisdom. The end result will not be a new list of rules to follow, but a fresh appreciation of your available options and their consequences.

How can this book promise perfection?

It offers a breakthrough definition: being "perfect" does not mean following a particular set of habits, practices, rituals and routines flawlessly. Instead, it means playing the game of continuous improvement. You will learn to relentlessly change and tweak your habits to fit the increasing volume of demands you need to process and complete each day. This kind of perfection is tough, because most knowledge workers face changing circumstances: doing the work of more than one person, handling modern technology and dealing with more information than ever before. Perfection, in keeping with the Winston Churchill quote in the opening pages, is a dynamic balancing act requiring permanent vigilance. I'll show you that some professionals are already there.

Is this complicated, and does it take a long time?

It's not complicated, but it does take some time. By the end of this book, you'll have learned a lot, and you will also have created a simple plan of improvement. This will help you take small steps to whatever destination you desire, helped along by your very own support system. While your improvement starts immediately, don't expect overnight success. The methods you currently use to manage your commitments were developed over several years in fits and starts. Unraveling and replacing what you already do is not a matter of magic – it's about applied knowledge (which saves time) and perseverance (which keeps you going). If you put in the effort as you read these pages, your reward will follow.

What can I use this for?

You can start by tackling immediate time-management problems or removing unwanted symptoms of time stress: both require skillful, self-diagnostic methods. On the other hand, you may want to accomplish a new target, goal or vision as you stretch your current capacity beyond today's limits. However, if you are someone who is just curious about the very latest thinking, you'll learn a lot about that, and also about yourself.

In all cases, you will discover there are physical, psychological and philosophical limits to accomplishing your daily goals while, at the same time, maintaining peace of mind. Unfortunately, the field of time management has experienced a growing trend of "I-do-it-this-way-and-so-should-you" thinking that oversimplifies the challenge of being productive. This book reverses that trend.

Where can I get the forms?

Download them here: http://goo.gl/Ohe9ju

Introduction

This is a book about you, but only if you happen to be someone who wants to get better at what you do.

You want to make the most of each hour of every day: get better at what we call "time management."

You're not alone – I'm a member of this group, and so are many others. Do you have big dreams of all the things you could do if only you had more time and capacity to fulfill your commitments? Your aspirations call you to further accomplishments, but you find yourself constrained. Perhaps you're frustrated by what you want to do but somehow can't achieve. It appears as if time won't allow you to reach your productive potential.

I imagine that if you've picked up this book, you have stopped wishing for more than 24 hours in a day. You have found yourself ready to make the most of the time you do have. Simple enough to say. Quite another thing to do.

It's just not that easy. Most people who pick up a book like this have gotten to the limit of how much they can use their own ideas to improve on their own. Perhaps you have too, and you're actively looking for other solutions.

The only problem is that the solutions available… well, to be frank, they suck. Conventional wisdom steers us all towards three stock answers: buy a new gadget, search out tips and tricks, or just copy someone else's blend of habits, practices, rituals and routines. Sadly, these don't work as well now as they did in the past.

Modern devices are small miracles, but even the guy who lines up outside the Apple Store for three days to get the new iPhone struggles. The connection between individual productivity and the size, speed or cost of the fanciest smartphone, tablet, watch or laptop is dubious at best.

Even though a lot of the tips and tricks on the Internet and in books are interesting, they easily become a distraction from our goal – making the best of each day while being at our productive best. We know that Michael Jordan didn't become a basketball great by Googling listicles on random websites. Perhaps you also suspect that people don't become efficient, accomplished professionals that way either. (A "listicle" is an article built around a list (of what are often lightweight tips), e.g. "The Top Ten Ways to Become a Great Basketball Player").

But what about copying or mimicking the behaviors of someone we respect? Is there a blogger, guru or trainer somewhere who has figured out the ultimate pattern of habits, rituals and solutions?

Maybe you don't quite buy into any of these solutions, even though you aren't sure exactly why they don't work. All you may know for sure is that more stuff comes at you each day with a rising expectation to stay on top of it all, chewing up more of your available time and demanding ever greater portions of your attention. New technology has become, in part, a delivery mechanism for *more*.

Some call it "progress."

However, as working professionals, our productivity hasn't budged (even though we can now answer our email from any point on the planet, at any hour of the day). The truth is, we're stuck at pre-fancy-new-technology levels.

To make things worse, we don't know why. Neither did I back in 2006.

Constant Spring, Kingston, Jamaica. 2006.

Another waste of my time. I shook my head and lifted my fingers from the keyboard.

Once again, I found myself blogging about the hours I had just blown at an inefficient local company or government agency. My mind searched for an answer: *What could I have done differently?*

It was a detour, I knew. A few minutes before, I had opened up my blog with a clear intent: to add another entry about bureaucracy in Jamaica.

But now, I had stopped typing as my head whirled with more questions. Should I have arrived earlier? Was leaving and coming back a better strategy? How could I have been more prepared? Did they make me late, or did I make myself late? Me? Or them? Or just "life in the tropics"?

I hated wasting my time, silently complaining: *There are too many damned days like this.* I moved my mouse to save the post and reviewed the last 20 posts. This blog, which was supposed to be all about my transition, now had eight entries on productivity and time management. *This stuff is way off topic.*

But I wasn't sure if I should be surprised. Born in the US to Jamaican parents, my life had involved moving back and forth between both countries: 18 years in Jamaica were followed by 21 years in the US.

Now, I had recently moved to Jamaica, where a chaotic business environment brought one surprise after the next. According to the World Economic Forum's Global Competitive Index I was moving from a country ranked third to one ranked 86th out of 144 countries in terms of its productivity. *I should expect some things to be different with an 83 point difference in ranking,* I reasoned.

But obviously, I had a problem. Even though I had taught productivity and time management programs in the USA and other countries previously, I had stopped several years ago when I got bored. The topic had gotten stale. Or, more accurately, I had gotten stale and moved on to other interests, believing that I couldn't become more productive. If I was already using the best techniques, I decided, what more could there be to learn?

What shocked me was the impact this new, hectic, unreliable environment had on me personally. I found myself running late. Forgetting to do stuff. Dealing with organizations that weren't reliable. Trusting people who were, apparently, incompetent. Watching the wonderful laidback environment that tourists love so much turn into an awful laidback environment where I couldn't get anything done.

At first I laughed at and refused to engage in the local practice of calling ahead to "confirm" a meeting. After a few mishaps, I realized its practical value as a method to remind the other person they had a meeting in the first place. This tactic was about making sure you weren't going to be the only one at the meeting. I had never had to do that in any part of the USA.

Humbled (and a bit humiliated), I didn't know what to do to cope with my failures. After all, I used to be the expert in the front of the classroom, not the novice without a clue. *Someone, somewhere must have solved this problem already,* I reasoned, so I opened a new browser window after carefully saving a half-written post.

Googling away, I searched for terms like "developing country time management," "extreme time management" and even "war zone time management." Hadn't someone figured out how to be productive in an unpredictable environment?

Maybe now, in 2014, such a book exists. But back then – nothing. Nada. Zilch. Just the same tired prescriptions I had given to others as a productivity workshop instructor:

"Follow these exact productivity practices. They work for me, and they'll work for you."

"You need the discipline to use these habits – find it, somehow."

"There can be no deviation from this method – if you do, you have no right to expect success."

Now, I felt a pang of guilt. My own mother had taken my productivity program years before and afterwards admitted: "I don't need this stuff. It's too much for me, son, I'm retired."

Later on, I'd tell people, "When your own mother tells you that your baby is ugly, it's probably time to listen!" In that moment, however, I had changed the subject, because everything I knew to say to rebut her objection sounded stupid. "Maybe that's why I am no longer leading these programs," I muttered.

Closing the window, I went back to writing my post on time wasting bureaucrats, but now, my anger had dissipated. They wouldn't be fired, so why write about them?

I leaned back in my chair, staring at the ceiling.

Two things were once again swirling in my mind. And then, a third.

First, I saw a rubric. I had used one during a short stint in a white-collar sweatshop. The State of California had contracted with a company in Florida to score its ninth-grade standardized tests. Located a few miles from where I lived in Miramar, I figured I had nothing to lose, so I applied and got accepted, probably because I held the required Master's Degree.

It turned out to be little more than a drudge, sitting in an air-conditioned office with a few hundred other graders, working on a computer, marking the English papers of fourteen-year-olds. Four hours in the morning, lunch, then four more hours in the afternoon.

"It's what management consultants do when business is slow," I joked to myself.

But during my single hour of training, I heard a word used over and over again that I had never heard before: "rubric." Or, maybe I had come across it and forgotten. When I got home, I had to look it up.

Today, Wikipedia tells me that a scoring rubric is a "standard of performance." My team of graders used a predetermined scale developed by experts to determine the level of skill a student demonstrated on a standard, handwritten test. Our managers hammered home the mantra: "Just follow the rubric!" They were serious, I discovered. Apparently, the software we used tracked our use of the rubric, and those who didn't follow it were soon asked to leave.

Second, I remembered a workshop a friend of mine had invited me to deliver earlier that year. He used something like a rubric, called a "competency matrix." The ones he put together for his training looked like ladders ranging from low to high levels of performance.

Thirdly, I realized that the vast majority of Jamaicans had never attended a time management class of any kind. Not that this is a special case – it's true for most of working adults around the world. But in Jamaica, it led to a deep gap between their skills and those of North Americans.

As these three thoughts bounced around, I said to myself, "I need a ladder – one that touches the ground. The real ground."

It would be a blend of rubric and competency matrix, for time management skills. At the bottom would be weak skills, and at the top, world-class skills.

Now, I leaned forward, staring at my imaginary ladder. I could see someone moving from one level of skill to the next, seeing the next step clearly and directly.

I knew from triathlon swim training that it was essential to focus on one skill at a time. Terry Laughlin, the Total Immersion swim instructor, made that clear in his books and videos, which I loved.

But then, a doubt entered: "How does that help me?" I paused and imagined that I could find space on this ladder that I needed to climb — a way to get better.

With that vague answer in mind, I clicked to close my bureaucrat rant and opened a new post. Out came my first ladder, on the topic of "Capturing," right in the middle of my blog on moving back to Jamaica, where it didn't belong. ("Capturing," as I described it then, is our way of "writing down new tasks.")

I started by writing out the worst behaviors and the best, at the bottom and top. Then, I filled in the gaps, coming up with four steps in all. As I described each level, I had to be honest: "I'm not as good as I think I am." But that didn't stop me. I was determined to reach someplace new.

The diagram below is a re-creation of the original, which is long lost.

Figure I-1

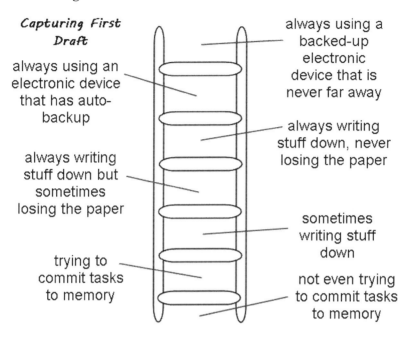

Capturing First Draft

always using a backed-up electronic device that is never far away

always using an electronic device that has auto-backup

always writing stuff down, never losing the paper

always writing stuff down but sometimes losing the paper

sometimes writing stuff down

trying to commit tasks to memory

not even trying to commit tasks to memory

When I completed the diagram, I sat back. This looked different to me. I had never seen a ladder of productivity skills like this one. I could also see my skills placed me somewhere in the middle – nowhere near the top.

It wasn't hard to understand why: some of my productivity problems in Jamaica existed because I had never bothered to perfect the skill of Capturing at the highest level. When I didn't Capture reliably, in the next moment, I left myself open to nasty surprises.

Fortunately, there were people I had worked with who had reached the top rung, but I had never seen the need to follow their example. Now, I could see why I needed to.

I flipped open a couple of productivity books and websites, thinking that I'd only succeeded in reinventing the wheel, but I only confirmed my first impression: I hadn't seen anything like this before. In fact, the pages I opened all focused on defining a single set of behaviors.

For example, one author had perfected the art of "Capturing" with a digital voice-recorder rather than paper and pen, which he would play back each evening before going to bed. Like others, he seemed satisfied to tell readers that only a single rung of practices existed: the one he happened to be describing. He barely mentioned the possibility of other rungs, or even future, improved practices that might be invented to extend the ladder of "Capturing."

"Finally, something new that I can use to get better," I said to myself. "Just because I can't easily find other ladders doesn't mean I shouldn't use it."

It was a start.

Eventually, over the next few months, posts on productivity started taking over my blog, and I had to start a new one. "After all," I reasoned, "I'm just fooling around. Once I run out of ideas, I'll stop. Or maybe others might come along and use them. Just a few months at most, and then that will be it." I was wrong. In 2014, I haven't stopped.

***

Maybe you're like me. You realize you're stuck but don't know why. I didn't know how to get unstuck, even though the symptoms seemed clear enough. In this way, I was like millions of professionals who want to improve their time-based productivity but don't know how.

You may also be facing a similar, perplexing life change that has brought all sorts of new commitments. You probably aren't Jamaica after living in the USA for over two decades. But you may be experiencing some of the symptoms of life changes – information overload, email overwhelm, time stress, a feeling of being out of balance, or a sense of always being in a rush. Perhaps it extends to missed deadlines and commitments that are falling through the cracks.

Why aren't there simple solutions to these problems?

In the chapters to come, I'll show you that simple solutions don't come easily to complex problems.

A Band-Aid is no substitute for open-heart surgery – and it's not the Band-Aid's fault, either. The heart is too complex system for such a simple solution. It takes years of training to understand its structure.

At the same time, the uninformed may see a YouTube video of a surgeon in action and accurately observe that the number of cuts being made with the scalpel to do a basic valve replacement surgery is fewer than 10. Given the fact that it takes more than 10 cuts to eat a 16 oz. Porterhouse steak, they'd mistakenly conclude that open-heart surgery, which requires fewer cuts, is easier.

Leonardo da Vinci once said, "Simplicity is the ultimate sophistication."

Bypass surgery is complex, requiring years of training to determine the handful of simple cuts needed to complete the procedure effectively. It's the reason why neither Band-Aids nor your steak eating skills could ever get the job done.

In the chapters to come, I'll introduce you to another complex system: the everyday combination of habits, practices and rituals you use to manage your time. But it's not just about some cool insights. One thing I learned from reading swim coach Terry Laughlin's book is that while you're sitting down to read its pages, you aren't getting better. You start getting better only after you close the book, make your way to the pool with a superb improvement plan and jump in the water to implement it.

By the end of this book, you'll also have in your possession a superb, Leonardoesque plan for improvement: simple, but sophisticated. As Justice Oliver Wendell Holmes, Jr. said, "I wouldn't give a fig for simplicity on this side of complexity, but I'd give my right arm for simplicity on the other side of complexity."

In Part One, you'll get the background knowledge you need to make this journey safely. The research I'll share might confirm some of your suspicions – you'll learn that time management doesn't exist, because *time cannot be managed*. Instead, you'll learn that all these years you have been managing something called a "time demand" an internal, individual commitment to complete an action in the future.

You'll also discover an astounding fact: you started creating time demands as a pre-teen, just after you discovered the concept of time (at around ages seven, eight and nine). By doing so, you sparked an awesome period of development that changed the course of your life. During the following years, you also began to craft personal methods for managing time demands, laying the foundation for every success you have experienced as an adult. I'll share research that reveals the fact that we can't escape the human need to create time demands and keep them alive: we need them to achieve our goals, aspirations and dreams.

Furthermore, your discovery of time demands will help you understand why gurus, academics and trainers have been so confused, even as you find a way to rise above the contrary advice that's been given by them over the years.

To back up this learning and sort out the knowledge from different disciplines, I'll link you to my Lab Notes, which are included at the end of this book. There, you can delve into the logic I used to arrive at these and other conclusions and sink your teeth into the academic research that backs them up. Where I used intuition in the absence of hard evidence, I'll let you know, so that you see where all of these ideas are coming from before you apply them. A few people may want to visit the source materials listed in the References, which include the sources most relevant to this book. My website's Library also includes references to the cover pages of over one hundred additional papers. See http://bit.ly/WLy6EY.

In Part Two, I'll take you through an actual improvement cycle in which you can start making real-time changes. We'll tap into your power to innovate in the area of time-based productivity, which you might have set aside in the last few years. Slowing down the rapid but forgotten process you used as an adolescent, you'll do an in-depth assessment of your current methods. In order to do this assessment, I'll explain what world-class behaviors look like through seven core skills: Capturing, Emptying, Tossing, Acting Now, Storing, Scheduling and Listing.

This is not just an intellectual exercise – you will define new targets and plans right away. At the end of the seventh assessment, I'll show you how to bring these plans together into a single Master Plan that's feasible and inviting, even though it may span several months or years.

While your plan at the end will be simple, it will be based on a sophisticated understanding of how human beings manage time demands, and more importantly, the results of your assessment. Your new self-knowledge will be the primary driver: prepare yourself to discover the complexity of what you do each day and, perhaps, the degree to which you skills were developed unevenly in the past. This, you'll find, is typical: for most of us, it's the product of a teenage mind working on its own without help of guidance. Rube Golberg meets MacGyver.

An accurate self-evaluation will let you take some important shortcuts on your path of improvement. You'll find yourself conserving time and energy as you focus on the handful of improvement activities that make the biggest difference, rather than trying to do too much at once. Your skill at defining a feasible Master Plan is key.

For some, the day you complete the plan will be a good time to lay down this book and take a pause, as Part Three looks at advanced topics that help you implement it. In these chapters, you'll take a deep dive into "the flow state" and the reasons why it's important to be aware of this high state of productivity. Then, I offer four advanced skills: Interrupting, Switching, Reviewing and Warning – that you may also include in your Master Plan. They also represent skills that were developed in your teenage years.

The last three chapters are meant to prepare you for real-world challenges. As professionals, we are bombarded with new productivity ideas, can't find the software and hardware tools we really need and face obstacles to being effective in the workplace. You'll learn how to navigate these issues.

As I mentioned in the FAQ, along our entire journey, we'll have a lot of help from researchers in multiple fields. As professionals, it's important we work with facts rather than anecdotes, balancing science with intriguing stories. Bringing findings from different fields together in one place is the only way to gain the insight we need to create a powerful Master Plan that doesn't ignore a single possible improvement.

To help pull this plan together, you will be completing several forms: the most recent versions are available by download from the following page on my book's website - http://goo.gl/Ohe9ju. You will use them to complete your self-evaluation, drawing a profile of the methods you use today.

As important as your Master Plan and current profile

are, you should finish this book with much more than a plan on paper. My ultimate goal is to give you a clean start in developing your time-based productivity skills. With it, you can fix problems, alleviate unwanted symptoms, and achieve unforeseen peace of mind. You can also use it to prepare yourself for a future that's likely to bring more time demands than ever before through new 24-hour-a-day technology that can never, *ever* be turned off.

What I want for you is a new beginning: some solutions to hard problems that give you a way to reboot your improvement efforts with a fresh set of insights and newfound energy. More than a mere method: a new mindset.

It's just what I wanted after running into problems in 2006: a way to begin again.

Francis Wade
2Time Labs
Kingston, Jamaica
2014

Part One

Understanding the Concepts

Knowledge-worker productivity is the biggest of the 21st century management challenges.

Peter Drucker

Chapter 1. The Big Picture

(In which you learn about the powerful forces in the world that push us to improve our time-based productivity... and why we can't escape them!)

Chicago, Illinois, USA.

In 2008, I started to notice a new kind of behavior.

I stood in the middle of the group, watching as six associates from McKinsey & Co. struggled with the new concept I had just shared. Our session on giving great coaching was going well, I thought, as they engaged with the idea and tried to work out a solution to the role-play we had just witnessed. But once again, I saw Brad, who was not much younger than me, glancing at his Blackberry. My brow wrinkled.

It had wrinkled earlier in a room that was overheated against the bitter cold outside. I had mentally prepared myself for the wind and snow, even before getting on a plane from my home in Jamaica, but I hadn't prepared myself for the stuffy, indoor heat of a hotel conference room – I had forgotten what that felt like even after living for almost 15 years in New York and New Jersey.

But it wasn't just the heat. I had already very gently warned him to put his smartphone away. But there he was, lost in a different world – cyberspace, apparently. The topic we were discussing was completely outside his awareness.

This time around, I simply stopped talking. After a few minutes, so did the other participants, and I silently directed their attention to Brad, whose eyes were locked in to his smartphone. After a few heavy moments, he looked up, apparently feeling the weight of the silence around him. "I'm sorry," he offered, shaking his head.

"Tough project?" I asked, with a touch of empathy that I hoped would help bring him back to the program we were in rather than the work he was missing.

"Unbelievably tough," he answered as he put his phone back in his pocket and joined the conversation.

Kingston, Jamaica, 2009

"I can't put it away," she explained. "I need to check it all through the day."

My confusion must have been apparent as she continued, now speaking to everyone in our time management class of about fifteen people. "About a month ago, I got a call from my manager. His boss in Canada called him to complain that I hadn't responded to email he'd sent about an hour before. He asked 'Doesn't she have a Blackberry?' So now, I don't go anywhere without checking my email."

"But you're in a class," I argued.

"It doesn't matter."

Stunned, I didn't know what to say. She was obviously going to be checking her Blackberry over and over again, missing key elements of the class and not learning nearly as much as she could. I moved on, trying to hide my disappointment. What I didn't know then was that this was only the beginning of the end.

For the first time, I had just lost the full attention of a workshop participant due to smartphone distraction and, although I didn't know it then, I would never have another class in which I could count on receiving 100% of each participant's attention. Sure, there had always been the odd distraction in the past, but this was different. She, like so many others from that point on, was required to be distracted while doing her job. She had no choice. It was a matter of keeping the job or losing it.

Since then, I have repeated my call for 100% attention in every workshop I have led. I routinely ask people to put away their smartphones, turning off all flashing, beeping, buzzing, blipping – anything that could interrupt their attention. More than 90% of the time, at least one person has refused or complained, spurring a classroom conversation that strikes the heart of the question: what does it take to be productive in today's workplace? It's obvious that things are changing quickly. Are we keeping up with the changes that increased workloads and technology are bringing every day?

I suggest that attending a training session while checking and responding to email is a behavior that answers the question. It's not hard to convince my trainees that a participant who checks email while class is in session is likely to miss something important. I drive the point home with some research that shows how exam performance drops when students use mobile devices while they are studying or attending class.

The real disagreement comes when I ask them to consider: "The way you and the people in your company use mobile devices is ruining your productivity." I ask them the following questions, in part because I am curious to hear what they think about a problem that isn't new to any of them.
- Does multi-tasking really work when it involves splitting your attention?
- Are you saving time by texting while driving? (At the time of writing this book, this practice is still legal in many countries and U.S. States).
- Did smartphone makers intend for us to use these devices to check email while talking with others?
- What happens to your concentration when you leave an intense task to check email for even a moment?

As we answer these questions and I share further research data, a chaotic picture emerges.

Employees are afraid. The recession has heightened this fear by limiting their employment options, making them more willing than ever before to fit in without complaining.

Jobs have become more stressful due to downsizing. As a result, many professionals are doing work that used to be done by more than one person. According to a CareerBuilder survey, 47% of workers have taken on more responsibility because of a layoff. 37% are doing the work of two people, and 30% feel as if they are burned out. This pattern makes unemployment statistics misleading. Even as the number employed has decreased, US productivity has increased as employees work harder, longer hours.

At the same time, many are scared of losing their jobs. They don't know if they can find different employment, and the chances are high that a new position will be just as challenging as the one they have. Others are anxious about missing an important message, and constant checking is how they prevent their manager's boss from coming down on them.

Also, most of us love technology. When our employers ask us to start using a new smartphone, we accept the gift of a new, powerful device willingly – the fresher and shinier, the better. What we don't see clearly are the strings attached. As one HR Manager said to me, "There's an assumption that when you get promoted, you are given a company smartphone in order to be accessible all the time."

She meant that you need to be accessible early in the morning, late at night, on weekends, during holidays, while you're on vacation, and when you take a sick day. She also added that, of course, these rules are unwritten.

In this chapter, we'll delve into all the questions raised by these stories and grapple with their combined implications.

***

It's obvious to even the most casual observer that life, especially in the workplace, is changing fast.

Research tells us that there are powerful forces operating in every single workplace around the world. These forces cannot be reversed by you or me – they are much bigger than we are, and our participation in the workplace requires us to be engaged by them despite the impact they have on our productivity.

For example, in the mid 1990s, many employees decided not to learn how to use email, especially in the higher ranks of companies. Today, in 2014, it's hard to imagine that any employee is given this option. "Using email" has become a skill as necessary as "using a telephone" used to be. Email skills, although they're no longer taught in classrooms, are an absolute requirement. The advent of this particular technology represented a force that was bigger than any individual, company or country.

It was inescapable, even though we probably didn't anticipate the scope of it when we received our first email message.

But other forces in the corporate air today are just as strong. While they may be categorized into broad headings such as mobility, information overload, messaging and cloud computing, I'll simply summarize some of the most recent data.

1. You are dealing with more email than ever before. The latest studies show that an average employee receives 130 to 175 messages each day from all sources, personal and private.

2. You are able to access email, plus a number of other messages and alerts, through a device that you increasingly carry 24 hours a day, seven days a week. The growth in mobile device use shows that in 2014, new devices are being adapted faster than ever before. The combination of message volume and mobility makes the professional world we live in unique in terms of time management.

3. In your company and industry, new expectations around your responsiveness to digital messages are fast being solidified. Employees report they feel pressured by their workplaces to be available outside of regular working hours, on vacations, holidays and on sick days. There is a quiet expectation that you will continue to increase your working hours by sacrificing personal hours. The only relief, according to a French study led by J. Bhatti, comes when you retire. Unfortunately, research from the American Journal of Epidemiology showed that "Doing more than 11 hours of work a day raised heart disease risks by 67 percent."

4. Your permanent, always-on availability to answer messages is altering your personal and work relationships.

5. The economic downturn has pressured employees to accept the new normal without much complaint. After all, others will take your job if you don't want it. Furthermore, as economies recover, hiring is expected to increase very slowly as companies look to replace pre-recession jobs with post-recession technology plus expanded human capability. Only half of the employees surveyed in 2006 by HR Solutions agreed that "Enough people are available in my work group to accomplish the necessary workload." Furthermore, a Human Capital Trends survey of HR executives by Deloitte showed that 57% say their organizations are "weak" when it comes to helping leaders and employees manage information, expectations and demanding schedules. This weakness may explain the result of a recent Towers Watson survey, which

showed that "inadequate staffing was cited by 53% of workers as the major reason for stress, while only 15% of senior managers thought this was so."

6. You process as much data in a day as your grandparents saw in a month. The recession hasn't helped – 57% of US workers strongly or somewhat agree to the statement "Since the economic downturn, the amount of information that I have to process at work has significantly increased," according to the October 2010 International Workplace Productivity Survey.

7. In a recent 2,000-person survey by Harris Interactive, 94% of employees admitted that when they get more than 50 emails per day, they are unable to keep up. In the same survey, one in five admitted that they feel as if they are already getting more each day than they can handle.

8. A recent study by a group of Swiss researchers showed that time pressure at work is causing an increase in near-accidents while commuting. Apparently, professionals have trouble turning off thoughts about work once they leave the office, which endangers their well-being, and that of others. Their study, which describes five other problems caused by time pressure, is described in further detail in my Lab Notes.[1]

9. A 2014 study by NPR/Robert Wood Johnson/Harvard School of Public Health showed that the number-one most stressful experience in the past month was "Too many responsibilities overall." It came in just ahead of "Problems with finances." Also, half of those who experienced a great deal of stress reported that the daily activity of "juggling schedules of family members" was the most stressful activity. A 2013 Pew Research Social and Demographic Trends Report found that 56% of working moms and 50% of working dads find it very or somewhat difficult to balance work and family responsibilities. The result of this stress turned up in a recent CareerBuilder Survey, which showed that two-thirds of American workers said they are not aiming for the corner office: 52% are satisfied in their current roles but 34% "don't want to sacrifice work-life balance."

These are some of the reshaped boundaries of the

modern workplace. For most of us, it hasn't been about transformation or achievement. It's been a struggle. In the face of what author Judith Kolberg calls "The Age of Endless" most of us have tried to keep our heads above water. We have tried working harder, working longer and working smarter – all of which are strategies that used to work. The fact that they no longer make a difference is disconcerting; we find ourselves in new, uncharted waters, at the intersection of new technology, more information and augmented expectations.

Having no idea what to do next scares us. It leads many of us to turn down promotions, limit the number of children we have, reduce our involvement in communities and churches, cut down the time we spend exercising, and purposely run deficits in our lives, believing that one day we'll catch up and re-balance our lives. Someday.

Unfortunately, we don't have time to catch up. Instead, we suffer from the following symptoms, all of which are related to "not having enough time" even if we don't realize it:
- Email inboxes full of unprocessed email.
- Feelings of guilt about not being able to catch up.
- An inability to stop ourselves from multi-tasking at moments when we know we shouldn't.
- Not getting enough exercise (or prayer).
- Scrambling to find information due to lack of organization.
- Being time-stressed.
- Turning down opportunities.
- Cutting back on necessary sleep.
- Waking up in the middle of the night remembering something we forgot to do.
- Running from one fire to the next.
- Watching as important commitments fall through the cracks.
- Seeing our reputation falter as we miss deadlines.
- Arriving late for appointments.
- Procrastinating.
- Taking time and attention away from loved ones.

We wistfully think to ourselves that these symptoms could be reversed if only we had more time or could somehow stop the clock. Unfortunately, that kind of wishful thinking doesn't help.

Instead, the circumstances call on us to develop the ability to "hot-swap": to change our way of doing things even as we must continue to do them. Some hot-swaps are easy, like changing a microphone while you are in the middle of a speech. Others are more challenging, like changing your sock while you're running. A few are impossible, like changing the motherboard on your computer while sending an email.

Somewhere between the extremes of "challenging" and "impossible" is the hot-swap that this book argues you must make at critical moments in your career. Today, you are using a combination of habits, practices and rituals that have gotten you to where you are now. But in the future, some of them are going to become completely obsolete, while others will need to be upgraded. While you are reading this book, for example, other people in your life (your boss, client or spouse) may be thinking up new ways to get you to do even more. They will need more from you. Faster. With better quality.

Unfortunately, we haven't been taught how to respond to such relentless demands. We have never really learned how to upgrade our habits, practices and rituals at will. We don't know how to manage (or more precisely, change-manage) our own personal development in the area of time-based productivity.

For most people, the easiest option is to simply find one of many productivity gurus. They offer books, programs and websites detailing their individual examples. After discovering, mostly through trial and error, that a particular habit pattern works for them, they codify it in a set of rigid rules. "Follow me," they say to their seekers. They promise that when you follow their precise behavioral prescriptions, you'll be able to share in their success.

For a small number of people, that works. They are able to replicate the guru's habit pattern and find success. Often, they share some of the guru's attributes (e.g. working style, affinity for technology, culture, age, or industry).

However, most of their followers, ranging from the ardent to the casual, have a hard time. Leaping from their current habits, practices and rituals to the guru's is tough. It's not because the guru is bad or even lazy: copying anyone else's precise blend of habits, practices and rituals when you have been using your own for several years is difficult for anyone. (I've observed that even a guru's small number of closest followers will admit to not quite following every piece of advice... human nature limits our ability to mimic the behavior of others. We're all different – there are no clones).

Instead, most people take bits and pieces from here and there, ignoring what doesn't make sense or is just too hard to learn. Unfortunately, most gurus frown on this deviation: It's a corruption that will lead to failure. "Do it all, or not at all" appears to be the mantra, as their programs subtly (or not so subtly) reinforce the need for followers to do everything as described, with no departure from the defined behaviors.

Those who do allow customization offer almost no actual advice on how to do so, leaving the learner to engage in their own process of trial and error. They must discover what can or cannot be tinkered with on their own.

Given the underlying need we have for custom solutions that fit us as individuals, it's no mistake that time management and productivity training via workshops, books or websites is hit-or-miss. One of the most influential studies of time management we'll examine in later chapters concluded that "Contrary to popular claims, time management training was not found to be effective." Dr. Therese Macan, the researcher who conducted the study, also concluded "the (failed) results call into question the assertations (sic) made by advocates of time management training."

If you add to our confusion the intellectual problem mentioned in the Introduction – that time cannot actually be managed – where do we look for solutions? According to Dr. Brigitte Claessens, a Dutch researcher, leading expert, and author of *Time in Organizational Research*, this is a real problem: "Of course, time cannot be managed in any sense. The only things people seem to manage [...] are their own activities [...] time management is a matter of managing one's activities, taking account of the time involved in it." In a prior study, she defined time management as "behaviors that aim at achieving an effective use of time while performing certain goal-directed activities."

Furthermore, in a 2004 review of time management literature, she and her co-authors note with as much regret as an academic can muster, "we found no empirical studies published before 1982." In the world of academia, that's a nice way of saying that before 1982, no one took the topic seriously.

Professor Laurie Hellsten continues this rueful tone in her own 2012 time management research summary entitled "What Do We Know About Time Management: A Review of the Literature and a Psychometric Critique of Instruments Assessing Time Management." In the opening paragraph, she writes:

"Lack of time is a common complaint in western society. In response, there has been a proliferation of books, articles and seminars on time management, along with their assertions, prescriptions and anecdotes (Macan, 1994, p. 383)." But what exactly *is* time management? Despite the epidemic of time management training programs... there is currently a lack of agreement about the definition of time management and a dearth of literature summarizing time management across disciplines."

To further complicate the issue, consider Einstein's assertion: "time is an illusion." Physicists disagree about whether time even exists. Obviously, that which doesn't exist (or is an illusion) cannot be managed.

Apart from the Claessens and Hellsten, few psychologists, physicists and philosophers have tackled the questions "Does time management exist?" and "Can time be managed?"

My research in all these areas has taken me to some interesting places - leading me to conclude that whether time exists or not, we can't "manage" it the way we do other things (like money, employees, and our physical environment).

But time, as a resource, passes by relentlessly in the background of our lives whether we attempt to act on it or not. "Good time management" is therefore a result, observation or assessment we make after the fact, not an activity we undertake directly.

In order to accomplish the result, we must manage other things: our actions, habits, priorities, commitments, energy, attention, choices, decisions, health, etc. These all add up to a result, which we judge for ourselves, concluding something about the quality of our time management skills in the past.

But what's happening outside of academia? While the question of time management's existence lies waiting to be answered by researchers, blogs, tweets and Pinterest pictures openly repeat the assertion that time cannot be managed. Participants in my programs now tell me so as well. In the past 12 months, there seems to be a groundswell of wisdom that is unmatched by academic activity.

Much of it has led to the notion that "self-management" is the proper replacement for time management. Self-management, according to Wikipedia, includes goal setting, decision-making, focusing, planning, and scheduling.

However, when we adopt this definition, we see that every kind of management (time, money, health, sports, etc.) includes an element of self-management. Replacing the term "time management" with "self-management" doesn't answer our questions.

Given the reasoning I shared earlier and the evidence of a new popular understanding, for the remainder of this book, we'll adopt Claessens' assertion: time cannot be managed.

However, I'll still use the term "time management" to refer to something I alluded to in the introduction: the management of "time demands." My continued use of the term "time management" is a rhetorical device — a way to keep our conversation going smoothly rather than make a pedantic point.

It's a tricky business for me to add to the "proliferation" and "epidemic" of books and programs Hellsten describes. My only hope is that Perfect Time-Based Productivity illuminates and coordinates the most helpful content to be found across disciplines so that you can, by the end, forge a simple plan based on the latest knowledge. (If you are interested in the question of whether time management exists, check out my "Big Ideas" page at http://www.2time-sys.com/big-ideas-time-management-exist/).

In the next chapter, we'll take a close look, through the lens of a number of disciplines, at what you have already been doing as a working professional to be at your productive best. You'll discover that there's a process you have been using each and every day that you may not be aware of: a point of view that will challenge much of the conventional wisdom in this area. I'll show you how to do an evaluation and compare it against best practices as well as data I have collected from past participants of my live programs. This information will help you build a realistic plan of improvement based on your actual needs, informed by scientific research.

***

At the end of this chapter, and each one that follows, I'll list a few one-liners that together reflect the contrary wisdom we just discussed. I invite you to save them for yourself and also pass them around in your social networks on Facebook, Twitter, Google+ and others. To access the complete file of all Remember and Share entries, download the file from http://wp.me/P3hu5l-ax.

.

Remember and Share

94% of employees admitted that when they get more than 50 emails per day, they are unable to keep up.
In a single day, you process the amount of data your grandparents did in a month.
Time cannot be managed, but time demands can.
Dr. Brigitte Claessens: "Time cannot be managed in any sense."
Professor Albert Einstein: "Time is an illusion." How can we hope to manage it?
Dr. Laurie Hellsten: "There is currently a lack of agreement about the definition of time management and a dearth of literature summarizing time management across disciplines."
"Good time management" is a result, observation or

assessment we make after the fact, not an activity we undertake directly.

Chapter 2. Who Do You Think You Are?

(In which you learn that you already have a functioning system in place and why it's helpful to build on this fact.)

Think about the best improvement you ever made to the way you manage your time demands. Got an example?

Many people stumble over this question, even though managing and executing activities in time is an activity we ALL do as functioning adults.

The reason we stumble is that we don't know "who we are" as professionals in the realm of time-based productivity. We don't pay much attention to how the job gets done – instead, our concern is primarily on the next result we want to achieve and the steps needed to close the gap. Rarely do we step back from the day-to-day fray to consider the means we are using, even though that should be the mark of a professional approach.

Let's meet two imaginary characters who also stumble: Julie and Michael. We will look at some of the questions they ask themselves and the improvements available to them.

Julie is stressed, in part because she is confused. As she sits at her desk, she feels the headache she's been nursing start to grow. "Is it because I have to decide right away?" she wonders.

She needs help fast. Her inbox has 2,500 messages sitting in it, waiting for her to find the time to deal with them, and she has put on 25 pounds as her gym membership languishes. Today, her boss told her: "It's time for you to find a time management course or book, and start getting better. The late delivery on your last project plus your tardiness this morning… well, these are more of the same. Other people are noticing."

But she hardly needs his help to notice. Long before he said anything, she had already decided to do something to address the problem. He's just the latest, but strongest, instigator.

Fortunately, he's a cool guy – he's promised to set aside some funds to help her fix the problem. "Where will I even find the time?" she asks herself, but sets that question aside. Right now, she needs to answer the question: "What approach should I use?"

Should she:
- Pick up a book from Amazon.com to find out what she should be doing to manage her time?
- Take a crash course in best practices?
- Surf around for bloggers and podcasters with tips, tricks and shortcuts?
- Hire a coach?

Up until now, these choices have represented the sum of options available to her.

This book introduces another option: diagnosing her current methods and comparing them against best practices so that improvement opportunities become clear.

Michael has always been driven by his curiosity. A personal improvement addict, he's read most of the books available. When he picks up a book like *Perfect Time-Based Productivity*, he tries to figure out what's behind the stuff he's reading, or hearing. "Where does this come from?" is the question that lurks in the background.

He's generally open to new content, looking for even a few nuggets of wisdom he can incorporate into his considerable base of knowledge. He's learned a lot over the years, so he's not looking for a silver bullet. Now, he's happy finding small improvements, but not just any old improvements: he wants potential solutions he can try in his life and implement permanently, even if they take a while to master. The same goes for new technology.

How should he conduct his search? Should he:
- Use Google to find the latest academic research?
- Browse life hacking websites to find cool tips and tricks?
- Read the first few pages of productivity books on Amazon to see if they have anything new to say?
- Look for first-hand accounts from other people who are trying new things via blogs, webinars, YouTube videos and podcasts?
- Read geeky websites that cover new technology so he doesn't miss the latest hardware and software offerings?

Up until now, his choices represent activities that involve a great deal of time and low probability of success.

In this book, he'll be exposed to the latest research in multiple fields that together tell a different story from the one he's used to hearing.

***

Both Julie, who needs an immediate solution, and Michael, who happens to be deeply curious, will find a unique way of thinking about time-based productivity in this book. They'll not only gain immediate knowledge about themselves, but they'll also learn how to be prepared for inevitable future changes. They are both about to learn that there never will be a final (or perfect) answer to the question of what professionals should do to boost their time-based productivity.

As you read through their stories, you may ask yourself: are you closer to Julie or Michael? Your personality will affect your approach to reading this book. Both approaches have shortcomings.

Julie's mistake is that she's often looking for quick solutions that don't require a lot of work. If there were a time management pill, she would take it. To get the most from this book, she must understand that it takes time to unravel the homegrown system she has put together over the years. She needs to keep in mind that improvement efforts are an investment that will pay off for the rest of her life.

For his part, Michael can get caught up in theory and cool ideas, sometimes leaving implementation for "later," which never comes. He likes the excitement of chasing and learning, which both give him a rush of dopamine. Unfortunately, better performance isn't fed by a sudden rush of new brain chemicals. It comes from systems made up of habits, practices and rituals.

"How boring!" he might think. But he doesn't know that implementation, in this case, isn't the final, drudge-filled step in a long learning process. Instead, it's more like Action Learning, in which the best knowledge comes from putting ideas into play for the first time.

Now, after this additional explanation of their faults, which is more like you?

As you can see, both of them have one important thing in common: they already have a way of managing their actions in time, their time demands, or their system of productivity. It was developed long before they picked up this book. So do you.

Where did it come from? How did it develop? When did its development take place? How does it compare to that of other professionals?

To find out, let's take our first deep dive and discover the answer to each of these questions, so that you can fill in any important gaps in your personal biography.

(A reminder from this book's Introduction: a time demand is an internal, individual commitment to complete an action in the future.)

***

When do children first start creating and managing their future commitments?

Initially, I thought I would find the answer to this question easily. Parents who understand the concept of time demands have no difficulty is giving an estimate: their children start developing future commitments between the ages of about 9 and 13.

However, the academic research isn't clear at all. A surprising number of researchers have assumed that time management skills are learned in adulthood, or don't even exist until someone receives formal instruction. Given the confusion around the definition of time management, perhaps that's to be expected.

After a search through the world of child psychology, I concluded that:
- A child who has not developed the concept of time cannot manage time demands.
- College freshmen enter college with a system already in place.
- Therefore, children start creating and managing time demands in fits and starts, beginning in their adolescent years.

In the Lab Notes, I outline the journey I took to arrive at these conclusions. As I played detective, I made some deductions to fill in gaps in available research.[2]

Where do kids learn these skills? To answer that question, we'll have to use a term that's become a favorite among psychologists in recent years: "prospective memory."

***

If you have ever wondered why your grandparents have a hard time remembering to do simple things in the future like visit a store or return a call, it's because they are experiencing a loss of prospective memory: the ability to remember to perform actions in the future. (Retrospective memory, by contrast, is our ability to remember facts from the past.)

Although our knowledge about prospective memory has expanded in recent years, there's a lot we don't know about its functions. Recently, a team of Swiss, German and Swedish researchers showed that prospective memory increases until adolescence, where it generally plateaus. At the same time, a number of other researchers have shown that it decreases in the elderly.

Also, the ability to use prospective memory varies widely from one person to another, a fact that was highlighted by Devolder and Lens, who studied 17 and 18 year-old boys. They showed that high GPAs in college are caused by more time spent studying, in part because the students viewed the future differently.

Time demands are a part of prospective memory, so we'll see what psychologists have to say about the way they are created and managed. Most of our prospective memory skills are self-taught. So are the methods we use to manage time demands.

As I hinted above, I've extended the finding that we all have a system a step further: my hunch is that these skills are self-taught by children in their adolescent years. While there's no academic research I can find to prove this notion conclusively, the general absence of organized training in time-based productivity indicates that it must come from another source. Perhaps people learn these skills from:
- An individual who deliberately taught them key skills from a book.
- Someone who role-modeled well-formed habits.
- A personality trait they were born with.
- Luck.
- The combined effect of people around them (i.e. "culture").

Unfortunately, answering this question once and for all

is far beyond the scope of this book! All we care about at the moment is that for the most part, children are left to their own devices as they learn to navigate a world filled with an abundance of time demands… or, to put it more accurately, a world *they* fill with time demands. Some succeed in this effort and some don't, but our lack of research in this area (plus the lack of clear definitions) means that we just don't know as much as we should.

If you're left wondering how the sharpest minds in the world might tackle this issue, here are a few hints.

Christine Bartholomew, a law professor at SUNY Buffalo, stated: "To better arm graduating students, law students must treat time as an essential component of practice-readiness. Unfortunately, most law schools ignore their students' time management concerns, despite growing calls for greater "skills" training in legal education."

In a recent Working Knowledge Magazine from Harvard Business School, Professor James Heskett writes, "How do we account for the renewed interest in these (time management) ideas? Is it an indication that our new managers are ill prepared to 'work smart'? (At the Harvard Business School, the philosophy has long been to eschew formal training in time management, instead overloading students purposely to force them to learn for themselves how to prioritize and become better time managers.)"

Astounding.

Does this attitude pervade U.S. education in general? Clearly, we need more answers, especially as pertains to average students who attend average schools with teachers unschooled in these concepts.

Parents often ask me, "What are you doing to help kids like mine?" So far, the only answer I have is, "I encourage professionals like you to be mindful and try to be great role models. Your kids need to see you making continuous upgrades, based on changes you are going through." Their faces often register sharp disapproval but it's better to show kids how to adapt to a changing world, rather than just tell them.

Or perhaps the disapproval stems from the fact that I probably won't extend my research in this direction. Instead,

I actively encourage other colleagues in this field to take the lead, perhaps using this book as a guide.

(And yes… for those who are curious… the fact that I don't have kids has something to do with my response!)

***

The bottom line remains the same: our skills at managing time demands are developed when we are children, without much guidance, and usually before we exit the teenage years. By the time we pick up a productivity book like this one, we have spent years practicing the habits we taught ourselves, hardening them into routines that don't require much conscious thought.

This important fact is overlooked by learners as well as those who I call time advisers: student support program leaders in colleges, academic researchers, gurus, writers, corporate trainers and business coaches. Is it a safe one to ignore? We'll begin to examine this question in the next chapter.

For now, let's assume the obvious: a habit that you have practiced every day since you were a teenager is hard to break.

Also, the fact that you taught yourself these skills means that you probably did a good job in some areas and a not-so-good job in others. The good news is that in *Perfect Time-Based Productivity*, we'll not only look at what you happen to have in place today, but we'll also compare it to best practices and the data I've collected.

The only reason we can make these comparisons is that our research at 2Time Labs has revealed that a common, structured method underlies the way in which human beings process time demands.

Also, we'll discuss the idea that while we self-create our own systems, they all share a few common design principles. Within this commonality, we can find, reuse and invent best practices.

Given this fact, where should we start looking for solutions?

(For the rest of the book, we'll use the phrase "time management system" to refer to the combination of habits, practices, rituals and routines we have self-assembled to help us manage time demands. Consider it shorthand for "time demand management system.")

***

As I mentioned in the Introduction, it rankled me that no one had written a book for professionals who need custom solutions, like those who moved to a developing country filled with unreliable processes. At the moment, the same is true for the advanced learner of time management skills who also needs a custom solution - they have already gone through all the "Productivity 101" books and websites written for the general public... including those geared for "Dummies" and "Idiots."

My annoyance only grew when I realized there was a repeated, subtle message: "You don't know much, and your current skills just aren't relevant. You don't need a custom system."

Back in 2006, I already knew that I had a system in place. What I needed was help to make it better, not a complete replacement.

Like you, I had spent many years assembling a system that, for the most part, worked for me. It had safely brought me to that particular point in my life and was part of the foundation of every single one of my professional accomplishments. To ignore that fact seemed foolhardy, even though I could tell that in some ways, it wasn't working.

Before moving to Jamaica, I used to promote this line of thinking in the training programs I led: "only an instant, wholesale replacement of the bad things you are doing with all the good things I am telling you is acceptable."

Even now, I wince as I think back to what I used to say as a trainer, especially as I recall my Mom's feedback.

***

What does this all mean for you, the working professional? Perhaps some of what we have discussed in this chapter rings true – you already have a systematic method for dealing with time demands, even if you have never recognized it. There might be flaws, but changing even small habits isn't easy, and it certainly doesn't happen overnight.

Earlier in the chapter, I mentioned that you might be like Julie, who knows that her system isn't working in some way, or like Michael, who doesn't have a pressing need but is reading this book out of curiosity.

We started by examining your current choices for improvement. Now, let's look at some of the reasons Julie is looking for answers and Michael is looking for ideas.

Julie the Problem Solver

If you're like Julie, you have some behaviors or symptoms you'd like to change right away. When we built a list of modern symptoms in the first chapter, you may have identified with one or two. You may have a different problem altogether that didn't appear on the list. Here's a more complete list:
- Email Inboxes full of unprocessed email.
- Not enough time with your family.
- Feelings of guilt at not being able to catch up.
- An inability to stop yourself from multi-tasking at moments you know you shouldn't.
- Becoming overweight (not finding time to visit the gym or develop and stick to a proper diet).
- Scrambling to find information due to a lack of organization.
- Being time-stressed.
- Turning down opportunities.
- Cutting back on necessary sleep.
- Waking up in the middle of the night remembering something that you forgot.
- Running from one fire to the next.
- Watching important commitments fall through the cracks.
- Seeing your reputation falter as you miss deadlines.
- Arriving late for appointments.

- Feeling as if you shouldn't be procrastinating as much.

Case Study: Rani - someone with a Julie-like persona

"I don't have an issue with time management; I just get too much email."

Rani happens to be an advertising executive in a leading insurance company who complained bitterly, "I never can get caught up on my email. I need an extra two hours per day." A short conversation revealed she was being buried by messages coming in too quickly for her to process, resulting in her spending weekends, nights and early mornings in her inbox, trying to catch up.

She knew logically that her complaints about getting more time wouldn't help. Taking time away from the rest of her life to answer email wasn't working, and she was continually distracted. For example, texting while sitting in traffic had become part of her strategy.

She had lots of symptoms, but to her, the problem had nothing to do with what she thought of as "time management."

On one level, she's right. Time can't be managed, and what she thinks of as "time management" doesn't exist.

However, she is also stuck with lots of unwanted symptoms and no solutions in sight.

You may be like Rani. You experience symptoms, but you don't think they have anything to do with "time management." Like her, you may have believed that the problem is a simple one that requires an easy solution (less email, more discipline, greater focus, or better gadgets). If so, you may find it challenging to read any further, because the upcoming chapters will complicate your life. Still, I think it'll be worth it. Here, you will learn the techniques that can get to the root causes of these problems.

At the moment, Rani doesn't see the whole picture: what's missing is the piece that connects her obvious stress and the process she taught herself to manage time demands that arrive in email messages. It's unfortunate, but the process she uses wasn't developed using any design principles or best practices. It's like giving a kid a piece of paper and asking them to convert it into a flying object. The child who crumples the paper into a ball and tosses it into the air accomplishes the objective, but crudely.

However, the youngster who wants to beat the 2012 world-record distance of 226 feet 10 inches would do things a bit differently. They'd study the principles of flight as they apply to paper airplanes.

Rani needs a deeper understanding of her problem that would lead her to far more choices. Armed with a knowledge of time-based productivity, she could make significant changes that could get rid of the unwanted symptoms she's experiencing.

While I can't promise that your problems will go away after you read this book, I can promise a greater understanding that you can use to get yourself unstuck while you discover the root causes of the time-based symptoms you are facing. As such, I won't be the one who solves these problems: you will.

Michael the Curious

Michael, as I mentioned, is looking for ideas, and if you're like him, you may not have a pressing issue you need to deal with. You probably enjoy learning and improvement. It actually feels good to use your brain, attention and energy to try to make things better. It's a process you enjoy so much that you spend your spare time tinkering with different aspects of your life.

Therefore, you didn't pick up this book to solve any particular problem, but you are open to doing things better, even if you are bit nervous.

Why could you be nervous?

Perhaps it comes from a concern that this book will invalidate your current system or knowledge in some way. A part of you might not want to learn that the months and years you have spent putting together a working combination of habits, practices and rituals is faulty, or worse, needs to be thrown out. You may also be fearful of getting caught up in the excitement of new ideas and end up making too many changes. Sometimes, it's a mistake to fix something that's not broken.

These are valid concerns.

The easy part to address is the notion that you might be convinced to throw everything away – the good news is that in this book, I recommend small changes at a slow pace. I don't want to develop a rash of converts to a new cause. Instead, it's to help you more effectively make improvements in the months and years to come. In this context, it's fine if you take several months or years to make the very first change suggested by what you learn in this book.

Further, the approach I take in this book is about honoring your progress to date. Any changes you make in the future need to harness your innate ability to motivate yourself, craft your own improvement plan and implement it.

There's a term psychologists use that we'll look at later – "self-efficacy" – that has to do with your perceived ability to effectively tackle a change in behavior. This book is about boosting your self-efficacy, because you're building on what you have already accomplished.

***

You probably recognize aspects of yourself in Julie, Michael, or both. In this book, I'll be speaking to both of them. The improvement process I'll take you through is the same and can be condensed into the following steps.

Step 1: Understand your current skills in terms of the behaviors you use right now.

Step 2: Set new targets for select behaviors, using world-class standards as the backdrop.

Step 3: Create realistic, conservative plans to close these gaps between current and target performance.

Step 4: Implement external supports to enable these plans to come to fruition in the form of new habits.

If you don't identify with either Julie or Michael, don't worry: it's not a requirement! You can still gain from this book.

Your Purpose

The best way to get the most out of this book is to first

determine the reason you picked it up in the first place. Here are some questions that might help:

- What would it be like to be someone who is continually improving his or her time-based productivity skills?
- What difference would it make to others in your life if you were to take away issues of time-stress and stop things from falling through the cracks?
- What would it feel like to be on top of all the demands on your time?
- Where in your life would greater coordination make a big difference?
- Would you be freed up if you knew that you were always doing your best?
- Are you tired of struggling along each day, barely surviving one crisis after another?

Take a moment and answer the questions that apply to you. I recommend writing down the answers in your diary or notebook.

How this Book is Different

Reading a traditional book is a linear experience: you get the concepts one at a time, and ideas build on each other like bricks in a wall. Therefore, as an author, I have to assume that you have read earlier concepts when I present new ones. This may create some problems if you skip around from one topic to another. In this way, *Perfect Time-Based Productivity* is like any other non-fiction text.

However, there are some differences between this book and others related to time management:

Difference #1: In the chapters to come, I offer a wide range of new practices. Choosing the ones that are right for you depends on your current starting point combined with the targets you set for yourself. I'll show you how to mix and match different levels of competency so that you end up with a custom-made habit pattern that meets your needs. We'll go through this process together in Part 2.

Difference #2: We know from the study of adult learning (andragogy) that merely offering new habit patterns to learners doesn't work. The reason? You already *have* habits, practices and rituals that you use every day. Also, you know that with even the best-made plans, humans have a difficult time implementing new habit patterns over old ones. We'll spend Part 3 looking at issues of effective implementation in individual lives and corporate communities while examining the unique role that new technology plays

These differences don't invalidate other books or programs you have learned from in the past. Everything you already know has helped you develop your current methods.

My job is to start with what you know and build on it.

If this sounds like a lot of work, you're right. I don't (and can't) promise instant gratification. Yet, this approach makes sense for professionals who must adapt to the blinding speed of technology-driven changes.

Let's move to the next chapter and look at why your system of habits, practices and rituals might no longer serve today's needs and what to do about that.

Remember and Share

Every functioning adult has his or her own time management system.

We each created our own time-based productivity system in our teens, with little or no formal training or coaching.

Individual time-based productivity systems vary widely in terms of quality.

Our homegrown time-based productivity systems are often uneven and overly complex.

Our habit patterns, once set, are hard to change.

Most people are unaware of their ability to craft a time-based productivity system.

Chapter 3. How to Set New Improvement Milestones

(In which you learn that both your failure and success are caused by your self-taught system, and why, in the end, it's actually OK.)

In the last chapter, you discovered that, even without any formal training, you have created a time-based productivity system that is all yours. We'll use the word "system" to refer to what you are using each day: an interdependent collection of habits, practices, routines and rituals that you execute daily without much conscious effort. You may have been using these recurring behaviors for many years, depending on your age and the duration of your career.

Perhaps you have made a few changes over the years. Some were conscious: principles you incorporated from a colleague or mentor who was clearly a high performer. Others were not as obvious, such as the behavior changes you adapted after buying your first smartphone.

But the fact remains: the system you use every day has its origins in your teenage years, even if you can't recall any of the learning you actually did. Now, as an adult, you can't return to the learning methods you used as a kid. Here's why.

Andragogy vs. Pedagogy, and then Heutagogy

When you are learning a subject like algebra for the first time, your teacher tells you exactly what to do in detailed steps.

However, the best teachers know that you don't teach a prodigy who has been studying algebra for three years the same way you teach an average child. In fact, kids hate to be taught the same thing twice. They get bored.

So do we, as adults.

As an adult learner, you aren't new to time-based productivity. In fact, to emphasize what you discovered in the last chapter, you already have a system that works in many respects. You used it rather effectively to create the time needed to reach this chapter, for example. By contrast, many other people don't have a system that functions well enough to get them through a single chapter of a book on time-based productivity, complaining that they "don't have time."

We are all subject to the following six principles of andragogy, based on the original definition popularized by Montana-based researcher Malcolm Knowles.

1. Adults need to know the reason for learning something.
2. Experience (including error) provides the basis for learning activities.
3. Adults need to be responsible for their decisions on education and involved in the planning and evaluation of their instruction.
4. Adults are most interested in subjects that have immediate relevance to their work and/or personal lives.
5. Adult learning is problem-centered rather than content-oriented.
6. Adults respond better to internal rather than external motivators.

Most professionals react to this list with relief. The second item in the list explains why we hate to be talked down to by "experts" who take an "I-know-everything-you-know-nothing" approach. Perhaps it's no mystery why so much time management and productivity training fails: it starts with an incorrect assumption.

Now, I wish I had discovered Knowles' insights or that Wikipedia list in 2006, when I started writing about time management. I felt a thrill: these principles had always been a part of my best learning experiences. I wanted everyone to know there is a better way to learn (and teach) than I had imagined. Since then, I have tried to weave the six elements of andragogy into each step of my training.

But there's more. Midway through writing this book, I discovered a subset of andragogy called "heutagogy."

If you think of yourself as a life-long learner, then you already know that you can't learn much solely by looking for the best teachers. Often, you don't have sufficient instructors, classroom opportunities and money to learn everything you need in the traditional way i.e. from someone else. Chances are, most of your learning takes place when you are alone, and you play the dual roles of instructor and learner.

According to Stewart Hase and Chris Kenyon from the University of Glasgow, heutagogy is a school of thought within andragogy in which individuals play both roles in this way, teaching themselves. It is the study of self-determined learning and looks to a future when, given the pace of innovation and the changing structure of communities and workplaces, knowing how to learn will be a fundamental skill.[3]

If this sounds like an independent form of andragogy, that's exactly what it is. It's also known as "meta-learning" or "metacognition": the science of developing your capacity to learn.

Writing this book taught me that I'm not the teacher/instructor/coach in *Perfect Time-Based Productivity*. You are.

If we ever meet in a live classroom in the future, then I might become a teacher/instructor, bringing my personality to your learning experience, answering questions, and engaging the group. But until that happens, I'm assuming that you are a heutagogical learner who can access only the words in these pages.

So, for the rest of this book, I'll make reference to the fact that you are both the teacher and the learner, coach and coachee, trainer and participant. My goal is to help you be more effective in BOTH roles. At different times, I'll speak to you in one role or the other to make my points.

Let's start to use heutagogical concepts right away by looking at the way you have been playing these two roles.

***

In the previous chapter, I mentioned the notion that your success in many things has been influenced by the quality of your time management system. In other words, during your teenage years, you performed well as "the teacher," instructing yourself as "the student" to learn a wide range of new behaviors. The fact that you did this without taking any formal training is breathtaking. (It's also not very well understood).

However, there is some bad news. Almost by

definition, your system is also the reason for any past time-based productivity failures. I listed the symptoms earlier, so I won't repeat them here. My research shows that we try to fix these failures using other people's advice in the following three ways.

1) Ignore and Mimic

This approach, encouraged by many gurus, involves ignoring our current methods altogether. Instead, we concentrate on perfecting a habit pattern learned from someone else. Success is defined by how closely we copy this new pattern. There is both benefit and downside to this approach.

The Benefit: It's easy to learn someone else's habit patterns if they explain them in enough detail. Usually, the logic of what they do is easy to follow. It makes good common sense. Also, there's almost no gap in time between learning and copying. You can start trying right away.

The Downside: The size and nature of the gap between where you are and where they are is unknown. You are forced to overlook it, perhaps hoping it doesn't matter. The problem is that it *does* matter, and you might waste a lot of time trying to implement practices that aren't important. Also, it disregards the reality that you possess strong habits that probably aren't easy to change. Perhaps when you were a teenager, this was true. However, as I'll show in the chapter on "Habiting," the assumption that ingrained routines are easy to change is dangerous for adults.

Lastly, when you commit yourself to copying someone else's habit pattern, there's a chance of falling behind the times, especially if the system you are trying to mimic is overly prescriptive. For example, a guru who advises you never to schedule anything more in your calendar than appointments with other people may never have updated this advice when paper was abandoned in favor of mobile/digital devices.

Informal research shows that this approach has a high failure rate because it's difficult to execute. Most people end up not following everything – just the parts that work for them, or the parts they like. As they make their own modifications, they may receive little or no guidance about what's essential versus nice- to-have. Some books make distinct "all-or-nothing" recommendations.

Some people completely abandon the guru and habit pattern they learned, but they continue making the same mistake by looking for a new pattern or new expert to copy. Also, a few stubbornly hold onto what they first learned, zealously turning it into a belief system. The world changes too quickly for these approaches.

When I moved back to Jamaica, I made both of these mistakes and suffered as a result. When I tell people that I'm writing a book to correct some of the mistakes I made, many assume that I am just writing another "Ignore and Mimic" book, which they know is not for them.

2) Understand and Mimic

This second approach is a modification of the first, in which you copy a set habit pattern defined by someone else. The only difference is that you make an attempt to understand your current systems before trying to mimic.

The Benefit derives from knowing your current skills at the start, which helps focus your improvement efforts as you try to close the gap between your current habits and those defined by a guru.

The Downside of following someone else's pattern is the same as in the first approach. In addition, it takes time and effort to analyze your own behaviors: some don't have the patience to do that. They want to jump right into new behaviors right away, and this kind of analysis seems to them to be a time waster.

It's possible to read this book and fall into this second category.

3) Understand and Flexibly Apply

Members of this group have decided to take the heutagogical approach, seeking to understand their current system before selectively applying the habits and practices suggested by others. Being a member of this group means investing some time to discover what you are already doing.

The Benefit: you're always moving between a deep understanding of what you currently do on one hand and of new learning opportunities on the other. You don't become stale or hit plateaus, and there are lots of shortcuts, as small steps in select areas produce the biggest results.

The Downside: developing an understanding of your current system requires an investment. It's more challenging to follow your own wisdom as you keep up with the latest thinking. It calls for self-reflection and openness to new approaches. The heutagogical approach isn't easy.

Usually, this third approach (Understand and Flexibly Apply) comes later in life after trying one or both of the first two. It's the one I advocate, whether you are like Julie or Michael, so I'll keep pushing you in that direction.

This isn't to say that there's no way to make progress using the first two approaches. There are pros and cons to each one, and you, as an aware learner, are left to decide which meets your needs. Even if you prefer one of the first two approaches, there's a lot to be gained from the rest of this book, as you'll see. You can still use *Perfect Time-Based Productivity* to dramatically improve the odds of accomplishing your goals.

Setting Your Own Goals

Using any of the approaches, you'll be working to accomplish your own goals. As you may recall, in Chapter 1 we looked at a list of symptoms:
- Email Inboxes full of unprocessed email.
- Feelings of guilt about not being able to catch up.
- An inability to stop yourself from multitasking at moments you know you shouldn't.
- Not getting enough exercise.
- Scrambling to find information due to lack of organization.
- Being time-stressed.
- Turning down opportunities.
- Cutting back on necessary sleep.
- Waking up suddenly in the middle of the night remembering something that you forgot.
- Running from one fire to the next.

- Watching as important commitments fall through the cracks.
- Seeing your reputation falter as you miss deadlines.
- Arriving late for appointments.
- Procrastinating.
- Taking time and attention away from loved ones.

Your goals may be related to these symptoms – things you'd like to change about your day-to-day life.

Or maybe you want to accomplish a particular vision or purpose that requires you to operate at a higher level. In other words, you don't have problems today, but your commitment to realize some big accomplishments in life brings with it a new set of problems, such as:
- "How do I apply for and complete a graduate program while being a full-time mother and wife?"
- "Can I run a marathon in the next twelve months without letting my work suffer?"
- "Can I accept that new promotion while keeping my commitment to never work on weekends?"
- "Should I volunteer for a political campaign while remaining a full-time student?"
- "Do I have the time to lead the church choir in addition to everything else I have going on?"

In any of these cases, the question is: how do you accomplish them using the third approach (Understand and Flexibly Apply) to improve the way you manage your time?

Take a moment to open up a new file on your smartphone or a fresh page in your diary or notebook. You may want to make this your go-to page for new ideas presented in this book.

Here's your first assignment: write a short list of the problems and issues you have today. Then, when you're done, speculate about the time-based challenges you might have in the future as more stuff gets piled on your plate.

Ask yourself: Why are these important? What is the present and future role of technology? How many roles am I playing in my life and on the job?

***

Obviously, reaching your goals has something to do with how well your system works. For example, I have done a number of marathons and triathlons, and I explain to anyone who will listen that training for an Iron-distance triathlon is a problem of time management more than anything else.

This book will help you set and accomplish goals that may have been out of reach until now, regardless of your current level of skill. Whether you are a novice or expert, the solution is the same: an upgrade in your current time management system toward a new one that lines up better with your commitments. If you already have a great match between your current methods and today's goals, you can prepare yourself for future changes that will eventually upset that equilibrium.

To perform an upgrade effectively, I suggest you use this book to become a more effective teacher and learner of time-based productivity skills. (Remember, you must play both roles because you are self-taught). It's the only way to achieve the overall goal of continuous improvement that will make you resilient. In your teens, you learned – and then forgot that you were self-taught. But now, as an adult, you need to be fully aware of the improvement process you are using, optimizing your roles as teacher and student.

In *Perfect Time-Based Productivity*, we'll be looking to set up short-term milestones using powerful techniques borrowed from the best industrial training designers. Below, I'll outline some of those techniques.

Punt, Pass and Kick (PPK)

Each year, millions of 6-to-15-year-old kids around the United States compete to see who can put together the best combination of three football skills: punt, pass and kick. The winners in local, state and national competitions for each age group is the boy and girl who accumulates the greatest distance in all three disciplines combined.

Alex Folz from Spring Grove, Minnesota knows a thing or two about this contest. He recently broke the record to win the national title in the 53-year-old competition. The fact that the finals took place during an NFL playoff game tells you something about his ability to operate under pressure. Like most winners, he didn't just wake up one morning and enter his first competition. He practiced his technique in all three disciplines for several years and for many hours each week.

As sports aficionados know, punting, passing and kicking are just three of the skills that top football players must master in two specialist positions: quarterback and kicker. They are the fundamentals of mastery. Before and even during NFL games, you can often glimpse players rehearsing these skills even though they've practiced them countless times. As it says on the National Football League's official website for the PPK competition, "Training means practice, practice and more practice [...] Remind (players) that even the best athletes didn't become great overnight and that while training is hard work, the payoff is great."

It's not that the Punt, Pass and Kick competition necessarily produces perfectly formed NFL recruits. After all, not a single position on the professional football field requires all three skills.

But there is something useful about working on punting, passing and kicking at a young age. Those mechanics are important. They set the stage for other skills essential to other positions. According to the website, "The NFL developed the Punt, Pass and Kick program specifically for physical education teachers and coaches so that they may better teach the fundamentals of punting, passing and kicking a football."

Imagine, for a moment, that you recently signed up to coach a cohort of 10 year-olds for a local PPK competition. Before doling out any advice, you'd probably start by getting them on the field to evaluate their skills. Using the principles described earlier in the Understand and Flexibly Apply approach, it makes sense to gain some insight into what they already do well and where their strengths weaknesses lie. It's important for you and your trainees to know where to focus your time and energy.

As you closely observe each youngster attempting the three core skills, it would be useful to have some kind of behavioral guide to what you are seeing. If you visit http://www.Rcampus.com you can find a set of interesting rubrics developed to do just that. In the training and development world, these are known as *competency matrices* and can be used as evaluation and training tools, helping a coach clearly see what the next step of development might be for a trainee. Here's an example from their website of a training rubric for kicking, reformatted for clarity, used by permission.

Figure 3-1

Kicking a Field Goal - Rcampus.com /Powered by iRubric			
	Poor (1 point)	Fair (2 points)	Good (3 points)
The Kick	Did not even get to the uprights.	Was to the uprights but wide or hit them.	Made the kick.
Approach Steps	Took too many steps and approach was off line.	Approach line was fair with close to desired execution of steps.	Steps were correct with proper approach line.
Eye placement	Did not look at the ball through the kick.	Only looked at the ball through part of the approach.	Looked at the ball through entire approach and kick.
Timing	Was well past the desired time of 2.5 seconds, 3.5<.	Was almost within desired time, <3.5.	Kicked all within <2.5 seconds.
Arms	Did not use arms during approach or kick.	Used arms for only either approach or kick.	Used arms through approach and kick.

Notice you could use this rubric to quickly assess someone's skill level. As a first-time coach, you'd probably find this job aid invaluable. Properly used, it would help you dispense the specific advice each kid needs. You would avoid the mistake of treating a 10 year-old who has been entering PPK competitions for years as a novice.

In time-based productivity, however, you are the coach as well as the trainee. Having a competency matrix can dramatically shorten the time it takes to move to higher levels of accomplishment.

Unfortunately, in the field of time-based productivity, detailed job aids like these are quite rare. Expert instructors prefer to simply tell learners what success looks like at the end. It's harder to break down complex, highly developed skills into small steps.

Why is that? Sometimes the coach has outstanding talent and doesn't understand the struggle that average trainees undergo. On the other hand, they may simply have forgotten what it was like to be a novice. It's the reason why the best athletes sometimes don't make the best coaches.

How can you use this insight to be a great coach?

How to Play Your Role as Teacher / Coach / Trainer

Earlier, I indicated that I'd be relating to you as both the student and teacher. It means that I'm going to ask you to set goals, revisit concepts, make plans, carry out adjustments, conduct evaluations, and even reward yourself. Often, this role is carried out by a third party, but the fact that you are reading this book means you are probably a self-starter. Now, you get to be a self-teacher who actively guides your own improvement process.

It's exactly what you, as a professional, need to succeed, if continuous learning is your goal. Given the fact that your self-development skills have already been put to use in your adolescent years, it makes sense to continue developing them.

One particular and important skill to maintain is related to what calls Dr. James Martin[4] calls *"goal-setting,"* discussed further in the Lab Notes. It's important to set targets for yourself that are somewhat conservative.

However, during the course of the average productivity workshop, the very opposite takes place. What happens is easy to explain.

Most trainers and authors use the "Ignore and Mimic" approach described earlier, focusing only on new behaviors to be implemented. They don't talk to learners about how difficult it is to get rid of multiple bad practices while simultaneously learning new ones. The learner responds as we all would – with inflated expectations.

Within a few weeks, their hopes are dashed.

There's a provocative article by Daniel Markovitz entitled "The Folly of Stretch Goals" on the Harvard Business review blog. There, he shares some of the latest research on setting over-optimistic targets. It's backed up by Edwin Locke and Gary Latham, two experts on goal-setting theory, who show that goals turn into threats when they seem too inflated.

Karl Weick from Cornell applies the remedy in his paper "Small Wins." To replace the "frustration, arousal and helplessness" that gets activated, it helps to "recast larger problems into smaller, less arousing problems."

Upgrading your entire time-based productivity system is exactly the kind of "larger problem" that Weick is talking about. No credible source I have found in my research disagrees. However, lots of YouTube videos, listicles and podcasts promote time management "solutions" that promise miraculous results with little or no effort, in a matter of minutes, and often at a very low price.

Can peddlers of this snake oil ever be called "credible?"

Let's not follow their lead. Instead, let's appreciate the reality: changing your habits, practices and rituals related to time-based productivity isn't easy, even if you have done so before. But a complex, challenging undertaking can be made doable by breaking it down into achievable goals. This is why I'll recommend setting conservative goals.

I'll repeat this advice at every step: craft your improvement goals so they appear to be realistic, even comfortable. However, bear in mind that it's also a mistake to set trivial goals that don't capture your attention, or, to use researchers' language, fail to cause any "arousal." Getting this balance right is your job as a trainer/learner throughout this book.

If this sounds a little like I'm about to ask you to create your own improvement plan made up of multiple goals, you're right. The research overwhelmingly recommends helping adult learners guide their own learning. We'll take full advantage of that finding.

Before you can create an effective plan, I need to introduce you to the building blocks of time-based productivity so you can focus your attention on the right activities. A competitor in the PPK competition focuses on developing skills that move a football the furthest distance possible using individual effort alone. The only difference is that, in time-based productivity, we aren't propelling pigskin.

I'll show you that we are all trying to manage something I mentioned in the book's Introduction - "time demands" - safely from inception to completion. I'll show you 11 "rubrics" for evaluating your own skills, and much later, in the advanced topics, we'll discuss how to develop your own rubrics.

The rest of the book is devoted to your progress in setting and achieving your own improvement goals, regardless of which of the three approaches you use (Ignore and Mimic, Understand and Mimic, or Understand and Flexibly Apply). My assumption is that even when you're mimicking, you are the one who chooses to do so, meaning that the responsibility for your development remains in your lap.

In the next chapter, we'll take a look at the essential role time demands play in every professional's life.

Remember and Share

Because you initially created your own time management system without guidance, it's likely that you made a few errors.

Compare your current methods of managing your time against world-class standards to find gaps.

You are never stuck with the self-created system of managing your time that you developed.

Bring a continuous improvement mindset to your time management thinking, and keep getting better.

True / False? - It's best to copy someone else's time management system.

What are your goals for improving your time-based productivity system?

Heutagogy, the study of self-determined learning, is the best approach to improving your time management system.

Don't replace your attempts to follow one person's time management methods with following someone else's. That's just more of the same.

Your time management system is a complex, custom creation. Don't treat it as anything else.

Chapter 4. What's Happening Behind the Scenes?

(In which you learn that, for many years, something unseen has been running your productivity system, and you must learn to manage it consciously.)

"When I get into the car each morning, it starts. I start replying to email because stuff has already started coming at me. I try to use the stops in traffic, when it's less dangerous. Usually, the rest of the day is hectic. I respond to email, letters, text messages. Everything is flying at me from all angles. It's always crazy - I can never get home before 8:30 PM. I have to find a way to get home to my family so I can put the kids to bed."

I sat quietly, taking notes as my prospective client, Zachary, explained his dilemma. As a well-paid consultant in a major firm, he was highly trained and successful. He regularly outworked others around him, which explained his quick rise through the ranks.

"I'm being buried by all the stuff I have to do each day," he continued.

As I explored his issue further in subsequent sessions, I discovered that he defined his job by his ability to dispatch many different items. His position made the habit a requirement. He was convinced of that fact. Therefore, all he could do was catch some things and duck below others. Some would hit him while he wasn't looking.

"That's the best I can do," he sighed, "because there's no way I can keep up with it all."

He isn't alone. Many people think of themselves as waking up to face a solid wall of stuff that flies at them each day, like a bombardment of hail in a blizzard. Their job is to make the most of an impossible situation, trying not to get buried or frozen in the process. It's all a survival game in which the winner is the one who can stay alive without getting burned out or buried.

To other people in his circles, Zachary's just being busy, but as we take a look beneath the surface, we'll see another story that partly explains his state of relentless overwhelm.

A New Definition

In the pilot test of my two-day, live NewHabits program in 2008, I started by describing time management in terms that Zachary would understand: as a survival game. It starred you and me, intrepid professionals, as we fought against "the forces of evil" that caused us to do too much each day.

All we could do was struggle in our attempt to survive and maybe overcome them.

During the class, however, I was asked: "Explain some more... what's a time demand?"

I stammered out an answer quite different from the concise definition I now share in this book. I was hesitant to use the term because, truth be told, it was just a placeholder. I still needed to find the proper name for this concept, but I hadn't found a paper, book or website with the right answer.

When the pilot was over, I realized that students were using the term in the class. After years of searching for a better term, I gave up and created a training slide for "time demand" with a formal definition. "A time demand is an internal, individual commitment to complete an action in the future."

Luckily, the original, stumbling explanation I gave my pilot participants made some sense: it came from a concept I had used over the years that started with my formal training in Operations Research and Industrial Engineering. It continued with the time I spent working in factories at General Motors, Pitney Bowes, and AT&T, as well as my experience at other companies such as CSX Railroad.

The key insight I used was that in every industrial process, an object was transformed using external forces. When you're baking a cake, for example, flour, water, sugar, salt and other ingredients are transformed by the baker and an oven into something new and delicious.

Automobiles are made up of components and sub-assemblies formed from metal, glass, rubber, silicon and other materials.

When I was an undergraduate suffering through

winters at Cornell, dough, automobile parts, and other objects transformed through a process were dubbed with the same generic name: "widgets."

The way I was thinking about it in 2008, there had to be a "widget" in time-based productivity. I knew that learners weren't dealing with flour and metal: they had email, notes on paper, instant messages, postcards, phone calls, bills, memos... all arriving in an endless, incessant flow. They were processing all this stuff by Capturing, Emptying, Tossing, Acting Now, Storing, Scheduling and Listing.

To identify this widget, I used the term "time demand": the element that was always present in each piece of stuff a human had to deal with every day.

Six years after coining the term, when I finally condensed my definition onto a training slide, I wrote: ***"A time demand is an internal, individual commitment to complete an action in the future."***

"Better late than never," I whispered, even though seeing the words on the screen for the first time unnerved me. "I must be doing something wrong — eventually, someone will correct me and point out the research I've overlooked." *Maybe*, I thought, *I can keep studying and correct the error before anyone finds out.*

The Source of Demand

Somewhere in the middle of drafting *Perfect Time-Based Productivity*, I threw in the towel. But that only came after a final, tedious search.

The first dead ends I ran into were other people who used the same phrase in different ways. Fans of Peter Drucker might recognize the phase "time demand" from his foundational 1967 book, *The Effective Executive*. In the chapter entitled "Know Thy Time," he includes a sub-chapter heading: "The Time Demands on the Executive."

Brigitte Claessens, the Dutch researcher mentioned earlier, also uses a similar term in her previously-mentioned paper, "Time management: Logic, effectiveness and challenges." She writes, "Modern society places a variety of temporal demands on people's activities."

By the time I discovered these references, I had already defined time demands in the opposite way, almost. The way I saw it, a time demand is NOT something someone places or puts on you: it is the kind of demand you place or put on yourself. As such, time demands always come from inside you, the individual – never from outside.

This notion of personal responsibility is what psychologists call "agency." It puts me at odds with the popular use of the term, an idea you'll have to keep in mind for the duration of this book.

While I didn't get much help from others using similar terms, I did find similar concepts in use under different terms by academic researchers. I was thrilled: "Here we are, finally!"

Digging Into the Academic Research

During the past few years, out of view of the general public, there's been an explosion of psychological research in a term I introduced in the second chapter: prospective memory. As I mentioned briefly, unlike retrospective memory, which has to do with the past, prospective memory is about the future. It includes, for example, your plans for next weekend.

"Finally," I reasoned, "prospective memory is the answer."

After a long search through the literature I outline in my Lab Notes,[5] I concluded that time demands were sometimes stored in prospective memory, but the two terms were not synonymous. Along the way, I discovered the idea of an "implementation intention": A future task is defined in terms of when, where and how it will be accomplished. Usually, it's accompanied by a trigger or reminder.

Peter Gollwitzer, the NYU professor who introduced the term in 1999, showed that when a task is defined in this way, it's far more likely to be completed, which was good news. However, the definition was too specific – an implementation intention is a particular kind of time demand, not the same thing at all.

These insights into the psychology of memory represent the cutting-edge thinking about how we form goals and intentions, remember them, and act on them in the future. Along with hundreds of other academic papers, they form a substantial body of research.

However, after working with professionals to improve their productivity, I have a feeling that as useful as these ideas might be, they haven't yet arrived in the workplace. Here's why.

The Problem of Studying Memory Use

While psychologists have spent a great deal of time studying how memory is used, experience tells me that working professionals have little or no interest in developing the mind's ability to remember to do things in the future. A few take the occasional memory booster like "Rosemary Oil" (which has actually been shown to help prospective memory), but most have no interest.

This reality runs counter to what we are taught in school: that it's important to have an excellent memory.

Today, we reinforce this message in countless ways. Little kids who memorize the names of scores of dinosaurs earn a smile and a pat on the head. In school, memory retrieval is essential for exams and quizzes, even as we reinforce the notion that brighter kids have better memories.

As we age, however, two things happen. First, we have a lot more to remember as we take on marriages, kids, jobs, promotions, marathons, friends, relatives, hobbies, etc. It becomes harder to manage the sheer volume of items in both prospective and retrospective memory. Unfortunately, the practice of using memory to encode and retrieve time demands simply doesn't scale, like many practices we teach ourselves in time management.

The second thing that happens is that our capacity to access both kinds of memory starts to fade after age 30 – a disconcerting fact that's well established by researchers.

The research about "prospective memory" and "implementation intentions" is interesting, informative and important. But these terms are shorthand for academics, not practical tools for everyday use by ordinary people who are still thinking and talking in terms of "stuff" they have to do.

In fact, instead of trying to expand our use of memory,

professionals have already outsourced the task to their gadgets. In order to store and retrieve information, we use paper, PDAs, smartphones, tablets, computers, and the cloud. This trend is irreversible, and most professionals are more likely to invest in buying more memory than spend time learning how to expand the one they already have.

Unfortunately for those of us interested in practical time-based productivity, many psychologists are still focused on memory use (even though most professionals have moved on to electronic tools). The fact is, researchers haven't kept up.

According to Professor John Bauerlein of Emory University, studying any new technology (including smartphones as a supplement to human memory) is hard. In a recent PBS documentary, he said, "By the time you design a research study, apply for funding, implement the study and publish the results about the technology… what has happened… the technology is obsolete… we have moved beyond it… and so the technology and the practices that go with the new technologies… they keep outdistancing the research… the research can't keep up with it."

Academics find it much easier to study a slow-moving subject like human memory. This places academics far outside the concern of everyday professionals and their concern for time-based productivity. Further, research in our management of time demands requires knowledge of several fields of study, as I noted earlier. Obviously, the way we use technology to track time demands is a major factor. This aspect of working life must be addressed in order to help professionals be more productive.

But all isn't lost. As we'll see in the next section, the available research on memory can deepen our understanding of the true nature of time demands, even though it wasn't originally intended to do so.

Discovering Time Demands

Beyond the high-level definition of a time demand, what can we discern about its creation, management and death? How do human beings work with them to fulfill larger intentions? Is it even possible to live a fulfilling life without dealing with time demands on some level? Are there advantages to having the ability to process them in large numbers?

And above all else, why should we care?

Let's return to our definition: A time demand is an internal, individual commitment to complete an action in the future.

In my last book, *Bill's Im-Perfect Time Management Adventure*, the story changes when the protagonist discovers time demands. Everything pauses, and then he starts heading in a new, fruitful direction.

Why did he find the discovery of time demands so important?

Bill, like many participants in my programs, realized or guessed that time cannot be managed and views with suspicion anyone who believes that it can. Participants listen to people who talk or write about time management and realize intuitively that researcher Bridgitt Claessens and motivational speaker Earl Nightingale are right: time cannot be managed.

In *Bill's Im-Perfect Time Management Adventure*, Bill's sudden moment of clarity is the same as the one I see in workshops – a moment when the energy shifts. The reason is simple: it's like seeing an x-ray of your hand for the first time or reading a description of your personality written by an acquaintance. It's an event that opens a door in your mind and brings new possibilities.

That is, when a person distinguishes a time demand, a "psychological object," for the first time, he or she sometimes recognizes, in an instant, its role as a bridge between actions and commitments. It's a token, like a playing piece in Monopoly, that represents many important things at the same time.

In my work, I've learned that time demands have the following properties:

Time demands:

- Are inescapable. Fully functioning adults must use them to fulfill their goals.
- Are discrete. They exist as separate entities.

- Are defined in the mind (therefore, they are psychological objects). They often include important information, such as when, where and how an action is to be completed.

- Are created at a particular moment in time, and vanish upon completion at a future moment in time. Therefore, they have a finite lifespan.

- Disappear once the action they describe is taken. In the 1930's, the Russian researcher Bluma Zeigarnik showed that incomplete time demands continue to interrupt our thoughts until they are completed, while completed ones have almost no effect.

- Are not ends in themselves: they are not supposed to be kept alive indefinitely. Instead, we feel a sense of accomplishment as we watch them disappear. Completion brings us one step closer to achieving our goals.

- Are objects we want to keep alive because they come from our most important commitments. We care about getting them done, or they wouldn't exist.

- Are fragile and easily to mismanage. When allowed to languish, they sometimes cease to exist altogether.

- Are subject to our attempts to keep them from being lost. We use an array of tools to prevent this from happening (e.g. prospective memory, paper, gadgets, databases, administrative assistants).

- Are used as a way to solve the problem of getting stuff done later. When we realize that we need to complete an action but can't do it immediately, we create a time demand in an instant.

- Are created only by humans. As Daniel Gilbert puts it in *Stumbling on Happiness*, "The human being is the only animal that thinks about the future."

- Are created in response to a trigger: either external or internal. Examples of external triggers include a television show, a conversation, a meeting or something we read online. An internal trigger might be an idea, insight or a new goal that we commit ourselves to accomplishing. These triggers, which always take place before the time demand is created, are themselves sometimes confused for time demands.

- Cannot be forced upon someone using outside force. No one can enter our minds and program time demands. There is no situation or event that can automatically and instantly force their birth. This differentiates time demands from tasks, which can be "assigned" or "given."

- Are individually created. While groups of people may pool time demands to create projects, they start off being owned by one person at a time.

- Enter a dormant state after they are created, until they are activated either by the action they prescribe or a reminder of some kind.

- Disappear from the conscious mind when they are well managed. Instead, according to research by Baumeister and Masicampo that we'll examine in later chapters, time demands are handed over to the subconscious mind.

- Are not explicitly taught as a concept, but we do observe other people working with them. Most of us are unaware of the definition at this time.

Many of these assertions haven't been formally researched, but I've found hints in various fields to support most of them.

What's clear is that time demands are limited by our minds, our biology, and the laws of physics. At the same time, functioning adults must create time demands to get work done. People who don't use time demands aren't being effective.

What happens to a time demand after it's created? In the next chapter, we'll look at the actions you take to manage them on a daily basis, a process we must understand in order to make improvements skillfully. This knowledge is essential.

Surgeons are at their best when their understanding of the human body is complete. Only then can they make the right interventions and take the best shortcuts possible to heal the human body.

Like them, specific knowledge allows us to take significant shortcuts and make the most of interventions we undertake. By the end of this book, the plan you create to improve your time-based productivity will allow you to find the smallest possible group of changes you can make to reach your goals, saving you time and effort. Unfortunately, like many areas of human endeavor, you need to know an awful lot in order to simplify your choices and select the handful of changes that make the biggest difference. This unavoidable paradox lies at the heart of *Perfect Time-Based Productivity*.

Christine Bartholomew, a researcher from the SUNY Buffalo School of Law mentioned earlier, advocates this level of self-knowledge in her 2013 paper, "Time: An Empirical Analysis of Law Student Time Management Deficiencies": "… (one of the) key components of teaching time management [is a] focus on the specific aspects of time management students lack. The goal is strong markers on all the subscales, as each represents a different, essential time management skill. Accordingly, assessment is necessary before remedying defects: effective time management requires an understanding of what the specific student deficiencies are."

The fact is that human beings use complicated, Rube Goldberg-like methods to manage time demands. In the absence of clear guidance at an early age, we carve out complicated habits, practices and rituals. In spite of those circumstances, they work, to some degree. Like little MacGyvers, we find a way to get by with just a few resources. (Tragically, some people don't, and their lives suffer as a result).

One source of challenges is that, as I discovered in my research on prospective memory, time demands are difficult to see clearly. To my knowledge, I am the first to describe them in detail. In the following two paragraphs, I'll discuss two models we'll be using interchangeably throughout the rest of this book. Both are imperfect, but we need them both to accomplish our goal of properly managing time demands in order to maintain our peace of mind.

The Simple Model - Seeing Time Demands as Physical Objects

In this view, we see a time demand as a physical object that can be moved from one place to another after it's created. Therefore, it could sit in your schedule in the form of an appointment, an email message that calls for you to take an action, or even a long-term item on your "bucket list."

In this view of the world, time demands can be found

wherever you happen to store them for later use.

Also, you can move them around whenever it suits you. For example, you can move one from a Post-It Note to a To-Do list in Google Tasks.

This is the model I use in my public training programs: it's easy to think of a time demand as a kind of building block that can be used to build some of the bigger accomplishments we care about, such as projects, careers and marriages. It's also the one I used to envision a time demand as a kind of widget.

In remaining chapters, we'll use this model primarily. Unfortunately, like many analogies, it's an oversimplification.

Like the analogy of an atom as a kind of miniature solar system, it helps us grasp a few basic properties that are easy to visualize. Unfortunately, when the time comes to learn quantum physics, we come to see that this model is quite limited, and the analogy, like all teaching models, is flawed, limited and imperfect.

A similar reality applies here. The "time-demand-as-a-physical-object" analogy is also imperfect. Here's a more complex alternative to the Simple Model.

The Advanced Model - Time Demands as Biological Entities

The Simple Model is useful, though flawed. The fact is, a time demand isn't actually a physical object that can be moved away from its source, so there's a limit to how well that comparison works. For some purposes, we'll need a different model that retains the fact that time demands also have psychological and biological properties.

Psychologically, a time demand belongs to a class of psychological objects that includes everyday items such as values, promises and motivation, according to theorist Kurt Danziger. He explained that these objects are mental constructs that don't exist in nature, are created for a specific purpose and are defined in a way that covers an important aspect of people's conduct that we can all understand. Examples of similar constructs include "motivation," "depression" and "procrastination."

Time demands are naturally limited by the ways the brain works. For example, when we die, all our time demands instantly disappear. Also, while we're alive, brain diseases like Alzheimer's and Parkinson's directly affect our ability to process them.

While we don't know everything about how the brain stores time demands, it appears that the process begins with a stimulus, some part of which is detected by senses. The hippocampus and frontal cortex are the first to respond, and they both help decide which information gets stored or not. (Obviously, not everything we sense gets saved for later).

To retain memories, the brain fires impulses along nerve cells and across synapses using a blend of electric impulses and neurotransmitters. Pathways used more often grow stronger over time. Therefore, with each addition, the brain rewires itself, growing and shrinking connections in a phenomenon called brain plasticity.

How this activity plays out in storing and retrieving conscious and sub-conscious memory is unknown. A time demand is more likely to be stored as a mini-network of neural elements rather than a single piece of information found in one physical location. Ida Momennejad and John-Dylan Haynes from the Berlin School of Mind and Brain showed that several regions in the rostral or anterior prefrontal cortex encode prospective memory, and different processes are used depending on the task load on the brain. When any of these brain functions are impaired, our ability to retain and manage time demands is impaired.

Earlier, I implied that a time demand doesn't leave its place in our minds. However, it also doesn't stay the same. It undergoes dramatic state changes during its lifetime. Like a fruit on a tree, it grows and matures in response to what happens in the real world, starting with its birth and ending with its "death." It has a lifespan that can be measured with a stopwatch or calendar. At a very young age, we discover its fragility and realize that without proper care, a time demand can disappear or "die," just like a living organism.

Given the finding that time demands participate in every single one of our goals, aspirations and intentions in life, bar none, we develop a concern to keep them alive: it's one that we take to our deathbeds. It's so important to us that when this capacity diminishes with age, depression sometimes results.

Obviously, creating and keeping time demands alive is an important activity that affects the quality of our everyday lives. Understanding their nature, and how they must be manipulated, will help us achieve our overall objective of attaining peace of mind in the midst of all that we have to do.

What are the key characteristics of time demands?

Let's follow the life of a simple time demand. It may start with a single trigger, such as a short trip to the refrigerator, which reveals that the milk is finished. Without much conscious effort, your mind instantly creates a time demand. From our prior discussion, we know that this time demand is delicate and will "expire" if we allow it to languish.

In the instant we create the time demand, our mind also adds some additional information, such as:
- Content of the task: to purchase a gallon of milk.
- Conditions of satisfaction: skim milk, not whole. A preferred brand versus another brand that went bad the last time you bought it.
- Duration: it should take no more than 20 minutes.
- Likely time of execution: probably between 5:30 PM and 7:00 PM, before the time when the store typically runs out of milk.

Some are satisfied by storing this information in their memories. Others add it to a paper list. How much gets written depends on a number of factors we'll explore later, if it is stored outside our memory, that is a major transformation. It's one of those external activities we mentioned before that changes the state of its existence. Before writing down the item on a list, it existed in a particular way, and after being added to the list, it became *different*. Earlier, we used the example of fruit on a tree. Consider the effect of water, sunlight and fertilizer on a young fruit – it also becomes different.

The paper list, for example, can be used as a cue (e.g. it's stuck to the front of a fridge where it's hard to ignore). Let's imagine that two days after this action has been taken, the note is removed and discarded after one of the following events has happened:

1. The owner has decided not to pursue the time demand because an extra box of milk is discovered in the refrigerator.

2. The owner has executed the time demand, which causes it to vanish from prospective memory. Its completion may spur the creation of new time demands, such as the purchase of Oreo cookies. There's often a feeling of accomplishment and satisfaction, which can sometimes be heightened by the act of crossing it off a longer list.

3. The owner has blocked out time on a calendar to get the time demand done. The slot from 6:00-7:00 PM next Wednesday is chosen as the perfect time to pick up the milk.

4. The owner has decided to add the task to a To-Do list.

5. The owner sees an advertisement on television. Apparently, there's a new kind of skimmed milk from the same company that has a dose of growth hormone said to make humans taller. The owner, who happens to be 5 feet and 2 inches tall, decides to buy this new variety, which can be recognized only by identifying its scientific name on the list of ingredients. The owner scrambles to write down the name in order to use it to buy this miracle beverage.

6. The owner has unintentionally neglected the time demand. After a while, it ceases to exist, as the entire family loses its appetite for milk after finally becoming vegan. At some point in the future, a new time demand might be formed: to purchase a gallon of almond milk.

As each of these real-world actions takes place, the time demand undergoes a number of transformations as it makes its way from birth to death. Additionally, you must continuously apply internal energy and attention to keep it alive, track its existence and update its status based on external events.

Your ability to manage time demands so they don't fall through the cracks is all-important, as is your ability to complete them in order to meet deadlines. Having a system of habits, practices and rituals to handle the volume of time demands you create each day is essential, which is why, in our teens, we self-create our own methods.

It can be argued that The Advanced Model creates a more nuanced, accurate picture of reality than the Simple Model. I recommend the work of J.A. and M. Burgess for those who wish to take a deeper dive into this topic. Their e-book, "Micro-Promises: A Theory of Promises," shares some breakthrough thinking on how to think about commitments while taking a rigorous, scientific approach to psychological objects. A few months ago, they published a book covering many of the same ideas - *Promise Theory: Principles and Applications (Volume 1)*.

As intriguing as the Advanced Model may be, it's a relatively new concept here at 2Time Labs. For six years, we've used the Simple Model in classrooms, which is one reason why it's our model of choice for the remainder of this book, apart from a few mentions of the Advanced Model.

> A fantastic body of research on another kind of psychological object – promises – is being undertaken by Jan Bergstra and Mark Burgess. They have pioneered the use of a mathematical vocabulary to investigate the way we make commitments to other people. Their thinking is freely available for download in their "Book of Promises," which exists in the form of an unpublished manuscript entitled *Micro-Promises: A Theory of Promises*. This section on the Advanced Model was inspired by their book (from the point view that a time demand might be a kind of promise made to oneself).

Beyond Time Demands

Fortunately, most of what we do each day isn't driven by time demands at all, according to recent research. In an oft-cited study listed in the Lab Notes, women who specified when and where they'd perform a breast self-examination were twice as likely to fulfill their intention than those who did not: a jump to 100% from 53%. Clearly, creating time demands can boost task completion.

However, a number of women didn't form explicit task plans but still carried out the exam. They had already created this particular habit before the study started.

Habitual behavior largely determines what we do on a regular basis. A study from Duke University showed that 40% of our activity each day is repetitive, taking place with a kind of effortless, unconscious automaticity. It essentially replicated a study led by Dr. Wendy Wood, in which "participants performed almost 50% of their behaviors without thinking about them."

Earlier I mentioned that it takes energy and attention to keep a time demand alive after it's born. Habits, by contrast, require little energy (or none at all). Instead, the action is sourced from a different place altogether: our neuromuscular memory, which includes our limbic system. This topic is one we'll look at when we explore the chapter on consciously and mindfully forming our own habits – a skill called "Habiting."

In the next chapter, you'll use your new knowledge of time demands to understand what we as humans do to manage them on a daily basis. You'll start to unlock a major mystery – the set of specific techniques you have been using.

Remember and Share

Time cannot be managed. Free yourself from trying. Leave confusion behind.

If time management is impossible, what should replace it?

Go beyond self-management, and discover how you manage time demands.

The actions you take every day come from time demands or habits – nothing else.

You can't improve your time-based productivity skills without understanding the underlying theory.

A time demand is an internal, individual commitment to complete an action in the future. It's also a psychological object.

Time-based productivity is about the management of a psychological object using engineering principles to achieve personal and business results.

Discovering how you dispense with time demands is the beginning of managing yourself with skill.

Is a time demand a psychological object with physical properties? Or biological properties? Surprise: it's both.

Want to or not, everyone is doing it: creating, managing and completing time demands.

Why does it feel so good to cross a completed item off a list? It's because that item is a time demand that you made to help yourself accomplish stuff in life.

Daniel Gilbert in his book, *Stumbling on Happiness*: "The human being is the only animal that thinks about the future."

A time demand is NOT something someone places on you; it is the kind of demand you place or put on yourself.

A time demand always comes from inside you, the individual – never from outside.

Chapter   5.   Introducing   11 Fundamentals and 3 Definitions

(In which you learn there is a generic process that every human being uses to juggle time demands).

"I had no idea that's what you do."

The room was quiet as Rick spoke, while the Just-in-Time team stared at the diagram on the wall. The dates on the diagrams read 1992, so most companies were still using overhead projectors and plastic slides. The room was dark, except for the light being splashed up for us to see. We were in an AT&T Factory that was undergoing tough times, so the company wasn't spending any cash on new-fangled multimedia projectors.

Mandy replied sharply: "Well, someone should have told you."

More silence, which got so heavy that Laura, the facilitator, jumped in: "Well, it's a good thing we found out now. Rick, it's clear that you thought Mandy was checking the contents of each shipment against the purchase order before she put the goods away. Mandy, it looks like you thought Rick was doing it on the dock. Each of you was only acknowledging receipt of the goods into your separate areas, not certifying the quality or quantity. Now, it looks like this might have been the cause of the problems we talked about earlier."

Both of them looked at her in disbelief – as long-time supervisors in the factory, every single piece of raw material first came through their hands. Rick was in charge of the dock, while Mandy controlled the stockroom and the warehouse. Without their delicate coordination, the entire factory would come to a standstill, bringing the production of circuit boards to a halt.

Between the two of them, they managed almost thirty employees. A number of those spent their days fixing problems that had originated in other places. Now, it was clear to all in the room that the source of this particular problem wasn't one of these mysterious "other places." It was right here in this meeting, within the limits of this cross-functional team.

Laura wasn't too surprised – she knew what happened every time this exercise was done well. Team members were allowed to discover the gaps, rather than be told what they were. She had uncovered the problem in separate conversations with Rick and Mandy, but she knew that they had to find it for themselves, together, in the right setting.

"Let's set up a little task force to deal with this particular issue," she offered. With numb looks on their faces, Rick and Mandy agreed, which was the cue for the rest of their direct reports to nod in agreement. A few of them jumped in with comments of their own.

"I knew something was wrong when Smith Industries sent us that incorrect part and we didn't find out until it failed in sub-assembly."

"I don't know why we didn't look at this process flow before. It's obvious now, isn't it Rick?"

"I think we've been lucky not to have a major problem here. I'm glad that we now have this baseline. We can change this process, right?"

In response to the question, Laura nodded "Of course. We just have to do it cautiously so that we don't disrupt the factory's operations. We can't have another shut-down, right?" Around the room, heads nodded in agreement. In the past year, the factory had lost 2 days of production due to quality problems and untold hours trying to find parts that were listed on the database but couldn't be found. Now, at least, a clear cause had been found, and the blame game could stop.

"We'll also need to make sure this doesn't happen again by including process reviews like this one in your cycle of regular meetings."

"Amen to that, sister," echoed Mandy. "Who knows what else we're messing up around here without even knowing why."

***

In the last chapter, I defined the term "widget" as the core element in a process that is transformed by outside forces. In this AT&T factory, a widget might be anything from an empty circuit board to a power supply that at some point could be connected to it. Laura, the facilitator, led the team through a standard examination of the process currently being followed by the receiving dock and warehouse by looking at the flow of materials through each area. It's a job for a team, not an individual, due to the broad reach of activity that spans two or three departments. She knew that once the widgets were clearly identified, it wouldn't be hard to figure out the process that flowed from the arrival of the trucks at the start of an assembly line.

We also looked at what can happen in the life of a simple time demand – picking up the milk. While most of us can relate to that example, let's look at what happens in the office on an unusual day, the morning after your last day of an extended vacation. You arrive at your desk to greet a barrage of stuff flying at you from all directions, including:
- Email messages, only a few of which are urgent... but which ones?
- Voicemail - you notice that your inbox is full.
- Papers on your desk, including minutes from three meetings.
- Post-It notes stuck to your monitor by colleagues.

Your immediate thought is, *I wish I had never left!*

It appears that there's more stuff for you to do than you ever imagined. Your mind does a quick calculation of the time required to recover from your vacation and asks itself, "Why didn't I wait until later to go on vacation? It will take two weeks just to catch up."

Is that last statement true?

Let's start by understanding a crucial distinction: there's a big difference between potential time demands and actual time demands. Before you read those meeting minutes, all they represent are potential time demands. Only when you read them and create new commitments do they become actual time demands. In other words, time demands do not exist until you bring them into being.

Also, a large pile of printed or electronic stuff doesn't necessarily translate into lots of potential time demands either. In fact, after you go through all the materials, you may find that many things were cleared up in your absence, leaving you with only two time demands lasting less than ten minutes each.

Alternately, you may return to find an inbox that's mysteriously empty, except for a single message with a single paragraph: "Sorry, your entire department was laid off in your absence. You need to wind things up and prepare for your new job in Bangalore, India." One email like this might initiate 300 new time demands that add up to a complete life change.

This is the reason why software intended to automatically find time demands would never work. Though Microsoft developers envisioned it in the 1990's, they failed to realize that there's no instant correlation between the words in an email message and the time demand you decide to create. Think about it: even an email you send that's ignored by the recipient can lead you to create a new time demand: "contact the person via phone instead."

It's easy to make this mistake of failing to separate time demands from the stuff that doesn't matter. Unfortunately, separating the signal from the noise around it takes some work on our part: the two kinds of information don't come neatly tagged. Instead, we have to wade through electronic and paper barrages of email messages, tweets, status updates, text messages, instant messages, faxes and letters to find the potential time demands that really do matter to us.

In a time when so many complain of information overload, this is much easier said than done. I imagined there had to be a shortcut, perhaps using academic research. Someone, somewhere must have studied the process that human beings follow to dispense of time demands.

Using Available Research

My original exposure to time demand management processes came in the early 1990's from companies that manufactured planning products. *DayTimer*, *DayRunner*, *Filofax* and the *Franklin Planner* were some of the popular brands at the time, publishing activity diagrams that described how their products should be used. After I returned to Jamaica and went looking for answers on their sites in mid-2006, I found that little had changed over the years. They were, of course, well past their heyday by then, having been steadily replaced by electronic solutions. I couldn't find anything to help me manage a greater volume of time demands.

As I extended my search to the academic literature, I couldn't shake a picture I had in mind of a person acting like a little factory, processing one time demand after another. Within this factory was an imaginary assembly line that transformed these "psychological widgets" one by one. Laura, along with other process improvement specialists like me, has a tendency to overlay flow diagrams onto many everyday tasks that others don't notice, such as driving on the highway or buying groceries.

While the model I had was clear in my mind, my search was fruitless. Instead, the approach taken over several decades by psychology researchers had actually obscured the answers.

It didn't take long to find out why. A large number of refereed articles on the topic of time management referred to a single 1994 paper by Therese Macan from the *Journal of Applied Psychology* entitled "Time Management: Test of a Process Model." It's based on her thesis, written in response to Alan Lakein's popular 1973 book, *How to Get Control of Your Time and Your Life*. Her article has been cited over 300 times and is one of the most important papers in the field. In it, Macan draws several powerful conclusions, but right at the heart of an otherwise stellar project lies an error. The "process" she describes in her paper's title, based on modern understanding, isn't actually a process.

In my Lab Notes[6] I explain that in fact, what she described is a combination of a cause-and-effect chart and correlational diagram which doesn't match up with our understanding of business processes. It's a coincidence of history: her work in the field was being conducted at the same time that Michael Hammer, the reengineering expert, was popularizing the term and vastly expanding our understanding of the Business Process Management (BPM).

Unfortunately, scientists in the field of psychology who have built on her work did not recognize this distinction.

They refer to her "process model" frequently, but never seem to distinguish that she is not describing a process, but a set of correlational relationships.

For example, the Plan-Do-Check-Act improvement cycle is a favorite process of engineers and managers. It has also been the backbone for time management processes described in non-academic books and training. However, as influential as it is in those circles, it is almost completely missing from the academic research, which has focused on soft, emotion-based outcomes like "Perceived Control of Time" — a measure of how in control of time someone feels.

In fact, Macan writes in her paper: "I propose that time management behaviors are not linked directly to these outcomes (less stress, more efficiency, healthy employees and effective organizations) but instead operate through a perception of control over time. Only if time management behaviors provide a person with the perception that he or she has control over time will the outcomes be manifested. Thus it is not the time management behavior per se that affects these outcomes but the perceived control over time that these behaviors afford an individual."

Pause for a moment to consider what she's saying, because this paper is one of the most influential in the field of time management and applied psychology. To paraphrase her finding: "If you don't believe or feel as if you have control over time, you'll fail."

At the start of this book, I addressed the fact that time management doesn't actually exist. Alan Lakein and Therese Macan went a step further… but in the opposite direction. Lakein promoted the notion that not only could time be managed, but also that *control* over time was necessary for success. Macan's research 20 years later tested his idea that feeling in control of time was important. However, she never publicly questioned the underlying philosophy… *Is control over time even possible?*

Such a question may have been well outside her scope as a psychologist, but her popularization of Lakein's book and rigorous research laid a foundation for other academics who have followed her lead without testing the core philosophy by asking, *Is control over time possible?* After all, it's possible to feel

as if you have control over something when, in fact, you
don't.

Today, outside of academia, you'd be hard-pressed to
find anyone who promotes the idea that time can be
controlled. The average participant in my live workshops
already knows this – time has a life and existence of its own.
Many of us who lived through the Year 2000 Problem (also
known as the Millennium bug) discovered that we had no
control or influence over time. The date could not simply be
delayed until we got our act together.

Over the years, our perception of time has changed.
Now, we relate to it as like we do the waves of an ocean
swelling and breaking on a beach. Time and waves are facts
of life that must be accepted: they can be neither controlled
nor managed.

However, many academics are still studying "perceived
control of time" as if it were a real possibility.

Brigitte Claessens, the Dutch researcher mentioned in
the first chapter, has stood out by bringing contemporary
management thinking to academia. She concluded in 2004
that "[...] there has been little research on how people decide
which tasks to perform and which tasks to complete during
their workdays."[7]

In a 2012 survey of time management literature at the
University of Saskatchewan, Laurie Hellsten further
highlighted the gaps Claessens identified. She summarized the
problem in a nutshell: "Despite the epidemic of time
management training programs, there is currently a lack of
agreement about the definition of time management and a
dearth of literature summarizing time management across
disciplines. Furthermore [...] there is a lack of a theoretical
model of time management." Her article also reveals the
apparent lack of research interest in distinguishing the
processes that professionals actually use on a daily basis.

The reason? Apart from the two causes I have
discussed so far (the popularity of studying prospective
memory and the tendency to build on Macan's research and
ignore practical processes) I can only guess at a third possible

cause. I suspect that it has to do with the difficulty of performing such studies.

It's just hard to observe what people do with time demands and even harder to track them as they make improvements.

Unlike widgets in a factory, psychological objects cannot be observed directly. This makes them difficult to measure, so they fail to gain the interest of modern academics, who are mostly interested in empirical findings that they can subject to statistical analysis.

Also, because we manage time demands using homemade brews of habits, practices and rituals, change happens slowly. It might take months or years to study the progress of a group of people in a controlled experiment. In my research, I have only found a single study in this field in which researchers took a multi-year approach: they tracked the time management behaviors of a cohort of students from their freshmen year through graduation four years later.

Furthermore, studying time management practices in today's world requires knowledge of technology, which can be hard to keep up with.

After surveying hundreds of research papers, it appeared as if I was at an impasse. The discipline of process management simply has not yet made its way into psychology and prospective memory. In a last-ditch effort, I tried heading in the opposite direction: "If the psychologists haven't discovered the world of process management, maybe I can find an expert in process improvement who has explored time management!"

Here, I ran into a complete dead end.

While industrial engineers are heavily trained in tracking the simplest actions needed to complete complex tasks, the bulk of the research done in the field is in production environments where the widgets are physical objects. Some have ventured into the world of information engineering, working with digital widgets, but they approach them similarly as they would physical objects.

A time demand, however, does not exist in the tangible world. There might be a few industrial engineers who are interested in studying psychological objects, but sadly, I have concluded that they don't act on that interest.

The truth is, modeling the process that human beings use to manage time demands is a tall order, even though we all follow similar processes. Perhaps this is the reason why Hellsten adds, "there is no agreement regarding the skills and behaviors that constitute time management." She continues: "Given the widespread use and acceptance of the value of time management behaviors, it is unfortunate that only a modest amount of empirical research has been conducted."

Unfortunate indeed, but understandable. Every researcher who has attempted to measure how we manage or control time must have eventually realized that there was a bigger problem afoot – the very thing they hoped to measure and study was, upon deeper examination, impossible to do.

This may explain a phenomenon that is obvious from a short examination of the 120 papers currently listed in the public library of time management research papers on my website. Academics tend to dabble in time management – they write one or two papers before moving onto other subjects. Maybe that's because they realize the foundational assumptions of time management are weak.

To date, Claessens is the only researcher I have found to bell the cat, asserting openly that time management doesn't exist. It's remarkable that there has not been a definitive paper on this topic.

I can only guess why: a proper answer requires a researcher to draw conclusions from a wide number of disciplines, and in academia, such interdisciplinary cooperation remains rare. According to Ethan Watrall in his article "Building an Interdisciplinary Identity in a (Mostly) Non-Interdisciplinary Academic World," "most universities are based on a model of one scholar = one discipline."

***

Outside of academia, I remained hopeful that I could find an interdisciplinary approach. I was lucky to find that IBM has examined the question of what takes places in the life cycle of human tasks. Deep within the documentation of their WebSphere Process Server for Multiplatforms, Version

7.0, they include a state transition diagram for to-do tasks that models all the possible ways that tasks can be handled. It is used to support the software sold for use in mainframe computers.

This was a practical document written by software engineers, but it was hard to expand it past its narrow purpose of informing other engineers.

Even further afield, outside academic and research labs, there was a lot of activity. Most of it was driven by self-help authors, trainers and coaches who speak to a business audience. They included a number of process diagrams in their books, programs and websites.

It was telling that they rarely mentioned academic research. Most made liberal use of stories – recently referred to as "anecdata" on the Harvard Business Review blog. If they did collect hard data, they shared neither the process not the results.

Although their solutions were process-oriented, which is what I desperately wanted to find, I balked at their detailed prescriptions. Part of the reason was that they were based on individual experience. To put it simply, each of the authors I read had described the process they personally used to manage stuff coming into their lives. During the course of their teaching, they elevated their process as the ideal standard and recommended that readers or learners follow suit.

The curious mind could not help but ask, "Why?"

While some authors and trainers are better known than others, none of the books I uncovered offered evidence to support the assertion that one size fits all. Many actually went a step further, and also recommended against alternate approaches they had not seriously tried themselves. This sometimes caused interesting spats around the Internet when one group of followers engaged with another.

The problem wasn't only methodological. They also had not warned their learners: "Be wary of my specific recommendations, as they have been tested only by me and perhaps a few clients. My system may not apply to your circumstances." If this statement were included at the very beginning of programs and books, it would help.

However, just admitting that "one system doesn't fit all" is just the beginning. It leads to a more difficult question that learners naturally ask: "How do I craft a solution that fits my particular needs?"

When I struggled to answer that question for myself, I thought my circumstances were unique: After all, I had:
- Recently moved to a developing country.
- Taught time management programs in the past.
- To tweak what I was already doing, not replace it with something new entirely.
- A yen to use the latest research wherever possible and enable access to it via the Internet.

I was wrong. Each of these peculiarities translate into four general realities that many professionals share when they try to improve their time-based productivity:
- "I have just undertaken a big change in my life that has brought on a lot of new time demands."
- "I have read a lot about time management and helped others with ideas about how to improve."
- "I already have a way to manage time demands that works, for the most part. I need only a partial improvement, not wholesale replacement."
- "I don't want stale ideas that I have already tried - what's new?"

Fortunately, combining academic research with the processes that authors and trainers have devised yields some fresh answers. However, given my objective to generate practical insight, I applied a filter I nicknamed the "Trainability Test."

The concept was simple: if an interesting finding could not be translated into behaviors that could be used to train or coach someone else, then it would not be used. It led me to discard several promising but under-developed concepts that would only confuse a learner who was looking for practical advice.

After applying the Trainability Test, I discovered that what remained was quite simple: a single narrative told from multiple angles by experts, authors and program designers whose work had never been brought together in one place. Here is the common story that underlies their hard work.

A Generic Process We All Share

Many books make the same point in different ways: "You need to understand how a system works in order to use it for your own benefit." The example that stands out is that of Michael E. Gerber and his book, *The E-myth Revisited*. It is a cult classic among entrepreneurs in which Gerber outlines the functions that every startup must perform in order to be successful. They include Leadership, Management, Lead Generation and other key skills that an entrepreneur needs to learn to run a company that can stand on its own two feet.

He describes how sustainable success is a matter of building capacity in each function, even if you're a solopreneur. When you start your own business, you may be strong in a few skills, even many, but usually not all.

I found his approach realistic, and inspired by the idea that this kind of knowledge makes a big difference, I started to pull together the behaviors I had gleaned from multiple sources.

My first post, written on my personal blog, addressed the folly of trying to shoehorn everyone into the same system of habits, practices and rituals. This I knew from my personal experience, with my Mom's advice ringing in my years.

My second set of posts was done a flurry as I laid out drafts of the 11 fundamental behaviors that every human being uses each day to manage time demands. I used the same format I had seen in the rubrics I mentioned earlier, borrowing heavily from the competency matrices I had used in training. The result was a rough ladder of skills for each of 11 fundamentals, ranging from novice to expert.

To explain how they fit together, let's revisit the fact I noted in Chapter 4, that time demands have a lifespan. They are created in the mind at a particular moment, and they disappear when the action is completed. Between these two milestones, we humans take a number of actions to keep them alive. I have labeled these actions "The Fundamentals" and they represent the process we all use to manage time demands, directly or indirectly.

The 7 Essentials Used by Human Beings

I break the 11 Fundamentals into two groups: 7 are Essential, and 4 are Advanced. Here is an overview of the 7 Essential Fundamentals, which have to do with the way we process time demands. (The remaining Advanced Fundamentals are described in Part 3.)

Figure 5-1

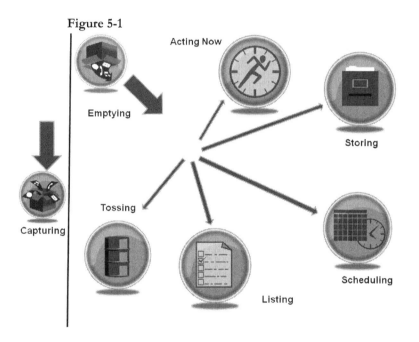

In the above diagram, the arrows show the flow of time demands, while the round icons depict the 7 Essential Fundamentals. Not surprisingly, the flow of time demands starts in the mind, when a trigger leads to the creation of a commitment.

Right after it is created, we do our best to save it for later execution by acting on it with the first fundamental, Capturing.

Capturing - the initial act of saving or recording a potential or actual time demand in memory, on paper or in some digital or analog format. The locations you use to capture both potential and actual time demands are called

Capture Points. For example, incoming email that hasn't been read includes a potential time demand. When you write a note to remind yourself to do something later, you are recording an actual time demand. Both your email inbox and the notepad are Capture Points. (Chapter 6 has further details).

Emptying - at some point after a time demand is created, you remove it from its temporary storage in a Capture Point. (Chapter 8) As you do so, you simultaneously act on the time demand in one of only five ways:

- **Tossing** - revoking a time demand, which is the same as deciding not to do it at all. (Chapter 9)

- **Acting Now** - completing the time demand while Emptying. (Chapter 10)

- **Storing** - converting some piece of information in a time demand for later use at an unknown time. (Chapter 11)

- **Listing** - placing a time demand on a list. (Chapter 13)

- **Scheduling** - adding a time demand to a calendar / schedule. (Chapter 14)

Once these five fundamentals have been executed and the act of Emptying is completed, then it's safe to stop processing time demands and start getting them done. In this mode of execution, you are either "Flowing" or "Habiting." That is, you are executing a task in the flow state, with full attention, or using an already ingrained habit to complete it. (Neither Flowing nor Habiting is a fundamental, but they are powerful skills I will describe in later chapters).

The 4 Advanced Fundamentals

There are also 4 Advanced Fundamentals, which are activities we undertake to influence the way we execute the 7 Essential Fundamentals. Therefore, they have only an indirect effect on time demands.

- **Switching** - the act of completing one time demand and choosing to start another. (Chapter 17)

- **Interrupting** - the act of being reminded to end a time demand immediately in order to start a new one. (Chapter 17)

- **Reviewing** - proactively checking your system to identify where there are broken processes or a backlog of time demands. (Chapter 18)

- Warning - getting advance warning from your time management system that something is about to break. (Chapter 19)

From these short descriptions, you may already have some idea of what each fundamental is about, and you may already see some gaps in the model. One reviewer, for example, suggested that "Delegating" might be a fundamental. If you do have ideas or feedback, please visit the forums on the website for this book and share your insight with others who have been exposed to this model. (http://perfect.mytimedesign.com/forums)

I have discovered that together, these 11 Fundamentals cover the activities that we humans use to manage time demands. We experience some real limits to what we can do with them, because of our psychology, how our brains work, the physics of time, and the way processes work. By the end of this book, you will have an in-depth understanding of these limits, the consequences of having a particular level of skill in a given fundamental, and the power of doing a self-evaluation. Remember, our goal is to build a feasible plan for improving your skills. Most of it will be made up of changes in these 11 Fundamentals.

Self-Diagnostic Results

In the past few years, I have seen hundreds of people use these ideas to evaluate their own skills. Here is an example of a completed evaluation form (called a Tracking Template) that shows an individual's skills in the 11 Fundamentals.

Figure 5-2 - Tracking Template

	White Belt	Yellow Belt	Orange Belt	Green Belt
Capturing	① ✔ ③	① ② ③	① ② ③	① ② ③
Emptying	✔ ② ③	① ② ③	① ② ③	① ② ③
Tossing	① ② ③	✔ ② ③	① ② ③	① ② ③
Acting Now	① ② ③	① ✔ ③	① ② ③	① ② ③
Storing	① ② ③	✔ ② ③	① ② ③	① ② ③
Scheduling	✔ ② ③	① ② ③	① ② ③	① ② ③
Listing	① ② ③	① ✔ ③	① ② ③	① ② ③
Interrupting	① ✔ ②	① ② ③	① ② ③	① ② ③
Switching	① ② ✔	① ② ③	① ② ③	① ② ③
Warning	✔ ② ③	① ② ③	① ② ③	① ② ③
Reviewing	✔ ② ③	① ② ③	① ② ③	① ② ③

Key
① Just Starting Out
② Automatic Behavior
③ Practicing for Some Time

This form uses a belt system borrowed from the martial arts, starting starts with the White Belt and progressing through Yellow, Orange and Green Belts. The fictional user above has a fairly typical set of skills, as described in the self-evaluation. Her overall belt is White, because her lowest single skill happens to be White.

In the next few chapters, you will be doing your own evaluation, gaining what might be a first-time understanding of how your fundamentals stack up against those of the world's most productive professionals, who collectively display Green Belt skills. You'll evaluate your 7 Essentials before creating a Master Plan. Then, you may also assess your skills using the 4 Advanced Fundamentals, which you can use to modify your plan.

Along the way, you may discover that your skills are unbalanced in some way. When they complete their profiles for the first time, most people realize obvious opportunities for improvement. It is a natural outcome of being able to see your behavior with a new level of understanding.

In the chapter on putting together your first master plan, I will share the results of the data we have collected from students in my live training programs, so that you can compare with other learners.

As you do your evaluation and make the comparison, I'll encourage you to lay aside any assumptions you may have about your current level of skill. Most of us naturally overrate ourselves, feeling that our skills are above average.

The better the knowledge you have, the lower the tendency to self-inflate: a few studies have shown that after being trained, people actually deprecate their time management skills. Jeremy Burrus, whose paper is listed in the References, explained this phenomenon to me in a podcast using research he led at a New Jersey high school. We like to think we're better than we are, but when we receive proper training, our self-evaluation skills improve. That leads us to give ourselves lower (but more accurate) skill ratings. Be aware of this tendency, as it might happen during your self-evaluation.

Also, as you do your evaluation, you'll probably see that your system for managing time demands is more extensive than you thought: it includes every Direct Message on Twitter, Instant Message on Skype, comment on Reddit or piece of feedback on iTunes. All potential sources of time demands are included, including any new service that has a social component (and therefore an inbox for messages).

Also, your system also includes all points where you store time demands, such as calendars or schedules on your smartphone, task lists on your Mac, cloud storage on the web, files on your tablet, etc. Getting these elements to work together as a coherent whole is an ongoing design challenge that I hope this book will help you confront.

Although app, device and website advertisers may say otherwise, the power of your system is not in the technology you use: it resides in the use of the right principles. We'll look at the design rules for turning the world's best principles into habits, practices and rituals you can use to adjust and upgrade your current methods. You will find that the best starting point is not a product review on Mashable or Amazon.com, but self-evaluation. As you perform it, I'll encourage you to make specific plans for improvement that may require new technology. If you already have a lot of technology at your disposal, we'll focus on using it effectively.

Recently, I have seen a new phenomenon: a heavily armed professional arrives at the program with a laptop, tablet and two (or three) smartphones. Without the right principles in place, such firepower only gets in the way.

If acquiring new technology isn't the point, then what should you set as a vision for what you want to accomplish?

Your Pseudo-Goal

The study of andragogy helps us understand why multiple adult learners may take the same class but have different goals leading to a wide range of end results. To help make things simple, in my time-based productivity training, I ask learners to set their own goals, but I refer to only a single goal: Peace of Mind.

A pseudo-goal is an improvement objective that learners are asked to assume for the duration of a class (or book). It's a convenience, acting as a placeholder for more detailed goals that you undoubtedly have. For the remainder of the book, therefore, we will use "Peace of Mind" with the understanding that it's just a convenient stand-in for your own goals.

So, in upcoming chapters, as I suggest different improvements, you must NOT take my word for it and simply accept one change or another. Instead, I ask you to perform an internal Peace of Mind Test using our pseudo-goal by asking yourself: "What impact does this change have on my Peace of Mind?"

In other words, based on your goals, you need to decide whether or not a new behavior makes sense, and if so, when. Your own internal standard needs to be the ultimate yardstick, even if I seem very convincing or imply that "Everyone is doing it, and so should you."

This Peace of Mind test is important. Obviously, I don't know your circumstances, and you remain the final judge of what works, doesn't work or is even worth trying.

After all, the improvement plan you'll be putting

together isn't for my benefit. It's for yours, and you need to be rigorous in looking out for your own best interests every step of the way. This is the only way I can help you develop the decision-making muscles needed to navigate a world of multiplying time demands and changing technology.

So, take out your diary or notebook and take a moment to write down answers to the following:
- What are the end results I want from reading this book?
- What are some of the best ways to express my goals?
- What will people around me notice if I achieve the outcomes I want?
- What unwanted aspects of my life would I like to remove?

You may describe a feeling like freedom, joy, or energy, or a result such as productivity, efficiency or economy. You could even choose numeric targets or a goal related to a measure of the number of errors you make each day. There may be a problem you are trying to fix, or a symptom you are trying to get rid of. Perhaps your boss or spouse has been nagging you in some way to address a time-based productivity issue?

Whatever it might be, take a few minutes to write or type it into that diary or notebook you created.

Also, if the Peace of Mind Test isn't your cup of tea, then devise a test of your own right now, and give it an appropriate name. Write it down also.

After you are done, click over to the next chapter focusing on the first fundamental: Capturing. We'll not only cover this particular fundamental, but I'll show you the process and the forms to use to improve all 11 behaviors.

Remember and Share

Every human being on the planet creates time demands and tries to keep them alive.

A time demand is an individual commitment to complete an action in the future.

Time management doesn't exist, but time demand management cannot be escaped.

Have you diagnosed your time-based productivity system lately?

Great time management needs a blend of psychology, engineering, management, adult learning and more.

Don't start with new technology — start with your own gaps, revealed in a great self-diagnosis.

The best diagnosis of your time management skills is one that can be captured on videotape.

Once you can diagnose your time management skills, you'll be shocked and humbled by what you find.

Fact: people who are trained to diagnose their time management skills are likely to deprecate them.

Are you over-estimating your time management skills? Don't assume; instead, diagnose and discover.

Human beings are limited in how we manage our time by the laws of physics, our psychology, and process management rules.

Each human being processes time demands using 7 Essential Fundamentals: Capturing, Emptying, Tossing, Acting Now, Storing, Scheduling and Listing.

The Trainability Test: focus on behaviors that can be effectively taught or coached.

Part Two

Steps to Upgrade Your Time-Based Productivity

Adapt what is useful, reject what is useless, and add what is specifically your own.
Bruce Lee

Chapter 6. Capturing – Securing Time Demands for Later Use

(Where you learn how we use a variety of methods to make sure that once time demands are created, they don't disappear).

"I just thought you didn't like me or something."

Lawrence (I've changed his name) sits in a chair facing me, and our knees are almost touching. We are seated in a 200-person group in a Connecticut ballroom, and each person is huddled with someone else: someone with whom we have each experienced a significant interaction during the past six days.

It's cold, even though the weather is warm. Controlling the air conditioning has been a problem all week, and I'm missing the mountain and sea breezes of home, which cool everything naturally on most days.

He's about 10 or 15 years older than I am – a military man. We are among the handful of men in the room. All of us are here for a nine-day intensive led by Byron Katie, the author of self-help bestseller *Loving What Is*. The process we have been taught involves taking a stressful thought and rigorously writing it down. That's the first step in subjecting it to a series of four questions that challenge its reality.

In this exercise, we share from our lists of stressful thoughts, but now we are focusing on thoughts about each other. I have written the following (which I have altered to ensure confidentiality):

"I think Lawrence is:
- Petty for criticizing the lady at the lunch-table for her poorly-applied makeup.
- Self-centered for not asking me about my background.
- Not strong enough to stand up for what he wants.
- Trying to avoid me because I talk too much."

I read off each item and explain why I think he doesn't like me. Maybe we had spent the last few days hanging out because there were so few men in the room, and all the women seemed so... enlightened. After he goes through his list, we each pick a single thought to work on.

By now, we are veterans of Katie's process, which we have used every day in different scenarios. Lists like these are no longer terrifying to consider, let alone share. I pick my thought – "Lawrence doesn't like me" – and apply the method we are perfecting, asking four questions.

I go through them slowly, asking and answering the questions as he listens, starting with "Is it True... that Lawrence doesn't like me?" My voice catches a bit as a world of childhood memories flood in. I remember all the times when I thought that I wasn't liked. There was the morning playing football at my friend's house, the time at cricket practice after school. Arguments with an ex-girlfriend. Not winning a big competition.

The truth is, Lawrence is just a reminder of all that stuff – an innocent trigger.

At this point, I'm used to using these insights because Katie's questions have instigated them all week. While they are simple to the extreme, even obvious, the answers I entered the program with have given way to them, revealing responses that tell the truth of who I am.

All this takes place during a week when I never actually talk to Katie once except to wish her "Good Morning" or "Good Evening." There's no magic in her or the questions. But for 200 people in her training, evaluating stressful thoughts in this new way brings discoveries that make a profound difference.

Lawrence shares his list, and at the end we do one of those awkward man-hugs. Relieved that the four questions have worked again, we walk away with fresh insights about how our minds really work to keep us from other people, many of whom just want to get closer.

When the weekend is over, I feel refreshed. The fact that I did this for myself with a technique I can use over and over again each day feels exciting. The consistent practice over 9 days hasn't made me an expert, but I have grown in leaps and bounds through using the same technique over and over again.

***

This chapter is perhaps the most ambitious in the

book. Here, I'll start giving you the means to evaluate your current time-based productivity skills. Like my experience at Katie's workshop, I want you to walk away with an awesome evaluation, conducted with a brand-new set of lenses. And, more than anything else, I want you to feel as if you can repeat a self-evaluation whenever you want.

I'll start by teaching you about Capturing – the first fundamental we'll tackle together. As soon as I show you its intricacies, I want you to evaluate your own skills and start to plan your improvement steps (in the next chapter). So, this chapter is no dress rehearsal. It's the real thing.

Why You Won't Have Produced Actual Improvements By the End of This Book

In at least one way, *Perfect Time-Based Productivity* is no different from any other productivity training, book or website in at least one way. When you turn the last page, you should not expect to be different just because you read some words. The reason is simple – reading words is different from practicing new behaviors.

Julie Dirksen, an adult learning expert and author of Design for How People Learn, drove this point home for me in a recent podcast. There is a big difference between helping someone craft a plan for improvement and them engaging in the actual practice they need to implement it. Trainers must be clear about the result they are producing.

So do self-trainers… like you.

By now, I hope you agree: it's crazy to expect habits developed over several years to change by the time you finish a book. The next two chapters will, instead, show you how to make a high-quality plan that will get you moving into action, developing new habits, and letting go of old.

Your plan will consist of behavioral changes that might start out as experiments but, over time, end up as permanent new habits, practices, routines and rituals that take little or no energy to execute. As this happens, you'll launch yourself into a world of new results, accomplishments and… Peace of Mind.

Or not.

The truth is, success is not guaranteed. However, every time you try something, you'll learn whether it works or not. You can use that information your next attempt a success. Like the week I spent in Connecticut with Katie, your skill at discovering and implementing new behaviors via skillful diagnosis will increase with practice and self-knowledge.

Putting together a great plan isn't easy, so we'll take it slowly in this chapter as we focus on first understanding Capturing and then evaluating and improving your Capturing skills in the next chapter.

Breaking Down the First Fundamental: Capturing

A year ago, Bob was promoted to project manager. His new team has been working together for a few months on what they've been told is a minor project. So minor, in fact, that no one in the upper ranks of the company seems to have noticed a recent two-month slip in the schedule.

During one afternoon update meeting, the CEO walks in with Bob's boss, surprising everyone. After some curt pleasantries, she takes over the meeting.

"Your project has suddenly moved to center stage. Given the failure of the upgraded technology we wanted to use in other areas, this project is now our number-one priority in the corporate strategic plan. I am here because I am concerned about efficiency... how well things are moving along on this project. We need some results quickly."

As is her custom, she sets the agenda and drives the discussion, handing out tasks in a flurry of commands. Bob needs to record them in some way.

Unfortunately, he's brought nothing to the meeting to write on, and his smartphone is at the shop with a cracked screen. Today, he's only brought his old feature phone, which has a numeric keypad and can only do basic functions such as phone-calls, voicemail and text messaging. As he scrambles he realizes he's in a bind – there's nothing in his vicinity to write with, or on.

What is Bob's best option under the circumstances, given the fact that he's recently received a warning from his boss about being more efficient with his time? Should he:

1. ... ask someone to take notes for him?
2. ... use his cell phone as a way to save voicemail messages for later?
3. ... borrow a pen and paper from someone in the room, interrupting the meeting?
4. ... try to remember each task that he's assigned?
5. ... leave the room for several minutes and run the risk of appearing "inefficient"?

What would you do?

***

Of course, there is no right answer to Bob's dilemma. His only choices are bad ones, and they all have negative consequences. At this point in the meeting, he has already failed in the fundamental of Capturing: the act of recording a time demand in memory, on paper or in some digital or analog format. He's missing a reliable place to store these time demands.

As his mind creates time demands in the meeting, he has no reliable place to capture them, meaning that some of them will probably fall through the cracks. Given the high-profile nature of the project, that would be a disaster.

He needs a Capture Point - a place to store time demands in the moment after they are created. There happen to be two kinds: manual and automatic.

Manual Capture Points

Manual Capture Points require our active involvement and engagement. The simplest manual Capture Point is memory. One of the lessons we learn as kids is to remember to execute time demands later by creating mental reminders. As long as the number of time demands is small, this technique, which we learn between the ages of 9 and 12, works quite well. According to brain scientists, it takes place in the frontal lobe of the cerebral hemisphere. In other words, this part of the brain serves as our very first Capture Point.

For Bob, using memory as a Capture Point is just one of the options available to him, and it's probably the one he has practiced the most over the years.

Many of us, however, graduate to using other Capture Points when the predictable occurs: the number of time demands we have to process exceeds the limits of our prospective memory, first by a little, and later by a lot. We determine that a change in practice is needed. We might start by noting what everyone else is doing, and we teach ourselves to use one or more of the following techniques:
- Writing on a paper pad.
- Scribbling on Post-It notes.
- Typing into a smartphone.
- Sending a self-addressed email.
- Assigning the item to an assistant.
- Saving a memo in a digital voice recorder.
- Scribbling a note and sticking it on the fridge
- Making an entry using software like Evernote or OneNote
- Recording a voice memo using Siri and voice recognition technology

Each of the manual Capture Points in this list works to some degree. Their effective use depends on the individual's ability to develop consistent habits, practices and rituals, as you don't just need to have Capture Point nearby – you must also use it right away in a reflexive manner. Supplemental activities are also required to maintain Capture Points.

For example, someone who uses Siri or other voice recognition technology must also develop the routine of managing iPhone battery life. This may mean having a charger available at all times, remembering to charge the phone at night, and using the latest apps to reduce consumption.

> In the past three years, I have switched my Capturing methods from the use of a paper pad to a Blackberry and then an Android smartphone. For me, data entry evolved from the use of a pen to a keyboard and then to a screen. This final switch has been the most difficult, as my fingers struggle with the lack of tactile feedback.
>
> These three ways of Capturing require different habits, which is why I carefully study my choices before switching technologies. I'll discuss that topic more in the chapter on New Tools.

Bob could have escaped the dilemma he found himself in during the meeting if he had developed the habit of carrying a manual Capture Point at all times. While "at all times" may exclude time in the shower or taking a swim, he would have a plan of some kind. If he can't ask for help from someone else (who can send him a text message) then he might create a physical reminder. I have switched my watch to the other wrist as a sort of crude Capture Point.

Watch-switching might do nothing for you, however: You'll have to create your own backup plan.

Automatic Capture Points

By contrast, automatic Capture Points such as your email inbox don't require your active involvement or attention. Time demands flow into these Capture Points 24 hours a day, seven days a week, whether you are awake or asleep. As a professional, you set them up as a place for other people to leave potential time demands for your attention. When you do so, and share their existence with the public, you make an implicit agreement: its contents will be checked on a regular basis.

For example, when you set up a mailbox, you send a signal to the world that everyone else understands: you are open to receiving mail and packages at your address. You promise to accept whatever arrives and process it in some way.

New technologies for automatically capturing potential time demands are emerging more quickly than we can adjust our behavior. Some locations include:
- Post office boxes / letterboxes / mailboxes
- Your chair, where your boss left you a note
- Paper inboxes on your desk
- Beeper or text message inboxes
- Voicemail
- Email inboxes
- Messages left for us by an assistant
- Tweets sent as Direct Messages
- Facebook messages
- Instant messages
- Skype messages
- Linkedin messages
- Researchgate messages
- Many, many others.

The great thing about automatic Capture Points is that we don't have to lift a finger: they are always on and asynchronous, operating without needing our attention. They make it much easier for us to interact with the world, acting as our way of saying "send it to me so I can see it later." Thanks to sound technology, most of them are fairly reliable.

Back in our grandparents' time, the number of automatic Capture Points was limited to only a handful: for some, only a post office mailbox. But today, new technology adds fresh Capture Points at every turn. It's rare to join a social network without automatically receiving a brand new, unwanted inbox. Many of the ones I have been assigned can't even be disabled.

Today, therefore, we have a new problem. The new unwanted inbox, of course, adds to our cognitive load, and it also adds a new time demand: "Check new inbox."

We can sometimes mitigate this problem with a device, software or service that allows single-point access to all Capture Points. For example, messages can be routed to a single email inbox like Outlook or Gmail or read on a single device like a smartphone. Programs like "If This, Then That" can be used to monitor rarely used mailboxes, sending a message when the odd email arrives.

Aggressively limiting the number of proliferating Capture Points while barring the creation of new ones can help preserve your Peace of Mind.

Mastering the combined use of manual and automatic Capture Points is, for today's professionals, an inescapable requirement.

Let's examine the Capturing technique by comparing low skills with high skills.

Extreme Methods Illustrated by Wally White and Greta Green

As I mentioned in Chapter 4, we create time demands in response to triggers or stimuli. In that moment, a background commitment becomes activated, which leads to the creation of a time demand. As I mentioned before, studies have shown that there are real limits to prospective memory, of which time demands are a part. Also, our capacity increases to a peak in early adulthood before it starts declining. Our memory just isn't a great Capture Point beyond a certain number of time demands, and its efficiency varies depending on the individual and over time.

To help us draw the contrast between different levels of skill, allow me to introduce you to two more fictional characters: Greta Green and Wally White. They are composites of people I have worked with directly or discovered through my research, and in the chapters to come, they'll help us understand the full range of behaviors that make up each of the 11 Fundamentals. As you may expect, Greta is a perfect example of someone with Green Belt Skills, while Wally is constrained by his White Belt skills.

Greta happens to be a skilled practitioner of time-based productivity, flawless in her management of time demands. She manages a seemingly superhuman number of them effectively, handling multiple responsibilities, which include a number of complex tasks. Further, she's always looking for ways to increase her capacity.

Wally, by contrast, is a novice in terms of these skills. His system is built on practices that allow him to manage only a small number of time demands successfully. Typically, these are short-term activities that are few in number: he has a tendency to suffer and become stressed when the number of his commitments exceeds a particular, comparatively low threshold.

As you can imagine, they lead very different lives, and people see them differently. Greta has developed a huge base of trust with her colleagues, who see her as utterly reliable with an apparently perfect memory. (On this point, they are dramatically mistaken, as you'll see in a moment).

Wally is a nice guy who gets things done as long as they are few in number, relatively small, and therefore not too important. His manager has learned to give him small tasks, one at a time, in hope that he will grow into bigger roles where he can manage more complex objectives.

Don't question the motivation of either character, however. They are both highly committed and work hard, sometimes putting in long hours. While Wally looks at Greta with a sense of awe, she sees a younger, less experienced version of herself in every interaction with him. She can still remember what it was like to rely on her memory.

How Wally and Greta Do Their Capturing

Wally rarely writes anything down for later use. He has used his memory extensively since he was 8 years old, when he amazed his parents and older siblings with his ability to remember all sorts of facts and figures. He has always been precocious, parlaying his memorization skills at a young age into superior grades. In fact, he's a Yale graduate and didn't have to study at all to graduate *cum laude* in history. He can't understand why his memory seems to have gotten worse lately, as increasingly important time demands have disappeared off his radar with alarming regularity. He has never thought much about his time-based productivity skills, always believing that his I.Q. of 160 would pull him through tough spots.

He assumes that he's well above average in terms of his time-based productivity, in spite of some recent evidence to the contrary. Unfazed, he believes this is a temporary situation and expects a quick return to his old, productive self sometime soon.

Greta is, in conventional terms, not as smart as Wally. Her community college degree earned part-time over six years isn't her main calling card, and many things in life come to her slowly, after a considerable amount of hard work.

In fact, when she was a teenager, she noticed that her friends in class seemed smarter, able to hold onto every fact with ease. She tried to be as good as they were at remembering things, but it never seemed to work. Early on, she decided that she'd need to write everything down in order to keep up. At first, it meant taking good notes in class. Over time, she learned to supplement her prospective memory with a small black diary, then a big black diary.

Now, her friends and family never see her without her smartphone. She uses it to hold on to every idea, promise and commitment. Even the small stuff, like making a grocery list, is something she records. In her mind, memory is almost an enemy with respect to tracking time demands. She'll use it only as a last resort. Even though she does much of her capturing on paper, she likes tools like Evernote, which capture in the cloud from any number of devices.

According to anecdotal data I have gathered from hundreds of evaluations, Wally tends to be somewhat younger than Greta, who has learned more than a thing or two about Capturing from bitter experience. Wally is also oblivious to the advances of age and the impact age has on short-term memory. He knows that his grandmother regularly mixes up names, recent past events and future meetings, but he hasn't connected the dots and can't see that ever happening to him.

If you were to take the two extreme capturing behaviors demonstrated by Wally and Greta and place them at opposite ends of a continuum, you would probably decide that most people, including you, fall somewhere in between. A good diagnosis will help you see exactly where you are right now.

Why You Need a Self-Diagnosis vs. The Other Kinds

Most doctors believe that it's a bad idea to encourage

people to self-diagnose. In medicine, an expert-centric treatment model has stood for ages. When medical knowledge was a scarce commodity, it was the only feasible option.

However, in today's world of amazing information availability, a new idea has emerged. Albert Bandura coined the term "self-efficacy" in 1977 to refer to learners' belief in their ability to improve, engage in new behaviors and accomplish goals. It recognizes that the way they feel, think, behave and motivate themselves is a critical factor in their learning.

Who, then, should evaluate the health of your current time management skills? Should I (in my role as author of this book) visit your office, follow you around for a day, and give you a diagnostic report a week later? Or is it a better idea to boost your ability to do an accurate diagnosis, and also your self-efficacy, by showing you the subtle processes that an expert diagnostician would use?

Thomas Leonard, often considered the father of life coaching, founded Coach University in 1992. I was fortunate to enroll in his program as the career exploded into the popular consciousness. While I don't recall the term "self-efficacy" being used in his teleclasses, he was clearly committed to the goal of coaches having an explicit goal of building client capacity: helping clients improve themselves without further help. At the time, this seemed to make logical sense: I didn't realize then what a breakthrough concept this was.

Many coaches and trainers realize that building a learner's capacity makes their role redundant. It's better for repeat business to help them just solve problems one at a time, forever keeping them at the same level of development.

Now, more than twenty years later, it's more obvious that learners should not only know how to do their own evaluations; they also need to develop the ability to construct their own improvement plans. I have learned a lot about this topic from Julie Dirksen, the adult-learning expert, and I recommend her book *Design for How People Learn* for a more thorough discussion about how to design training that builds the learner's capacity in multiple dimensions.

As the teacher and the learner, I encourage you to
adopt the skill of doing self-evaluations, using the tools I'll
share with you in this book. In the next chapter, I'll guide you
through the process of doing a self-evaluation on Capturing.
Then, I'll give you the information you need to do your own
self-diagnosis of the other 10 fundamentals. In the chapter
"Habiting," you'll learn how you can expand your self-efficacy
in any area of your life by developing your own evaluation
tools. I'll show you the approach I used to develop the
materials in this book as an example.

Remember and Share

Capturing is the process of storing time demands in a safe
place for later retrieval.

A Capture Point is a location for temporarily storing time
demands.

Capture Points can be automatic (for potential time demands)
or manual (for actual time demands.)

You mind is a terrible Capture Point... unless you don't have
much to do each day.

How can you make sure you never need to use your memory
as a Capture point... ever?

Great time managers develop the habits of carrying a Capture
Point at all times.

Develop the habit of instantly diverting every time demand
that you create to a Capture Point.

You don't need to have the best time management skills –
just the set that suits your circumstances.

People who are great at Capturing never allow a single time
demand to slip through the cracks.

Chapter 7. How to Complete a Self-Diagnosis

(In which you learn how to diagnose your skills in the 11 Fundamentals.)

Let's begin your self-diagnosis by looking at the "Cheat-Sheet" I have developed for Capturing (Figure 7.1). In each sheet, I use the martial arts ranking system to distinguish different levels of skill. As a reminder, White is the lowest skill level, followed by Yellow, Orange and Green.

(In my belief that there will always be new levels of skill to discover, I have left the higher belts undefined, including the Black Belt level. I'll also share why I don't possess the highest belt in a later chapter).

I have learned from trial and error that a good diagnostic tool for time-based productivity skills should help people do the following:
- Evaluate skills quickly.
- Pick out immediate opportunities for improvement by focusing on observable behaviors.
- Resist the temptation to inflate skills.
- Craft a path for continuous improvement that takes months or even years to complete.
- Return to the diagnostic tool repeatedly, whenever life brings change.
- Leave room for future technology and innovation.
If you see a way to improve any of the diagnostic tools in this book, do drop a comment in the forums on my website – http://perfect.mytimedesign.com

---

Here's a summary of each of the four sub-skills to be used in your evaluation of your skills in Capturing.

Sub-Skill #1 - Carry a manual capture point (other than memory) at all times: Greta always has one with her.

Sub-Skill #2 - Capture manually: Greta not only has a manual Capture Point with her at all times, she uses it every time without fail, rarely reverting to memory.

Sub-Skill #3 - Consolidate automatic Capture Points: Greta sees this as an ongoing problem she needs to stay on top of. She seeks out and uses the technology to make sure that no inbox is left unattended.

Sub-Skill #4 - Maintain a backup routine: Greta has a plan for capturing in situations in which a manual Capture Point isn't available. She often asks other people to send her text messages, for example, as a reminder. Richard Branson, who is a big fan of the skill of Capturing, is known for scribbling in his passport, according to an article on the Virgin site entitled "Always write down your ideas." (He's a big advocate of walking around with a notebook in your pocket, so this must be part of his backup plan!)

Wally, on the other hand, uses his memory out of habit, and has multiple email inboxes that he uses now and then, whenever he feels as if he's in the mood. This leads to lots of miscues, as his friends invariably send messages to inboxes that he doesn't check.

Greta's habits often appear silly or even obsessive to others, but her objective is not social approval. Instead, it's to ensure that she maintains her own Peace of Mind by never using her memory as a Capture Point.

It's not too hard to imagine that Greta is able to process a much larger number of time demands than Wally. As a Green Belt, her commitments almost never fall through the cracks, and she wastes less time scrambling to remember or recreate promises. To others, she has the memory of an elephant. Little do they know, she doesn't. Her "memory" doesn't rely on brain cells but – it's an efficient combination of paper, a smartphone and the cloud.

Lastly, Greta is probably someone you'd prefer to work with. Wally is sometimes so unreliable that his manager sometimes has to keep track of his new time demands. Also, as Wally's prospective memory skills decay, he may be setting up himself for failure. A 25-year-old, single White Belt who perfects the habit of using memory to capture time demands may unwittingly sow the seeds for future problems: his life may change to include a spouse, a few kids, a mortgage, and his first promotion at work. At that point, his memory system is likely to fail.

Completing Your First Cheat-Sheet

To get through the evaluations that remain in this book, I need to provide a few tools. In this chapter, I'll go over them in detail, and in future chapters, I'll refer to this explanation. A clean version of these forms can be found in Appendix 1 of the paperback version. Electronic forms can be printed or filled in directly online. You can download the PDF at http://goo.gl/Ohe9ju.

Figure 7-1

Capturing Cheat-Sheet

Behavior	White	Yellow	Orange	Green
Carry a manual Capture Point at all times	Rarely or never ☐	Sometimes ☐	Often ☐	Almost Always ☐
Use a manual Capture Point instead of memory	Rarely or never ☐	Sometimes ☐	Often ☐	Always ☐
Consolidate automatic Capture Points	■	Starting ☐	Occasional ☐	Sustained ☐
Maintain a flexible, backup method	■	Starting ☐	Sometimes in place ☐	Always in place ☐

Current Belt ☐   ☐   ☐   ☐

Rank yourself in each of the line items listed above. Each of them relates to one of the four sub-skills we went over earlier.

One of the key principles to use is that of making conservative evaluations: we humans have a tendency to inflate our self-rating. I have included research about why this is counterproductive in my Lab Notes.[8]

Rather than falling into the trap of over-optimism, you can borrow an idea from athletes – "The Goldilocks Principle" – to create your plan. They know that it's a mistake to become either over or under-excited as they start a game or prepare to sprint. Both the extremes are counterproductive. Instead, they need be excited at a level that's above normal, but between the extremes: "just right."

This means, as you carve out plans to improve your Capturing skills in this chapter, you need to be conservative... maybe even a little pessimistic. Plan to go slower than you might expect and put in place more support than you think you'll need. Assume that failure is right around the corner, not to depress yourself, but to implement mitigation steps.

Being a little bit pessimistic also gives you some room for quick improvements, which can help develop positive momentum. According to Ray Williams in articles published in the *Financial Post* and *Psychology Today*, "Recent neuroscience research shows that the brain works in a protective way, resistant to change. Therefore, any goals that require substantial behavioral change, or thinking-pattern change, will automatically be resisted." Instead, he offers a book by Aubry Daniels who "argues for small improvements and incremental targets [...] and regular positive reinforcement."

Here are the steps to follow in the process of self-evaluation:

Step 1. In each row, check off the answer that best describes your current reality.

Step 2. Give yourself a Current, Overall Belt. It should be the lowest belt of all the ones you have checked in the Cheat-Sheet.

Many people resist the logic of the second step, arguing that if they are a Green Belt in three disciplines and a White Belt in one, they shouldn't be a White Belt overall.

The reason I made that rule is partly to maintain a high standard and also to help people focus on their weak spots. For example, if you are learning to drive and pass everything on the test except parallel parking, it's a good idea to accept the failure in order to spend time perfecting this skill. The same logic applies here: the lowest belt is your weakest link and might be the one that you need to focus on the most. It's better to highlight it clearly so that you can improve it.

Further, it's important to keep some perspective. As I mentioned before, you are both trainer and trainee. In the former role, you don't help yourself by setting a low standard that's easy to achieve, fooling yourself in the process into believing that you are better than you really are.

Also, remember that the point of this entire exercise is not to give yourself the highest belt possible. Instead, it's to rid yourself of a real, unwanted symptom (if you are like Julie) or to prepare yourself for a future upgrade (if you are like Michael). Coming away with an inflated view of your skills doesn't help you achieve the true Peace of Mind you are after.

As I tell participants in my live programs, I'm not going to come and visit you in the office, demanding to see your self-evaluation. At the moment, this is between you (as teacher) and yourself (as learner). Holding yourself to a high standard will only help.

If you have difficulty holding yourself to account and would benefit from having an objective, but supportive point of view, I recommend getting a coach. If you are looking for someone who is trained by 2Time Labs, contact me through my training website, www.mytimedesign.com. (If you are a prospective coach, I invite you to do the same).

Crafting Your Improvement Plan

As you were completing your assessment, you may have gained a few insights into possible areas of improvement. You can already see what you'd like to change. What's important is to decide how quickly to make those changes.

For example, moving from being a White Belt to a Green Belt is not a simple matter of purchasing a paper pad or an iPhone. How long will it take to move to the next belt? As you can imagine, there's no right answer, and you are the only one who can make an informed estimate.

Your improvement plan, therefore, starts by setting a series of targets spaced out over time. In the previous chapter, we met Bob, the project manager who was surprised by the arrival of his CEO in a regular update meeting. He's weak at the skill of Capturing, so let's use him as an example by looking at his Cheat-Sheet and the process he follows to create an improvement plan. As you can see below, he's currently a White Belt overall.

Figure 7-2

Capturing Cheat-Sheet

Bob

Step 1 – Current Evaluations

Behavior	White	Yellow	Orange	Green
Carry a manual Capture Point at all times	Rarely or never ☑	Sometimes ☐	Often ☐	Almost Always ☐
Use a manual Capture Point instead of memory	Rarely or never ☐	Sometimes ☑	Often ☐	Always ☐
Consolidate automatic Capture Points	■	Starting ☑	Occasional ☐	Sustained ☐
Maintain a flexible, backup method	■	Starting ☐	Sometimes in place ☑	Always in place ☐

Step 2 – Overall Belt

Current Belt ☑   ☐   ☐   ☐

The four immediate improvements he can attempt are shown in the diagram below.

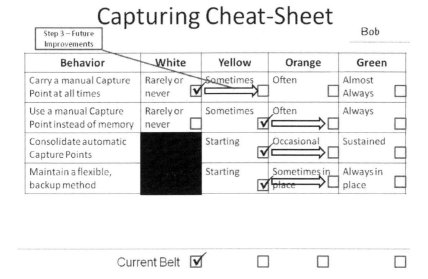

Capturing Cheat-Sheet

Bob

Behavior	White	Yellow	Orange	Green
Carry a manual Capture Point at all times	Rarely or never ☑	Sometimes ☐	Often ☐	Almost Always ☐
Use a manual Capture Point instead of memory	Rarely or never ☐	Sometimes ☑	Often ☐	Always ☐
Consolidate automatic Capture Points		Starting ☑	Occasional ☐	Sustained ☐
Maintain a flexible, backup method		Starting ☑	Sometimes in place ☐	Always in place ☐

Step 3 – Future Improvements

Current Belt ☑   ☐   ☐   ☐

Figure 7-3

Following the arrows, he may decide to bring the first discipline up to the Yellow Belt level, or he might improve one of the others.

Let's imagine that he decides to become a Green Belt by the end of the year. To accomplish this goal, , he'd use the Planning Form below to do something quite simple: stretch out his improvement goals over time so that each step looks doable, realistic and conservative.

Figure 7-4

Fundamental: ____Capturing

Current Belt Level: ____White   Date:__Jan 1, 20 ____

Target 1

Yellow	x
Orange	
Green	

Take a paper pad with me wherever I go (Often)   New Habits
Hardly use memory (Often)
Start a backup capturing system (Sometimes)

Target 1 Date: _   1-May

Target 2

| Orange | x |
| Green | |

Almost always have a paper pad with me   New Habits
Have a backup system in place sometimes

Target 2 Date: _   1-Oct

Target 3

Never use memory and always have something to write on   New Habits
Keep consolidating inboxes
Figures out a backup system -- always in place

| Green | x |

Target 3 Date: _   1-Jan

His current belt is entered at the very top, along with today's date. Then, he has entered the improvements he wants in three consecutive time periods in order to move up from his current belt to the next. His chart looks reasonable, but at this point he's a bit wary: this is, after all, the first Planning Form of 11.

At the end of the day, Bob has a plan for improving his skill at Capturing that requires him to focus on a small number of practices at any one time. By following this approach, he has increased the odds of succeeding. Also, his plan meets his goal of achieving Peace of Mind, not only as an end result, but as an experience he hopes to have at every point during the improvement cycle.

Take a moment now to fill out your own blank Cheat-Sheet and Planning Form available from my website, or use the copy in the Appendices. Keep them in a safe place.

Congratulations! You have completed a plan for upgrading this fundamental.

Including Plans to Upgrade the Other Fundamentals

Having set up a plan to improve your skill at Capturing, you may wonder how you will include changes in the other 10 Fundamentals. The answer is simple: this particular plan for changing your Capturing is a temporary one that you'll change once we merge all your plans together into a single Master Plan in Chapter 17. It's a simple process to follow using the design rules I'll explain later.

To keep track of your overall belt in each of the fundamentals, I invite you to use the Tracking Template, provided below – the same form I shared a few chapters ago. At the end of the class, Bob's Template looked like this. As you can see, his skills are uneven, which is typical.

Figure 7-5 - Tracking Template

	White Belt	Yellow Belt	Orange Belt	Green Belt
Capturing	① ✓ ③	① ② ③	① ② ③	① ② ③
Emptying	✓ ② ③	① ② ③	① ② ③	① ② ③
Tossing	① ② ③	✓ ② ③	① ② ③	① ② ③
Acting Now	① ② ③	① ✓ ③	① ② ③	① ② ③
Storing	① ② ③	✓ ② ③	① ② ③	① ② ③
Scheduling	✓ ② ③	① ② ③	① ② ③	① ② ③
Listing	① ② ③	① ✓ ③	① ② ③	① ② ③
Interrupting	① ✓ ③	① ② ③	① ② ③	① ② ③
Switching	① ② ✓	① ② ③	① ② ③	① ② ③
Warning	✓ ② ③	① ② ③	① ② ③	① ② ③
Reviewing	✓ ② ③	① ② ③	① ② ③	① ② ③

Key

① Just Starting Out

② Automatic Behavior

③ Practicing for Some Time

Take a moment to fill out the first row in the chart for your skill at Capturing. By the end of the book, you'll have a complete profile that, as I mentioned, you can compare against the data I have collected in my classes.

When you do that comparison, you may believe that the purpose of this book is to push everyone to become a Green Belt. That's understandable.

However, it's not a goal I happen to have.

This is your show: based on your evaluation, you are the only one who can set realistic targets. I can't sit here in my office in Kingston and presume to know what's best for you, in your life, to achieve Peace of Mind the way you want it.

You may decide that Orange Belt skills or Yellow Belt skills are all you need. You will NOT be a "loser" for deciding that Green Belt skills aren't necessary.

Someone can be a White Belt and be quite happy. If you are a retiree, for example, and you already tracked time demands for several decades, you may decide that White Belt skills suit you just fine.

You also may be unhappy because you are experiencing some of the adverse symptoms identified in the first chapter. If an upgrade in Capturing is what you need to remove these symptoms and re-establish your Peace of Mind, then you may be on the right track.

My point is that you have the freedom to set your own goals and accomplish them at a rate that works for you. Don't forget who the teacher/coach/trainer is in *Perfect Time-Based Productivity*, and don't abandon the heutagogical model.

With that in mind, finish your plan for Capturing. Make sure it suits your needs. Take the extra step of sharing it with someone else who is willing to help – maybe it's someone who can listen to you explain your plan to confirm that it makes sense, or maybe he or she is willing to remind you when it appears you may have drifted away from it. As I'll show in the chapter on Habiting, this kind of sharing is important.

In the next chapter we'll focus on Emptying, which is more difficult in terms of implementing new habits, practices and rituals. It's not easy to process time demands stored in Capture Points. But before we move into the next chapter, take a moment to jot down any new insights you gained in your diary or notebook.

Remember and Share

The Goldilocks Principle of goal planning means setting targets that are neither too ambitious nor too boring.

You don't have to have the best time management skills — just the right set to suit your circumstances.

Sometimes, the best kind of evaluation is one that you do of yourself - #PTBP

Chapter 8. Emptying – The Most Difficult Skill of All

(In which we see that your mind, which so eagerly creates a new time demand, finds it challenging to decide what to do next.)

"Wait, maybe it's not in this pad, but written on the one in my office. Or the one at home..."

I'm in a meeting with Marsha, a busy executive in a mid-sized insurance company. The meeting has paused while she searches for an action item she wrote down during our meeting two weeks ago. It happens to include the specific improvements goals she decided to implement in the project, but now she can't recall the exact figures. We need them to move on in our discussion.

First, she flips open the blue steno pad she carries with her at all times. "I know it's here somewhere..." she mutters as she flips through multiple pages. "Hmm," she says aloud, "maybe it's in one of my other pads. I'll call my secretary."

Fifteen minutes later, her secretary has searched her office, the office attendant has searched her car, and her son has searched her bedroom at home. Apparently, there are at least five blue steno pads in which Marsha records everything of interest, a habit she learned as a ten-year-old. The fact that it's always blue makes people think she's using the same pad, but she's not.

"I'm sorry, I know it's in one of my blue pads."

The rest of us are sure she's right. We remember seeing her write down the item, following her usual habit. The problem is that with so many pads floating around, she has no idea which one it's written in. It's as good as lost.

***

Sam, an IT employee of Marsha's company, wakes up each morning to the sight of 2,900 email inboxes. Part of his job is unusual. He helps colleagues dig themselves out from the avalanche of messages that sit in their inbox. It's not for fun – the firm tries to keep its storage costs down by limiting the size of each person's inbox. As he scans a report of their usage over the past 24 hours, he explains:

"It's not as if these are bad people. They just don't realize yet that their 50,000-message backlog is a result of bad habits, not the people around them. Other people in the same office get the same amount of email, but their inbox is clean." He stopped for a moment and then continued. "They just don't get that they are responsible."

He continues, his voice dropping quietly: "Marsha is a prime example. I dumped her inbox just two months ago, giving her a fresh start. She came back to me just last week. What she's done has hardly helped – look." He points at the report on the screen. "She's already back up to 1,500 in two weeks. It's like declaring bankruptcy but never changing your spending habits!"

"Well," I joke, "at least I know why she never seems to be able to reply to my email. It's not personal!"

He shakes his head and then clicks over to another tab on the Yahoo! page. "Here's my favorite," he says as he shows me a report he's bookmarked. Apparently, a third of those surveyed would rather clean a toilet than clear up their email inboxes.

***

In this not-so-fictional account, Marsha is the kind of employee who was promoted because she was far more efficient than her peers. Over the years, her managers have rightly perceived her habit of writing everything down as a sign of efficiency. In fact, she's a virtual Green Belt in Capturing, according to her self-evaluation.

Marsha's case is a classic. Her decades-long practice of capturing everything makes sense, but her habit of processing the items written in those books occasionally, haphazardly and partially means that the collection has come to represent a huge backlog of unprocessed time demands. As the backlog has grown, so has her stress-level. Others around her have lost confidence – when she writes something in her blue steno pad, they capture it, too... because she's likely to lose track of it. When they send her email, they follow up on Whatsapp an hour later to make sure she sees it. Seasoned insiders know that a call to her secretary is necessary when she needs to take immediate action.

Unfortunately, she has fallen victim to a syndrome that afflicts many professionals. It's the individual version of what Robert Sutton calls "The Problem of More," in which a solution that works on a small scale no longer works when the numbers grow. In engineering, it's known as a "scaling problem," and it shows up again and again in time-based productivity.

When she was dealing with a small number of time demands, her habit of writing everything down and processing it "later" was the perfect habit. Now that she's an executive who must process a huge number of time demands, she's understandably confused – unsure as to the reason why so many things are falling through the cracks.

A few weeks following our conversation, Marsha's CEO exploded in a meeting with a top client when she repeated her "I-don't-know-which-blue-pad-I-wrote-it-in" routine. "Would you get your act together?" he hissed between clenched teeth, clearly embarrassed at her display.

Victims of Unintended Consequences

danah boyd (whose name is always spelled with lower case letters) is a Microsoft researcher who spoke to the issue of email management in an interview on *The Verge*.

"I'm of an era where [...] the notion that 'You've Got Mail' was exciting. Everything about email – we would race home after school and be like, 'What's on email,' and this is great. It was like little gifts from the heavens. My relationship to email is not like that these days."

Back in the mid-1990s when email was just starting to catch on, most people were like danah, treating email as a miraculous privilege. In those days of single-digit-per-day email volumes, it was normal to let messages sit in your inbox if none of them required immediate attention. With the low rate of incoming messages (often less than 10 per day), the "Skim-and-Leave" tactic we taught ourselves worked well.

Also, as kids, our parents taught us a useful principle: "Put things where you can see them so you won't forget them." In other words, we learned that you might not forget to execute time demands if you include visual cues. If you had to remember to take the Algebra textbook to school the following day, you learned to leave it by the door the night before. Research conducted by Peter Gollwitzer and others is clear: visual cues work well.

However, research by Steve Whittaker at Sheffield University shows that there's a limit: "Visual reminding is compromised when there are too many inbox messages. As the number of inbox items increases, older outstanding items are overlooked when processing new incoming message." In other words, visual cues work for small numbers of large items, but for large numbers of small items, it fails.

Now that email volumes have grown for most people, the visual benefit of the "Skim-and-Leave" tactic is failing. 2014 research conducted by the Radicati Group shows up to 180 email messages are sent per day, per user, a number confirmed by other studies.

Some get twice that number. Further, the report by the Harris Interactive poll mentioned earlier showed that the average person can bear only 50 emails per day. This number only increases with the number of other electronic devices we use. It's not surprising that the Skim-and-Leave strategy has stopped working.

Unfortunately, the Marshas of the workplace often don't see the bigger picture, and (as Sam mentioned) the part their habits, practices and rituals play in causing their dilemma. Instead, when they open their email each morning to see tens of thousands of old inbox items, they blame their lack of discipline. Or motivation. Or their workplace. Or their culture. Or their tendency to procrastinate.

Why Emptying is So Very, Very Hard

Seeing the overwhelmed email inbox problem as one of Emptying sheds a different light.

Emptying is all about moving time demands from capture points. To recap, once time demands are created, they are immediately stored in manual or automatic Capture Points. At some point in the future, they are Emptied, which means removing the time demand from a Capture Point.

Now however, let's add another characteristic to the

definition of Capture Points; they are intended to be places of temporary storage only, making them a place of triage.

The term "triage" originated in the medical field and is derived from the French verb "trier", meaning to separate, sift or select. Wikipedia defines it as the process of determining the priority of patients' treatments based on the severity of their condition. While incoming patients to a hospital wait for the process to be completed, they are typically placed in a specially designated area, often in an emergency room. Once they have been triaged, they are assigned to different areas of the facility, leaving the waiting space free for new patients.

Another point of triage used to "separate, sift or select" includes the everyday, mundane kitchen sink. In the modern household, it acts as a place to "capture" dirty dishes, cutlery, flatware, glasses and bits of food. Kitchen sinks aren't designed for permanent storage: that's the job of a cupboard.

Here are a few more examples of points of triage:
- A loading dock in a factory
- An office reception area
- A postal mailbox

These are all temporary staging areas that serve the same purpose. Emergency room nurses, homemakers, receptionists, dock workers and postmen will all tell you if asked: these points of triage are not meant to be infinitely large. They are controlled zones that are designed to handle a certain, small volume of incoming items or people while they are being processed. When they become overloaded with too many items, it becomes impossible to use them for their intended function.

Industrial engineers in factories have been studying the operation of these points of triage for decades, where they are known as "buffers": temporary storage areas whose purpose is to smooth out the flow of inventory between stations in an assembly line.

Unfortunately, we were never taught to treat our email inbox like a point of triage or a kitchen sink. Once again, most of us are self-taught... to our detriment, in this instance.

Instead, we use the Skim-and-Leave strategy. Imagine

what it would be like if you applied that strategy to your good, old-fashioned paper mail.

It would mean walking out to your postal mailbox, skimming through all the items, opening a few envelopes, and placing the contents in our pocket. Then, imagine putting all the rest of the unopened mail, plus the empty envelopes, back in the mailbox to deal with "later." As an occasional practice, this might work. If it becomes a habit, you're likely to receive an angry note from the mailman.

Now imagine employing a "Skim-and-Leave" strategy with your kitchen sink, habitually washing a single dish or two to use now, while leaving the rest for later. This doesn't work, either, as parents of teenagers who try this technique can testify.

With regard to email, however, we lack the visual cues inherent in a kitchen sink or postal mailbox. Unless your company has an aggressive IT department, you probably don't have a clue how close you are to the digital limits of your email inbox. In fact, as time progresses, these limits are diminishing due to the rapid decrease in the price of storage space and the rise of cloud computing. The impending availability of infinite storage space makes it easier for us to abuse our inboxes by treating them as permanent places of storage rather than temporary points of triage.

Unfortunately, there is another cost to this unwitting decision.

Case: Elaine

Like a few people who attend my workshops, Elaine has tens of thousands of messages in her inbox: over 40,000. What does this backlog represent?

She never intended this to happen - it's the natural result of the Skim-and-Leave strategy she has used for many years. Instead, she is highly motivated with good intentions, but it doesn't matter. Her inbox still tells a sorry tale.

When incoming email arrives, she skims it quickly, deciding whether or not to delete it as Spam. As a result, none of the messages are sales pitches for Viagra or get-rich-quick schemes. The opposite is true: almost all of them represent real time demands. She knows this from glancing at each one briefly before moving on, deciding that there's a time demand in there somewhere, but she can't get to it right away. So, she leaves the email message in her inbox, "where she can see it," until later.

This glance is not as simple as it seems, however: it converts a potential time demand (in unread email) into an actual one. It adds a small obligation to her cognitive load.

Each of the 40,000 messages she has skimmed and left behind represents at least one new actual time demand. In other words, she has promised herself the same thing 40,000 times: "I'll get back to this later."

If you are thinking that this takes tremendous energy, then you are right. David Rock, a brain scientist, describes in detail the high cost we pay by trying to divide our attention between multiple obligations. Every time she checks her inbox for new messages, she's confronted by the sheer volume of incomplete promises she's made, plus the likely consequences of not addressing those that are (or have become) important and urgent while she has been putting them off.

Further, each of these time demands represents a decision she must make, plus a level of urgency and importance she must determine. According to Rock, "prioritizing is one of the brain's most energy-hungry processes." There are five functions used in prioritizing: understanding, deciding, recalling, memorizing and inhibiting. "They use the prefrontal cortex intensively and require significant resources to operate." Unlike the basal ganglia, which is an older part of our brain that controls our habits and requires little energy, the prefrontal cortex is younger, in evolutionary terms. It "chews up metabolic fuel such as glucose and oxygen." He recommends, therefore, that we do this activity early in the morning before others that take up too much attention.

"Picturing something you have not yet seen [...] (takes) a lot of energy and effort," writes Rock, making prioritizing "the triathlon of mental tasks."

That's the reason why, to Elaine, the dreaded routine of cleaning a toilet looks easy in comparison.

To solve the problem (while keeping her job), Elaine

needs to confront the challenge head-on by upgrading her skill at Emptying. In her case, she must learn to move emails that contain time demands from her receiving inbox after reading them the first time - touching them only once. In other words, when she Empties her inbox, she needs to act on each message using the fundamentals introduced earlier: Tossing, Acting Now, Storing, Listing or Scheduling.

There's a big difference, for example, between moving all her messages into a temporary folder and leaving them in her inbox. (Gmail users who are skilled at tagging can achieve the same effect by applying different views).

While Elaine's particular problem centers around her email inbox, the solution – improving her Emptying – applies to all her Capture Points, each of which must be treated like a point of triage. Her Peace of Mind depends on her ability to Empty.

Briefly Revisiting the Advanced Model

The Advanced Model (based on seeing a time demand with certain biological properties) offers a different perspective.

To recap, in this model, time demands are psychological objects that spend their lifetime in our minds. During that time, their nature changes in response to our actions. From this point of view, Emptying isn't about removing time demands from Capture Points – it's about changing the status of a time demand when we take a particular action.

Bluma Zeigarnik, the Russian researcher mentioned in Chapter 4, found that incomplete tasks stay in our minds longer and with greater presence than completed tasks. Her work was recently extended by Florida State University researchers Roy Baumeister and Ed Masicampo, who discovered that the subconscious mind appears to "ping" the conscious mind continuously – a nagging reminder of the fact that a task remains incomplete.

This incessant pinging, and the nagging feeling that accompanies it, is called the Zeigarnik Effect.

Therefore, from the moment a time demand is created, it does more than simply sit in our minds waiting for something to happen – instead, it enters the subconscious where it distracts or bothers us until it's complete. Its very existence adds to our cognitive load.

Also, there are limits to the number of time demands we can maintain in our conscious minds and the resources we can devote to processing them in large numbers. Rock explains that our prefrontal cortex can only hold a limited amount of information. Most people have heard the rule of thumb discovered by cognitive scientist George Miller in 1956 – the mind can hold only seven chunks of information at a time, plus or minus two. New research by Nelson Cowan in 2010 paints a dimmer, updated picture – the number should be reduced to between three and five.

When these chunks happen to be time demands, the cognitive load increases dramatically. As we discovered earlier, time demands are often formed from multiple bits of information. Making decisions about how, when and where to act on each one isn't easy, even when they are completely distinct. (Most time demands do, in fact, compete with each other for limited space in the prefrontal cortex, which means that they are not completely independent.)

Rock refers to a field of study that focuses on these issues: "Relational complexity studies show [...] that the fewer variables you have to hold in mind, the more effective you are at making decisions." Consider the task of making 40,000 inter-related decisions, which is the problem Elaine faces. She's burdened by the effect they have in her subconscious as well as the limits of the human mind, which can process them only in small numbers. She experiences a bottleneck that increases her cognitive load, increasing her stress.

However, Baumeister and Masicampo's research also paints a hopeful picture. As I summarized earlier, their research shows that when concrete plans are missing for a task's completion, it "sometimes calls on the conscious mind to help by formulating plans." They also unveiled an important finding: that the "pinging" stops when incomplete tasks are "safely staged" for later action. According to them, "Thoughts of an incomplete goal will not interfere with current concerns so long as a plan has been made to see the goal through later on."

This is great news for Elaine – permanently removing the burden improves her ability to manage her email and the time demands they represent.

However, she might ask, "What does it mean to "safely stage" a time demand and to have a plan to see the goal through?" As an example, let's use one of Elaine's personal projects: her commitment to visit Spain on vacation in the next twelve months. Here are six different sequences of events that might take place right after the time demand is created.

Sequence #1: She commits the time demand to memory. At some point later, it gets reactivated by a random trigger – she sees an advertisement from a Spanish hotel, which leads her to call a travel agent. This is her default habit – an unsafe method to stage a time demand that keeps the Zeigarnik Effect alive and sets off the unconscious pinging that tends to drive her crazy.

Sequence #2: She mentally tags the time demand with high importance but low urgency. She hopes that when she later sees an email message from her travel agent, she'll be reminded of the action it represents. This method isn't a safe way to stage a time demand.

Neither of these two sequences is satisfying. They increase the Zeigarnik Effect. By contrast, here are four sequences that stop it.

Sequence #3: A friend happens to tell her that his recent trip to Spain was a waste of time. She changes her mind and decides to stay home instead.

Sequence #4: She sets an appointment in her calendar to call her travel agent about specials for travel to Spain. At the appointed day and time, she makes the call.

Sequence #5: She adds the task to her to-do list, focusing on the action she needs to take first.

Sequence #6: She creates a reminder on a smartphone app that beeps, vibrates and flashes lights at the appropriate time – a cue she can't possibly miss.

Of course, Elaine is not unique. The choices she has are examples of the ones we all have when we Empty. There is a structure behind her actions that none of us can avoid.

Emptying has the power to enhance our Peace of Mind when it's done well. It's an opportunity to bring our commitments, knowledge and experience to the forefront to help make critical decisions about our future.

How well you Empty, therefore, determines and shapes the life of a time demand as well as whether or not the action it calls for is ever taken. That has implications for the accomplishment for every single goal you set in life, including the commitment you have to work, relationships, family and health. You consciously create every single aspect of your life using time demands.

Imagine the strain Marsha and Elaine are under as they go through each day with the added pressure of the Zeigarnik Effect, symbolized by multiple blue steno pads and an overflowing inbox. If they could only upgrade their skill at Emptying, it could make a tremendous difference, opening up new possibilities for their lives.

However, the Simple Model is easier to work with, so let's return to it to describe the extreme behaviors used to Empty time demands.

Extreme Methods of Emptying - Wally and Greta

In my search for extreme Emptying behaviors through the lens of the Simple Model, I have found highly competent professionals who empty religiously and regularly. Like Greta Green, after Emptying, they leave their Capture Points void: containing nothing, and ready to receive new time demands.

Unfortunately, the average company has many more Wallys than Gretas. People like Wally rely on serendipity to pull up time demands from the recesses of their memories, which operate as their main Capture Point. For example, when Wally is asleep at night, all of a sudden, he sometimes experiences a "Pop-in" causing him to jump out of sleep. He's just remembered that he needed to send the Smith Report yesterday, in time for the executive meeting this morning. It's a random and stressful way of Emptying.

Wally's mind, his main Capture Point, is full of unprocessed time demands that, in keeping with the Zeigarnik Effect, keep disturbing him with continuous pings.

As he makes his way through the typical day, visual cues remind him, one after the other, of time demands he's stored in his memory. Collectively, the overall result is a feeling of being overwhelmed and burdened.

Occasionally, Wally sets up time during weekends to perform what he calls a Kamikaze Attack. He'll arrive on Saturday morning when it's quiet and try to catch up on unprocessed time demands in a single day: deleting, throwing away and organizing his office and electronic messages so that it looks pristine by Monday morning. Unfortunately, as I mentioned before, even though he's cleared a backlog, his habits, practices and rituals remain unchanged. That's a guarantee he will just go back to creating the same mess he had before.

Most professionals fall between the two extremes represented by Wally and Greta.

Greta places a high priority on the activity of Emptying and sets dedicated time aside each day to ensure the task is done well. This helps, given that it's probably the most significant and challenging fundamental. Email isn't a problem, and if it ever becomes one, she knows to re-examine her methods for Emptying in order to keep up.

The Zeroed Inbox

Greta has accomplished what's popularly called Inbox Zero – a particular goal of email management that many experts see as the highest standard. Merlin Mann coined the term, and it refers to the practice of Emptying your email inbox periodically so that it has zero contents. (Some get confused, however, believing that it means they should somehow keep their inbox empty at all times. That's a goal Greta has specifically eschewed).

To bring her inbox to Zero on a regular basis, she has learned to avoid performing the following habits:

- Skimming her inbox for important items and leaving the less important items for "later" (Skim-and-Leave)

- Checking her email inbox and other inboxes randomly, whenever she has a spare moment.

- Re-checking them again whenever she feels anxious, thinking she might miss something important

- Activating pop-ups, buzzes, flashing lights, dings, rings or envelope-shaped icons to create an interruption whenever she gets an email, tweet, Facebook message, SMS, etc.

She's unique but not alone. Greta is a far distance from the average professional, who is said to check email 9 times per hour and spend 28% of the day sending and reading messages. Perversely, many companies unwittingly reward employees who are "responsive," encouraging these numbers to increase by promoting the idea that the better an employee is, the faster they respond to email. In a bizarre reversal of our findings, some managers castigate employees who don't reply quickly enough, telling them, "You need better time management skills."

Greta has even gone a step further: she has also turned off automatic downloads of email so that she receives messages from the server only when she's ready to do her Emptying. In this way, she has full control of the activity and has eliminated the temptation to take a quick peek.

Mark Horstman at ManagerTools.com is a strong advocate of this approach. When I interviewed him for a recent podcast, he emphasized the fact that the most productive executives use this technique, based on his experience coaching thousands of managers. One of the principles they understand intuitively is that an email message is only a carrier of potential time demands, and a lot of the emails they receive don't include a single one.

Therefore, to ensure that they spend as little time as possible Emptying, they set sharp time limits to this activity. Following "Hortsman's Rule" (the idea that the time needed to do a task shrinks to fit the time allotted) helps them get all their Emptying done more efficiently, because they have made the commitment to complete the task in a short time frame, such as 30 minutes per day.

Unfortunately, even effective executives are often unaware of their own methods. Therefore, they don't properly pass them onto other employees who may run into problems aiming for the Inbox Zero goal. For example, if an employee is the only person in a department who Empties on a schedule and company culture favors fast email response times, he/she could get into trouble. My experience tells me that this disconnect between employees happens often. More often than not, however, the entire company from top to bottom is enmeshed in unconscious practices that kill productivity; we will explore this in the chapter on corporate productivity near the end of this book.

Effective executives like Greta know that there's more to improving one's productivity than learning a single new skill. She knows something Wally doesn't: the Zeroed Inbox is not the final answer. New practices and technologies constantly present exciting new possibilities and challenges (we'll discuss that when we look at new tools). As a result, she remains open to new methods that will help her deal with even higher volumes of email.

For example, Greta is always hunting for new apps that will help her consolidate all her email inboxes and every other Capture Point (her dream). She aims to shorten the time she needs to Empty, which would make her job just a little bit easier.

Emptying to Create a Plan

When Greta sits down to do her Emptying with all her Capture Points nearby, she does it in an uninterrupted, highly focused manner, as David Rock recommends.

She also makes sure not to end the session without achieving the Peace of Mind that comes from having a feasible plan for the day. According to researchers like Brigitte Claessens and Peter Gollwitzer, her success depends on that objective. Planning out when and where you intend to perform a particular action dramatically increases the chances that you will actually do it. It uses the idea of an implementation intention to its fullest.

The research is clear: daily planning produces better results. A study of college students over a four-year period, performed by Bruce Britton and Abraham Tesser, showed that the habit of short-term planning was a better predictor of GPAs than pre-college SAT scores. They looked at the ways students use daily lists, plans, schedules and goals. (Their study is one of the few to span the entire student cycle from freshman to senior years.)

Masicampo and Baumeister also concluded that "commitment to specific plans can free cognitive resources for other pursuits. In our studies, the amount of thoughts and attention that unfulfilled goals demanded was drastically reduced once a plan was made, and performance on other, irrelevant tasks was significantly improved."

***

There is an opposing school of thought, however. Its members argue that plans written up in the form of a daily schedule are a waste of time because things frequently change. Instead, the argument goes, only appointments with other people deserve to be in a schedule. The objective is to have no precise plans or knowledge of what you are going to do next unless other people are involved, instead leaving your decision until the last moment to provide maximum flexibility.

To you, the learner, this reasoning may have some merit, but when placed alongside the results I shared earlier, it can be confusing.

The fact is, this technique does work, researchers say... but only for professionals who don't experience time constraints and therefore don't need to plan ahead. The lack of constraints allows them to enter each day with an open mind, see what it might bring and respond accordingly. Although it means making multiple decisions each day about what to do next, they have the time and the freedom to do so. Some writers, including David Allen, author of *Getting Things Done*, seem to promote this approach: they recommend against making detailed daily plans for activities that don't involve others.

Research shows that people who resist detailed planning are likely to rate highly on the Perceiving (P) dimension of the Myers-Briggs Type Indicator (MBTI.) This personality attribute (extreme or moderate) represents over 40% of the population of the United States. It's defined as the preference to delay final decisions, keep options open and go with the flow.

In unrelated research, Stanford professor Philip Zimbardo has defined a different attribute altogether: "present time perspective." People with this trait believe that today's behaviors have a far lesser effect on future results than actions that take place closer to the result itself. As a result, they don't work well with deadlines, believing that it's just not necessary to do a lot of planning for the future, because even the best-made plans are subject to dramatic change. They like to keep things fluid and make room for spontaneous impulsive action at all times. This group looks a lot like the group of those who report a Perceiving/P preference in Myers Briggs as well as those who promote David Allen's approach.

Zimbardo contrasts that group with people who hold a "future time perspective." They believe today's actions are critical to fulfilling tomorrow's goals. Structured planners who often achieve complex results, they are highly goal oriented. As you might expect, they view those who hold a personal time perspective as lazy and undisciplined. By the same token, those who have a present time perspective see their counterparts as controlling, demanding and uptight.

Which kind of approach better describes yours? Are you accomplishing the Peace of Mind that you want with it?

Professionals with the future time perspective are more likely to be found at the higher levels of organizations than their counterparts. If you plan to rise in the corporate ladder, expect to demonstrate more of these behaviors. Here's a great resource you can use – the Time Intelligence Report, located at http://timeintelligence.co.uk/ to test your strength in each perspective.

If you are thinking of becoming more planning-oriented, I think the place to start is examining the habits you use right now. Do you wake up each day asking yourself, "What am I doing today, and when do I plan to do it?" In that moment, do you naturally respond by creating a mental plan of action for the day?

If so, I recommend that when you Empty, you take that plan and put it on paper or in digital form.

My recommendation comes from a simple observation: it's stressful to walk around with a plan in your head – a mental schedule. It's what Wally would do, and it leads to him feeling overwhelmed. When, for example, you have a day filled with surprises or emergencies, it's far easier to re-juggle your schedule in a visual digital or paper format that exists outside rather than purely inside your head. We'll explore this fact and the research behind it when we examine Scheduling.

On the other hand, if you don't experience time constraints, you may be:
- Artistic or highly creative.
- On vacation.
- Retired.

Whatever the case, it might work well for you to continue with the "present time perspective," ignoring the criticism of those who argue that their way is better. Remember, your time-based productivity system exists to serve your needs, not those of anyone else. When you complete your evaluation of the 11 Fundamentals, you'll take a look at the entire picture and decide the best way to move forward.

Evaluating Your Skills

Here's the Cheat-Sheet for Emptying, which comprises three core skills. Go ahead and evaluate your skills to discover your current belt level.

Figure 8-1

Emptying Cheat-Sheet

Behavior	White	Yellow	Orange	Green
Capture points are emptied on a schedule	Rarely or never ☐	Sometimes ☐	Often ☐	Always ☐
Capture points are periodically completely emptied	Rarely or never ☐	Sometimes ☐	Often ☐	Always ☐
Holds Kamikaze, cleanup weekends	■	Often ☐	Sometimes ☐	Never ☐

Current Belt ☐ ☐ ☐ ☐

Use the Planning Sheet from the previous chapter to create some new target behaviors for yourself.

In the next three chapters, we'll look at the first of the five options you can exercise when you Empty —

Tossing, Acting Now and Storing. This is a bit of a break from the heavy lifting we just did!

Remember and Share

If you receive average volumes of email, treat your inbox like a kitchen sink – only a temporary place of storage.

Treat your email inbox as a triage zone, and you'll never become overloaded by too many messages.

Don't walk around each day with a mental plan – take it out and put onto paper or into digital form.

Your system for time-based productivity needs to serve your needs, not anyone else's.

I just learned I have a present time perspective – I love freedom and flexibility!

I just learned I have a future time perspective – I love structured goals and tight schedules!

Inbox Zero doesn't mean that your inbox is always empty – just sometimes.

Empty your inbox when you process email and see your productivity and peace of mind soar.

Have your email practices kept up with the increased volume of messages you receive each day?

Lots of time-based productivity practices work well but don't scale. Be wary.

When you safely stage a time demand for later completion, you stop the Zeigarnik Effect from taking place, helping ensure peace of mind.

A recipe for stress: leaving time demands unsafely staged so that their incompletion can nag, ping and bother you. #zeigarnikeffect

Are you someone with a future time perspective or a present time perspective? Knowing makes all the difference.

Using your email inbox as a To-Do list works only for small numbers, according to the research.

You consciously create every single aspect of your life using time demands.

Chapter 9. Tossing – Lightening Your Load

(In which you learn that if you want to manage time demands in large numbers, you need to rid yourself of the dead ones!)

Judith Kolberg might not be a household name, but among consultants who work with chronically disorganized people, she's a lifesaver. She's known among Professional Organizers as the expert's expert, someone who helped identify and define what is popularly called "hoarding." She literally wrote the book on the topic – *Conquering Chronic Disorganization.*

Like most outsiders to the profession, when I first met her I had no idea who she was, as I explained in the foreword to her latest book. As a featured speaker at the annual conference of the Institute for Challenging Disorganization in Chicago, I was far away from my home in Kingston. She introduced herself, and we began talking casually, but the conversation quickly became serious as she threw one tough question after another, making me forget all about the finger food I had been eyeing after a long day on the road.

Kolberg discovered that people become chronically disorganized because they "think, learn and organize in ways that are unconventional." As a result, they end up in trouble, because the only tools available to them are conventional ones that don't serve their needs. It might seem easy for them to just throw a bunch of stuff away, but that turns out not to be the case.

Recently, she has made a pivot. In her 2013 book, *Getting Organized in the Era of Endless,* she focuses on dealing with the overwhelming amount of information we face each day. She describes the need to "filter and purge," defining those as critical skills for navigating the modern world. She dreams of a day when every piece of data can be tagged with an expiration date, when it would either prompt us to get rid of it, or better, delete itself.

The ultimate expression of this idea is a concept she mentioned in our 2013 podcast: setting up a digital "will" that prescribes the safe disposal of important information in detail.

Her work is potentially groundbreaking, breathtaking, and firmly built on the fundamental we will discuss in this chapter: Tossing. Research shows that some people keep a lot of stuff around because it helps boost their prospective memory – each item reminds them of something they need to do in the future. If this sounds familiar, it should. From our point of view, they are creating reminders of time demands in a way that doesn't scale, returning us to the "Problem of More" explained by Robert Sutton. We also used the example of "leaving-something-by-the-door" as a useful memory jogger that works with a small number of time demands.

***

Let's do a quick recap: time demands flow into Capture Points, where they wait until you are ready to Empty them. Later, when you actually sit down to do so, you choose between the practices, applying them one at a time to each time demand: Tossing, Acting Now, Storing, Listing and Scheduling.

Tossing means disposing of a potential or actual time demand from wherever it may be in your system. It is not restricted to the moments when you are Emptying, as you can engage in the practice at any time. Here are some examples:

- As you browse the Internet, you discover a new exercise fad. After reading a short article on fitness regimes, you form a time demand as you write on a paper pad: "Start Technique X exercise program." The following morning, when you Empty, you arrive at this particular time demand, which now appears to be a bunch of hype. You cross out the item and move on without a further thought.

- An incoming email mentions Viagra in the subject line. While you know, in theory, that each email message represents a potential time demand, you delete it immediately without reading it.

- You check your calendar for open dates for a conference call, coming across a meeting you no longer have to attend because of a recent reassignment to another department. You get rid of it and all related reminders.

- You need to update your list of projects: the recent

technology initiative is going to be cancelled after all. You cancel the project entirely and remove all traces of it from the list.

- A brief glance at your Android's address book reveals a number of stale contacts – people you intended to contact "one day." An hour later, it's all cleaned up, courtesy of your delete key.

In each of the above examples, you are Tossing: revoking any commitment you previously made to a time demand, actual or potential.

When Greta Green does her Tossing, the result is clear: no dead time demands are sitting around in her system to affect her Peace of Mind. Far from feeling guilty, she feels light, as if she's not wasting any space, time or attention. She's ruthless, understanding that each decision to "keep something around just in case" comes at a small cost that accumulates mental clutter.

Unfortunately, Wally White is plagued by stuff he's trying to keep in mind, leading him to feel as if he's burdened. The stuff he does have written down or digitized is mostly stale, as he's probably tried a number of diaries, devices and online technologies, mastering none. Therefore, they sit unused, storing time demands he actually still needs. For example, 15 Post-It notes surround his monitor. Five or so have actually fallen off and lay lost behind his keyboard. Only two are still valid: the dates for the others have long passed.

He also has an iPad he no longer uses for anything except movies, games and Facebook – but he does have a few project drafts sitting on there somewhere... he's not quite sure where.

In the last chapter, we met Marsha and Elaine, who maintain multiple steno pads and overflowing inboxes respectively. Both have abused their Capture Points for so long, their pads and inboxes are now filled with dead time demands, obscuring ones that are very much alive.

In extreme cases, Wally might be a hoarder, using physical objects to remind himself of time demands. This clutters his life and affects his emotional well-being, according to the Center For Emotional Health, which reports: "Individuals with compulsive hoarding tend to report difficulties in remembering the location of items and like to have items visible or have visual reminders. They often worry they might forget something and thus hold on to items as reminders. They have difficulty in utilizing broad categorization skills and find it difficult to make decisions regarding the disposition of possessions."

Also, new brain science research shows that hoarders aren't just lazy: their brains work a little differently, as fMRI readings taken from the anterior cingulate cortex and the anterior insula show.

***

The principle of getting rid of time demands that add no further value is not new. It's exemplified by the principles of lean manufacturing, in which waste removal is essential. Greta's system is "lean" and doesn't waste her energy or resources. By contrast, Wally's poorly managed system is an impediment that makes it harder for him to get anything done. He's often burdened just by glancing at old time demands, which clutter a number of his spaces.

The truth is, the only time he Tosses is when he forgets or suffers a catastrophe: his computer crashes or he loses his appointment diary. He has even flirted with the idea of declaring email bankruptcy by deleting his entire email inbox in order to start all over again. Whoever wants him can call him... an extreme and ineffective strategy.

When Wally does work up the courage to clean up obsolete time demands, compared to Greta, he does so reluctantly and slowly. He fears regretting the decision to delete, even if he logically understands that a backup exists somewhere. Getting rid of time demands on purpose is quite scary for him, but each short delay allows an unneeded time demand to stay around a little longer than it should, adding to the clutter.

Perhaps he should start by saying "No" more often. It would help, but as a White Belt, he doesn't possess a clear enough picture of his current time demands to make an informed, fact-based decision to turn down a new task. Therefore, he simply says, "Yes," taking the path of least resistance. (We'll look at this particular problem again in the chapter on Scheduling.)

Evaluating Your Skills

Here's the Cheat-Sheet for Tossing, which comprises three core skills. Go ahead and evaluate yourself to discover your current belt level.

Tossing Cheat-Sheet

Behavior	White	Yellow	Orange	Green
Tossing occurs when forgetting or losing	Often ☐	Sometimes ☐	Rarely ☐	Never ☐
Tossing occurs frequently, especially during Emptying	Rarely or never ☐	Sometimes ☐	Often ☐	Always ☐
Items are tossed immediately, without delay	Rarely or never ☐	Sometimes ☐	Often ☐	Always ☐

Current Belt ☐	☐	☐	☐

Figure 9-1

When you click over to the next chapter, we'll examine the choice to take immediate action while you are in the middle of doing your Emptying. This is an emotionally satisfying practice, but stopping your Emptying to pursue another task altogether represents a clear danger to your Peace of Mind.

Remember and Share

Sometimes, it takes courage to willfully abandon a time demand.

Revoking a time demand can be the start of a new freedom.

Once you capture a time demand, you don't have to complete it – just delete and move on.

Many people are hoarders because they keep too much stuff around as reminders of their to-dos.

At some point, physical reminders don't work and must be replaced by digital reminders. Are you there yet?

Aggressively get rid of dead time demands and feel your load lighten.

There's a limit to how much stuff you can keep around to remind you to engage in time demands.

Chapter 10. Acting Now – Gaining Immediate Relief While Avoiding a Dangerous Detour

(In which you learn that it feels great to complete a time demand right away, but there's a huge downside to doing so.)

"You're just not focused enough."

Erin's eyes blinked in disbelief. She stared hard at the table, unable to look at her boss, Martha. The swelling of her eyes told her she needed to get out of there fast, but that wouldn't work. This was, after all, a formal performance review session. How could she end up crying in her first-ever feedback session at Syscon Technologies?

A flushing heat spread up her neck anyway. Sad and disappointed. She had worked so hard over the year and hadn't expected such a low rating: "Sometimes Meets Expectations."

Suddenly, she realized that Martha was quiet. She looked up to see her offer a tissue and a caring expression.

"Good news is you can definitely turn this around. It's not a terminal situation!" Erin nodded, dabbing her eyes.

"I think you have just been too focused on making everyone happy, answering every call and responding to every emergency. But the problem is, you aren't the unit's Chief Firefigther. Your job is to design new software, not put out every fire." Erin stared.

"You somehow have got to find a way to follow your own agenda each day, not the one everyone else is pushing. Without a good plan, all you'll do is chase issues. You'll never accomplish anything long term. It's the reason you haven't taken those courses you promised to take."

"But," Erin started, "I've just been too busy."

With a conclusive tone, Martha paused for a beat before replying, "Right."

"I can't even get through email without having to fix some problem that pops up. It's not fair." As the words came out, she wished she could take them back. *Now she'll think I'm being some kind of brat*, she thought. Fortunately, Martha gave her a moment.

"Sorry, I didn't mean that. This is my responsibility. I know that. I just don't know what to do differently."

Martha pulled out a paper pad and a pencil then suggested: "Let's start by looking at what you can change about the way you interrupt yourself while doing your email." She emphasized the words "you," "yourself" and "your," causing Erin to straighten up in her chair. This was not the moment to play the victim.

***

It's an ever-present temptation for professionals... while you are Emptying, you recognize the opportunity for a "quick win." Why not spend a few minutes to immediately complete an easy time demand, rather than wait until later? How can it hurt? After all, you intend to resume Emptying in the next few minutes...

Unknown to most of us, located in our brains is an additional benefit from taking immediate action. The latest neuroscientific research shows that dopamine operates a bit differently than we thought. Up until now, the hormone was thought to be linked only to pleasure seeking. The truth is more subtle: dopamine is released in anticipation of reward — before the reward is actually received. It encourages us to search for and acquire the benefit of completing an action immediately. For example, when you are in the middle of an intense round of Emptying, the rush it provides appears to be the perfect escape from the heavy cognitive load you have been carrying.

Erin has developed the habit of consistently interrupting her Emptying in order to address an immediate issue. The trigger might be an email, a text message or a tweet. Sometimes, the issue isn't even urgent — it could be interesting, titillating, or intriguing — but acting on it right away satisfies her curiosity or gives her a good feeling. In each case, she responds by abandoning her Emptying to complete a time demand.

At the end of the day, however, she can't understand why she's so tired. She's been busy – she entirely skipped lunch – but it still feels as if she got almost nothing done. It took the conversation with Martha to bell the cat. Now she knows the truth: other people in the office are more productive, and now it seems it's because she's constantly jumping from one thing to another without completing anything. Her boss is about to teach her that acting while Emptying is a dangerous habit.

Wally White is just like Erin, but he represents an even more extreme case. He has tremendous energy, which he applies to a number of different tasks. However, he rarely Zeroes his Inboxes, because he's likely to stop Emptying in mid-stream to complete one time demand, and then another, and then another. When he finally returns to his Capture Points the following day, he finds himself in trouble — there is something important he missed seeing yesterday because it lay buried in an email message he didn't read. Because this happens to him repeatedly, there always seems to be something lurking in the shadows – a time demand he didn't quite get to before that becomes today's fresh, new emergency.[9]

What Wally and Erin don't know is that it's fine to interrupt Emptying in order to take the occasional immediate action, but Sutton's "Problem of More" also limits this practice. Giving in to the impulse to Act Now too frequently ruins their productivity because it doesn't scale: it works only in small doses.

Greta Green is, of course, subject to the same brain chemistry as everyone else, but she's found ways to work around it. Not too long ago, she used to be just like Wally and Erin, but now she uses upgraded methods. When she sits down to Empty a Capture Point, she sees the practice as a critical planning activity that she will not interrupt, except for an outstanding opportunity or emergency. In these moments, it's better to delay the gratification that comes from completing the task right away until she's finished Emptying all the way to zero.

However, she does "Act Now" at least once during every session of Emptying, taking advantage of an opportunity. It means she can take a few minutes to complete a time demand. For example, she receives a voicemail from her Mom asking for Aunt Milly's phone number. She takes action at once, immediately returning her phone call. During the call, she's hyper-aware that she's taken a quick break from Emptying – an activity she must finish to have a successful day.

This hyper-awareness sets her apart from Wally and Erin. She treats Emptying like a special activity. By contrast, Wally and Erin don't see its importance: it just feels like more stuff to do.

This is why it's a best practice to limit the duration of this particular kind of detour. Several authors, including David Allen (*Getting Things Done*), and consultants, like Dean Acheson, recommend that the time be brief and sharply limited. I use and recommend a five-minute limit, but you should set and use a standard that works for you.

Setting and sticking to a limit helps emphasize the fact that Emptying is far more important than Acting Now, unless there is an emergency. Our tendency to underestimate the time it takes to Act Now on a task is vast. It causes us to lose the script as well as awareness of our priorities. Keeping in mind the fact that you're taking a short and quick detour makes all the difference.

When you are Acting Now, it can be useful to set a timer to make sure you don't fall into this trap.

Evaluating Your Skills

Take a moment to rate yourself in the skill of Acting Now before you make some plans to upgrade each line item.

Figure 10-1

Acting Now Cheat-Sheet

Behavior	White	Yellow	Orange	Green
Think carefully before Acting Now	Rarely or never ☐	Sometimes ☐	Often ☐	Always ☐
Take less than 5 minutes while Acting Now	Rarely or never ☐	Sometimes ☐	Often ☐	Regularly ☐
Return to Emptying after Acting Now	Rarely or haphazardly ☐	Sometimes ☐	Often ☐	Always ☐
Stop to reconsider if 5 minute limit is exceeded	Rarely or haphazardly ☐	Sometimes ☐	Often ☐	Always ☐

Current Belt ☐   ☐   ☐   ☐

Now, use the Planning Sheet to chart a path from your current level of skills to the next.

In the next chapter, we'll look at the skills required to store important information for later use and make it available for time demand execution.

Remember and Share

Emptying is so important, it should only rarely be interrupted.

Within reason, limit Acting Now.

Remember to return to Emptying after your detour to Act Now.

Don't try to prevent Acting Now – it's a useful way to get stuff done.

Chapter 11. Storing – A Persistent and Increasing Challenge

(In which you learn that storing data required to complete time demands is essential in today's world of information overload).

As Wally White sits at his desk after lunch, he opens his email program. Looking at three important messages with attachments, he mutters under his breath, "At least they didn't send me more paper."

He glances over at the credenza of unsorted paper documents that fill both horizontal sliding drawers, forming an untidy, two-foot-high pile.

One attachment is the Johnson Project report, which had just arrived. It wouldn't be needed for several weeks. He weighs his options. Should he print it out like the old-fashioned guy in the office who prints everything? He quickly glances at his stack of documents corrects himself: *Bad idea. Global warming.*

Looking for options, he clicks around his computer's file directory: *Which folder should I use? Perhaps if it's on my desktop, I can find it later.* Closing all his open windows, he reveals his Windows Desktop – a cluttered mess of over 200 files, shortcuts and folders. "Forget it," he mutters.

After another pause, he thinks, *Okay – my smartphone.* Keeping the email unread could work... he has only 700 email messages in his inbox, which is far fewer than the worst people he has worked with. That way, he felt sure he'd have it available at the right time.

Several weeks later, he's in a meeting with Zana, the manager of the Johnson Project. She asks: "Wally, can you pull up that report? Do you have it here?"

"No," he replies quickly, "it's on my credenza. Give me a minute."

In no time, he's back in his office digging through the pile, which has now grown a bit taller. Something doesn't feel right, however. He's sure that he promised himself to stop using that pile until he'd gone through it... but on the very top is an item he put there yesterday. Confusing.

He checks his computer and cloud account, but no luck – there's no trace of the file.

Returning to the meeting a full 30 minutes later, he gives her a glance, shrugging his shoulders. She barely looks at him. A few minutes after he left, she had called a break and pulled the file down from the cloud.

The following day, he discovers the file attached to the original email. Wincing, he thinks, *That's all she'll remember when she does my 360 evaluation next week.*

***

If you have never suffered a similar problem, it might be only a matter of time. Many professionals face the challenge of storing information for later retrieval while simultaneously mastering evolving technologies whose use isn't optional.

Several months ago, I joined a project that used the popular program Dropbox. I'd had an account that I hadn't really used until then, but as I sat in a conference call, I found myself agreeing to upload and retrieve a number of different files. Once the meeting ended, I quickly visited the website to conduct an immediate crash course. A few words and videos later, I understood.

Perhaps you have already noticed: the process you use to store and retrieve information is fast becoming a critical skill.

Let's quickly recap what happens when the need to store critical data is triggered. When a time demand is emptied from a Capture Point, it's sometimes obvious: there's no way to complete the action in the future without having some piece of data available at the right time. It might take the form of a phone number, email address, password, necessary fact or mp3 file. Its availability depends on your proficiency at storing and retrieving what you need, when you need it.

In past decades, much of this data was stored on paper, but in today's world, technology offers a bewildering number of options.

Wally's dilemma is common. How do you store information related to a time demand so it's easy to access when needed? The answer seems to change with each innovation. Any specific recommendation I make in this book, for instance, could become obsolete in just a few months.

Obviously, the answer is not to lock onto a single technology or process and stick with it forever. For example, professionals who started their career using only paper and continue to rely on it are facing a challenge as its drawbacks become more evident. Here is a short list:

Paper is:
- Hard to duplicate and back up. When it's lost, it's often gone for good.
- Not scalable. Storing the equivalent of a Gigabyte takes up the space of an entire Encyclopedia Britannica. An iPhone has the same capacity as 16 trucks filled with paper.
- Fragile. It perishes in contact with fire and water. Plus, it often fades.
- Expensive to store, transfer, transport and access from storage locations like libraries and filing cabinets.
- Difficult to search through.
- Mostly sourced from trees, which are essential to the global ecosystem.

There are, of course, documents that cannot be digitized at all, such as a will. For everything else, however, there is a cost and a risk to using paper as a primary place of storage.

Greta Green has embraced the digital age and recognizes that paper has severe drawbacks. She scans whatever she can, as soon as she can, converting it to a digital format. Sometimes, she uses the scanner in her office, but most of the time, she just uses her smartphone to take a picture that's automatically saved to a secure location in the cloud.

This doesn't mean that she never uses paper – she'll print out a hard copy if she must. But once she uses the paper, she doesn't try to save it permanently. In fact, if she has to write anything down she scans the note right away. Fortunately, existing programs like Evernote, Dropbox and Google Drive make much of this activity easy for her to perform, and fresh new alternatives come out each year.

Her smartphone also doubles as a retrieval device – a portable screen to pull up information from the cloud. Other devices, such as her laptop and tablet serve the same purpose. Given the fact that her cloud server is also backed up, she doesn't have a "permanent" location for any information, including time demands. They are all precise, synchronized copies of each other.

She's practicing good risk reduction: the chances of a fire striking the location where paper is stored are much higher than the odds of multiple cloud failures.

It's not a bad principle to use the approach that reduces the risk of loss most. The principle is sound, even if only certain people can apply her methods due to bandwidth, cost and other constraints. Therefore, you shouldn't blindly mimic Greta's tactics: you must assemble your own methods using the same principles.

However, for large numbers of time demands that require lots of supporting data, it's clear that Greta's system is scalable. Wally may skate by today, but he's on the cusp of a disaster. As soon as the amount of data he needs to manage increases, he'll have a major problem. By contrast, Greta is using resources that are almost universally scalable and methods that travel with her anywhere in the world.

What Professionals Store

Professionals conduct business using addresses, calendars, task lists, project plans, passwords, email messages, pictures, audios, videos and other files of different kinds.

As I mentioned before, some documents must remain in their original paper form (e.g. a will, Social Security card, concert ticket, a birth certificate, title to a car, or a life insurance policy). Keeping the originals in a safe place and a copy somewhere is the best way to manage these items.

Now and then, professionals need to link an actual physical object to a particular event, such as a ticket to a concert that's scheduled far off in the future. If you plan to attend and don't want to scramble to find the tickets, it helps to create a link between the event and the point of storage, perhaps by making a note in your calendar: "The tickets are stored in the credenza, in a file called Temp."

Password management is fast becoming a key skill, and the old days of reusing a password or writing it down in the back of your diary are fast becoming obsolete. Professionals routinely look for, and use, the latest electronic or digital techniques to reduce the probability of being hacked by increasingly sophisticated outsiders.

Storing for Psychological Purposes

Apart from the example of the concert tickets, most of the information stored in the locations I just described is related to potential (rather than actual) time demands.

Greta keeps supplemental information stored so it can be pulled up when a time demand has started. That supplemental information may include:
- actions to be followed under certain circumstances – e.g. a checklist
- a collection of "Things I'll Never Do Again"
- a wish list of desired attributes in a future spouse
- a catalog of habits to change or a set of goals
- pictures of places to visit
- a bucket list
- a register of people you're waiting to get something from
- a "Someday I hope to..." list

The items described above serve different purposes, but they aren't meant to represent actual time demands – only potential ones. However, they can be transformed. For example, when an item like "Someday I hope to visit Spain" becomes a time demand after Greta decides to start planning the trip, what was only a potential time demand becomes actual, earning a place in her schedule.

Greta realizes that "information overload" isn't something that happens to you. Instead, it's something that you do to yourself by creating too many time demands. (For more on this topic, see my Lab Notes.)[10]

Evaluating Your Skills

Use the table below to evaluate your skills at Storing.

Figure 11-1

Storing Cheat-Sheet

Behavior	White	Yellow	Orange	Green
Scramble to find information	Often ☐	Sometimes ☐	Rarely ☐	Never ☐
Reduce paper by scanning	Rarely or never ☐	Sometimes ☐	Often ☐	Always ☐
Back ups are automatically done	Rarely or haphazardly ☐	Sometimes ☐	Often ☐	Always ☐
Store unique paper items for instant retrieval	Rarely or haphazardly ☐	Sometimes ☐	Often ☐	Always ☐
Save passwords, appointments, lists and contacts electronically	Rarely ☐	Sometimes ☐	Often ☐	Always ☐

Current Belt ☐   ☐   ☐   ☐

Once again, when you have completed your evaluation, create a plan for improving your habits in this area.

This chapter has focused on your skill at safely storing the information needed to complete time demands. But how do you make sure that you actually act on them at the right time (and thereby hit deadlines, meet your goals and allow your life to run smoothly)? We'll answer these questions in the next chapter, which deals with the universal problem of "doing stuff later."

Remember and Share

Paper storage is more risky than its digital counterpart.

Password management is fast becoming a professional requirement.

A professional's skill at managing information must change to keep up with new technology and increased volume.

Using your smartphone as a scanner is a great way to store information instantly and safely.

Information overload is a function of your commitments, not your technology.

Chapter 12. How to Solve the Problem of "Doing Stuff Later"

(In which you learn that it's easy to manage time demands in small numbers, but the more there are, the harder it gets).

Interviewer: Please join me in welcoming Rebecca Crossley to our show today.

Rebecca: Thanks for having me! I'm a keen listener to the 2Time Labs Podcast.

Interviewer: And congratulations to you on your promotion to CEO of Syscon Technologies. We understand that your father used to work there, and he played a part in your commitment to being highly effective, especially in the area of time-based productivity.

Rebecca: That's right. He's the real reason I'm a CEO today. He taught me everything I know, and when he ran out of stuff to teach me, he put me on to experts who could help me move to the next level.

Interviewer: Tell us about your journey from being a young engineer and how you made it as an effective time manager... even though we all know that time can't be managed.

Rebecca: I know – it's weird that we're still using that term every day, even when we know better. Well, my story starts long before Syscon. It actually goes back to middle school, when I wanted to do as much as possible – do well at school, play soccer, and take piano lessons. I realized that I'd have to do a better job remembering, so I looked for ways to develop a better memory.

Interviewer: How well did that work?

Rebecca: Not very well at all... I Googled every online game I could find to improve my memory, but I still couldn't remember to do my scales or get my gear together for practice ahead of time. Fortunately for me, my Dad, Bill, is a productivity nut. Someone even wrote a book about him. He sat me down one day and told me to start writing everything down in a list. After that, I became a list-obsessed. You could never find me travelling without my to-do list.

Interviewer: So that must be the secret of your success? Always having your to-do list with you at all times?

Rebecca: Well, not quite. That was a huge leap for me – developing the habit of writing down everything I needed to do. It wasn't until I became a freshman at Cornell that I started doing it 100%. I had so much to do that there was just no way I could survive without writing everything down. That worked until I switched to the engineering school.

Interviewer: You weren't an engineer from the beginning?

Rebecca: No, I thought I wanted to do law. I started out doing liberal arts. I decided law wasn't my thing and made the switch during my sophomore year. That's when I ran into a much heavier workload, because I was determined to catch up with the other folks in my class. Plus, I had a part-time job to help pay my expenses.

Interviewer: What more could you do?

Rebecca: Well, Dad wasn't around so I couldn't get his help, and besides, I wanted to get through college "on my own." Too independent, I guess. However, he got me an invitation to meet Graham Riley – people call him "G." He was a retired professor living in Ithaca and a friend of my Dad's. He's also a productivity expert, although I didn't know it at the time.

Interviewer: What advice did he give you?

Rebecca: Well, he showed me a lot of different things, but the biggest was the fact that I needed a better way to manage my to-do list. He showed me how to split it up into smaller lists, which I did. I went from having a list with 200 items, which was completely overwhelming, to nine or ten smaller lists that were much more manageable.

Interviewer: Is that what you have today?

Rebecca: Well, no. At the time, he also told me that I may need another upgrade later in my career and that if I ever ran into problems, I should give him a call.

Interviewer: It sounds like he was very influential.

Rebecca: Oh, he was. He kept in touch with me weekly for another ten years. I think he was repaying my father in some way. He always told me that changing my skills required a slow, gentle approach that should happen easily but with lots of support. Up until the week he died, he was a huge support.

Interviewer: I'm sorry to hear that he died. How long ago was that?

Rebecca: That was fifteen years ago. But it wasn't the end, thanks to my Dad. When G passed away, I had just given birth to twins, and that was about six months after being promoted to my first supervisory role. Within a matter of weeks, I was working nights and weekends, struggling to keep up. In fact, I wasn't keeping up. I was breaking promises to deliver all over the company, making me think I shouldn't have been promoted at all. I wasn't "Leaning In" – it was more like "Falling Apart."

Interviewer: Was your father able to help?

Rebecca: He sure was. He knew from working with G that there was another level of effectiveness to reach, but it would involve giving up my lists and replacing them with a single schedule or calendar that would help me keep track of time in addition to what I have to do.

Interviewer: Was that an easy switch to make?

Rebecca: Actually, I may be summarizing too much. All these changes must seem like they happened easily. They were tough, and the last one has been the hardest of all. In fact, Dad put me onto a coach who specializes in helping people upgrade their skills so they can handle more commitments successfully – she has been awesome. She really understood the importance of ongoing support, especially when the stakes are high. Without her help, I wouldn't be the CEO of Syscon today. But I also credit my father, and G, for intervening at just the right time. I may have gotten there alone, but it would have taken much longer and involved a whole lot more trial and error.

Interviewer: Rebecca Crossley, it's been a pleasure having you on the 2Time Labs Podcast.

Rebecca: Thanks again for having me.

(The characters in this story are all borrowed from my previous book: *Bill's Im-Perfect Time Management Adventure*. This scene takes place some 40 years after the original story).

***

Rebecca's journey isn't unusual, although expert assistance allowed her to progress faster than she would have under ordinary circumstances. Perhaps it reminds you of moments in your life when you made similar changes to your methods in response to a change in your circumstances and an increase in time demands.

In this chapter, we'll explore our boundaries when it comes to managing time demands – tasks that must, by definition, be completed "later." Rebecca went through a number of changes, which we'll examine one by one to discover what universal lessons they have for professionals.

To understand the transition she went through, let's return to a conversation we started in Chapter 2 about what we do as kids, developing our own methods of managing time demands. We learned from researchers that we discover the concept of time when we are between 7 and 10 years old. Later, in our adolescent years, we develop the ability to manage time demands.

What prompts us to create time demands in the first place?

It probably comes from a failure to get what we want. In the absence of research, I can only guess that there's a time when we learn that it's not possible to do everything now. Some of the things we want must be done "later."

For example, we may have learned that becoming a Punt, Pass and Kick champion couldn't be done now. We may also have discovered that getting it done later meant putting together and coordinating a whole bunch of time demands over a span of months and years.

Perhaps at the start, our parents or guardians managed our activities, and we simply took their lead. But as we came into our own, we set our own goals, which required us to manage our own time demands. Like Rebecca, we started by using memory as a Capture Point. Without it, there's no way to make plans.

***

In Chapter 2 we introduced the term "prospective memory." It's the kind of memory we use to track future commitments, including time demands.

Our default choice to use prospective memory is natural. After all, it travels with us all the time, it can't be left at home, and it never runs out of battery charge. However, like any other part of the mind, it requires energy to function, and there are real limits to the amount of information we can hold. Also, the use of prospective memory varies from one person to another, in part because we use self-taught methods.

For example, research done at a school in New Jersey by Jeremy Burrus (whom we met earlier) and his team at the Educational Testing Service showed that by the 9th grade, time management skills vary widely between students, along with the way they use prospective memory. Other studies show that as teens get a little older, they add distinct time management skills one after another.

However, when we're young, we don't spend much time thinking about our use of memory. We just use it. Academic success at that age is all about exploiting our growing ability to remember stuff of all kinds. The best students, by and large, have superior powers of recall. It's only natural, therefore, to use our memories at this young age to also track time demands in addition to the facts and figures needed to pass tests and quizzes.

This works for many young students because:

1. They have a relatively low number of time demands to manage. Unlike adults, they juggle primarily obligations to themselves and to a small group of people.

2. They have the structured support of teachers, the school system and their parents. It's difficult to forget to do your homework with so much *de-facto* help.

At this point in our lives, the negative consequences of using memory – or making a mistake – are low.

Of course, there are exceptions: Rebecca may have been one. She may have been the typical high performer in high school – student council president, third in the class, and co-captain of the debate team. This valedictorian, who eventually goes to Harvard, may be a bit different. She may be using her iPhone to write every task down, in much the same way that adults would. This precocious student already uses her smartphone to manage time demands (in addition to playing games texting).

But most of us aren't like her at that age. Instead, we try to perfect the habit of using memory to manage time demands. It turns out, according to research by Lia Kvavilashvili, that we try to remember at least two things using separate forms of memory: the fact that the time demand exists and the particular piece of information required to execute it.

The Breaking Point

Rebecca noticed long before her peers that her memory wasn't keeping up with her needs long before her peers, and, like the ultra-performing student council president, she tried to find an answer.

Most teenagers don't Google productivity solutions or have a parent who explains how to use a to-do list. Instead, they blame life – coursework, teachers, job, friends or family. Acting like victims, they harbor escape fantasies to simpler places in the world (like a beach in Jamaica) where pressures disappear because time demands (hopefully) don't exist.

A deeper analysis shows that without fully realizing it, they are trying to accomplish two things:

Goal #1: Augment their capacity to manage more time demands.

Goal #2: Reduce the number of time demands that slip through the cracks.

In support of the second goal, research completed by Victoria Bellotti and her team in 2004 showed that the big problem people have with task management is not establishing priorities. It's "making sure that the important tasks get done even if the unexpected occurs." Given the fact that the unexpected is always occurring, it's no wonder Rebecca had a challenge.

The advice that she received from her father to create a to-do list has been passed on for centuries. Benjamin Franklin is known for recommending his practice of keeping a combination list/schedule. It's as easy now to get started as it was then: just get a piece of paper and start writing.

However, today's teenagers are walking around with powerful technology that was unimaginable just a few years ago. Aided by the widespread availability of high-speed Internet access, they have hundreds of low-cost options available to them via different apps, programs and websites.

In fact, their devices have the capability to traverse the journey that Rebecca took over the years in just an instant. She made the jump from memory to a single list to multiple lists to a single calendar. Astonishingly, the average teenager now has access to the same productivity power that Rebecca has as a CEO.

Turning Points

However, before personal computers were popularized in the early 1980s, the only upgrade professionals could make was on paper. As a result, they bought memo pads, diaries, and Post-It notes.

Like many, Rebecca didn't completely switch away from using her mind. She blended memory and her to-do list in an uncoordinated fashion that wasn't perfect, but it was a huge improvement over using the mind by itself. It wasn't until she got to college that she made a concerted effort to stop using memory altogether.

In this book, we refer to these moments of duress when we need to make a change as "Turning Points." Unlike Rebecca, most of us don't have help making the required transition, so we make mistakes. We teach ourselves habits that don't work or cannot scale.

The first Turning Point Rebecca shared was the initial one – using memory to create and manage time demands. The second was a to-do list. Why did she run into problems with this new approach?

Curating a Long To-Do List

Unfortunately, as Rebecca became better at using less memory, her to-do list became unmanageable. Why does that happen?

Let's start at the beginning of a typical day.

As we discovered in the chapter on Emptying, most of

us wake up with a mental plan: a picture of what the day's activities will look like. (Once again, a few exceptions exist – we have already met a few professionals who have an extreme present time perspective and don't make plans.)

This plan isn't fixed: it changes several times each day.

In the morning, for example, we might review our calendar as well as yesterday's to-do list and decide to make some changes. We may also go looking for new time demands buried in email. Once we are done, we get to work on the first task.

When we are finished, we have a choice. What do we work on next? How to decide?

With a short to-do list, it's not too hard — we check the list while mentally comparing it against our plan for the day. However, when our to-do list is long, the task of checking becomes a burden. Instead of 12 items, we find ourselves reviewing 112. As the day progresses and surprises pop up, we find ourselves checking both our to-do list and our mental schedule, doing our best to prevent anything from slipping through the cracks.

Before long, we start to feel overwhelmed. There's just too much checking and re-checking.

Most of the expert and casual advice I've seen on the Internet has to do with cutting back on the size of the list. This won't work for most people; it only heightens the Zeigarnik effect (the nagging feeling that you're forgetting something).

As Rebecca demonstrated, there is a better approach.

Sorting a Single, Long List

Many people find this to-do list solution on their own. They sort and separate it into several smaller, more manageable lists.

Perhaps the best-known method was used by President Dwight Eisenhower. The technique, popularized by the late Stephen Covey, involves breaking a list into four buckets: urgent and important, urgent and not important, not urgent and important, and not urgent and not important. In this way, a single long to-do list breaks into four separate lists. When you are reviewing your to-do list, you need to check only one of four lists instead of all the items on all lists, as shown in the diagrams below.

Rebecca's To-Do List for Today

Complete the report
Stop by the gym for an hour
Eat lunch with new employee
Pick up milk on the way home
Attend monthly meeting
Send Vic new financials
Plan for Katie's birthday party
Watch Big Bang Theory

Figure 12-1

Important, Not Urgent	*Important, Urgent*
lunch w/ new guy financials to Vic	complete the report plan for Katie's birthday party
Not Important, Not Urgent	*Not Important, Urgent*
Big Bang Theory monthly meeting	pickup milk gym

As you compare the two methods, you may notice a slight drop in anxiety and even a small boost in confidence from using the four quadrants instead of the list. Why is this an improvement?

The Power of Tagging, Searching and Viewing

All Rebecca did was break her single to-do list into four

separate lists.

However, from an entirely different perspective, what she actually did was add an explicit tag to each task, using two attributes. Then, she applied a particular view using each of four tags. Confused? Let's look at what she does more closely, because it describes a key action we take when we create time demands.

In the first to-do list she developed, it's easy to imagine that when she created each task, Rebecca also subconsciously tagged it with additional information. Part of the information she included was how urgent and important each item is. We call these "implicit tags": a kind of psychological meta-data we add to time demands to help us manage them.

Let's revisit her to-do list, but this time, let's reveal the implicit tags she chose.

Rebecca's To-Do List for Today (with implicit tags revealed)

Complete the report (important, urgent)
Stop by the gym for an hour (not important, urgent)
Eat lunch with new employee (important, not urgent)
Pick up milk on the way home (not important, urgent)
Attend monthly meeting (not important, not urgent)
Send Vic new financials (important, not urgent)
Plan for Katie's birthday party (important, urgent)
Watch Big Bang Theory (not important, not urgent)

Implicit tags are defined by different "attributes" which can each take up different values. In this case, she uses two attributes, which each have two possible values.

Attribute #1 – Importance: consists of a range of two choices: "important" or "not important."

Attribute #2 – Urgency: consists of a range of two choices: "urgent" or "not urgent."

When she pulls this information out of her mind and uses it in a written or digitized list, she instantly has some new options. Now that they have escaped her mind, we call them "explicit tags."

She can look at:
- All items that are not important.
- All items that are urgent.

- All items that are urgent but not important.

Tagging with the attributes of the Eisenhower matrix instantly allows her to see these views. If she tried to see them with the original, unsorted to-do list, she'd find the job much harder, if not impossible. Different views allow us to focus on what we want while ignoring what we don't.

This is a simple example. My research shows that when we create time demands, we use a lot more than two tags. To illustrate, let's consider an easy task from her list: "Pick up the milk."

She created this time demand after visiting the fridge and noticing a half-empty box. Here's what it would look like if it were explicitly tagged with some of the attributes she had in mind when she created it.

"Pick up the milk" (not important, urgent) becomes "Pick up the milk" (not important, urgent, Kroughers Supermarket, inexpensive, this evening after work.)

In addition to the original two attributes borrowed from the Eisenhower matrix, she's also added three more: location, cost and time. This longer description takes us a step closer to the reality of what she does.

Now, the Eisenhower attributes (urgency, importance) begin to look a bit Spartan and perhaps less critical. Given her tight schedule, the most important tag in the list might be "this evening after work" which translates into a time between 5 and 7 PM.

In Chapter 4, I mentioned the fact that before a time demand is created, it has, at the very minimum, a description of the action, a duration and a likely start time. According to experts in Knowledge Management, who have been using such techniques for decades, these attributes can serve as useful meta-data. You may notice tags in email messages tracked by Outlook and Gmail.

Theoretically, it's best to include as many tags as possible in a description of a time demand. Practically, however, there is a limit to what our minds and currently-available software can handle. Many tags must be ignored simply because we don't have a good way to manage all the extra information, or time to devote to managing details we don't need.

Transitioning From the Use of Memory

Given these limits, what's our best option?

Let's start by asking the obvious: "Why explicitly tag time demands in the first place?" It might be true that even simple time demands are created with implicit tags like the examples I just gave, but how does this knowledge help us? Why should we turn psychological knowledge into written or digital data?

The first benefit is that with explicit tags, you don't need to examine an entire to-do list: just the slice you care about. This helps you focus your attention. For example, as she adds more explicit tags, Rebecca could assemble digital views that represent:

- Every item she needs to buy at Kroughers Supermarket.
- Tasks she hopes to accomplish between 5 PM and 7 PM.
- Planned purchases of more than $100.

When Rebecca uses one of these views, it lessens her cognitive load, which, as we discussed, helps her make better decisions. In fact, in the absence of tags, creating these views is exactly what our brain does when we ask it to sort through time demands. What we are trying to do, in effect, is relieve the cognitive pressure that increases with the number of time demands we have to manage.

In our effort to lessen the load and achieve Peace of Mind, it becomes clear that more explicit tagging is good, but less processing is even better. All this tagging, sorting and viewing should be done by software, not by us. We need a way to explicitly tag time demands that's quick, easy and painless.

Unfortunately, I'm not aware of more than a single software program that enables the kind of multi-attribute tagging I'm describing. Nozbe, a program for syncing tasks, teams and projects, appears to be the exception. There may be others, but you can explore Nozbe at http://nozbe.com.

Some programs (and training) offer a mix of labels, categories and contexts, which are all synonyms for tags.

I'll address our needs for better software briefly in the

chapter on New Tools. While we wait for better electronic solutions, here's what we can do today.

Tagging Using Scarce Resources

I have concluded that there's not much research into how best to use explicit tags with time demands. Here's my best guess about what we do, and should do, informed by my live workshops and background research in fields such as Human-Computer Interface Design.

Let's return to the purpose of tagging: We make a tag explicit in order to sort and view it in various ways. Tags work as handles – additional bits of information we use to manipulate time demands.

There is, however, a common thread we all share as humans. We care a lot about managing scarcity and maximizing our utility. It's a basic economic notion that applies to material resources as well as time.

Unfortunately, no one has studied "the economics of time demand management," even though the notion appears to be basic enough. If Rebecca could look at only one of the three views of her time demands from the list shared above, she'd pick the one that represents the scarcest resource, whether it's travel capacity, time or money.

If she could, she'd ignore the other views and turn her efforts to exploiting, maximizing or conserving the resource in some way.

Let's say, for example, that Rebecca limits her trips to Kroughers because she's noticed that the more trips she makes, the more likely she is to spend too much money.

For other people, the scarce resource might be their physical location, an idea promoted by David Allen, author of *Getting Things Done*. When you can view a slice of your time demands tagged with a particular location (e.g. the supermarket), it's much easier to do everything that can be done only at that location. I have used similar tags to ensure that when I'm travelling to a particular region of the world, I meet people who live there in person, taking advantage of the fact that I'm there for a short time. (One criticism of this method is that technology is making the need for geographic choices irrelevant. Between mobile telephony and ubiquitous Internet access, we don't need to define what can be done in a certain place as often).

Later in this chapter, we'll take a look at people who view time as their scarcest resource. The choice of what to see as scarce is up to us: the fact is, tagging takes energy. Therefore, we should manage only a minimum number of explicit tags.

While tagging is easy, each new tag creates a certain level of complexity, according to Brigitte Claessens, the psychologist we met earlier. She notes that "quantity, quality, resources and time" are attributes people use to regulate their daily activities, but she also warns that "the conflict between these attributes may explain why timeliness might sometimes suffer."

The task of finding and selecting the right tags is a matter of self-discovery. Once again, copying someone else's system won't work. It's the reason why so many professionals can see the logic of the Eisenhower method but don't happen to use it.

Doing Better Tagging

As you can imagine, you can use a number of possible attributes in addition to urgency, importance, place, time, and cost.

Here is a short list I have made from the explicit attributes I've encountered in theory and practice. It consists of a particular attribute followed by some of the values it might take. For each line item, try to write down a time demand that might use that attribute in your Diary. This exercise will tell you something about the way you create time demands and which attributes you naturally use when you create them.

Figure 12-2

Attribute	Possible Values
Caffeine Rush:	Peak, Low, None
Commitment:	Someday, Must, Urgent
Cost:	< $100, $100-$500, >$500
Creativity Required:	High, Medium, Low
Danger of Incompletion:	Red, Green, Yellow
Distance to be Travelled:	<10 miles, 10-30 miles, >30 miles
Energy:	High, Medium, Low
Mental Status:	Work, Vacation, Holiday, Weekend
Noise Level:	Quiet, Hum, Chaos
Person of Interest:	husband, boss, co-worker, son #1, daughter #1, daughter #2
Project Name:	ABC Project, XYZ Project, etc.
Temporal Tagging:	duration, plus all the open time slots in your calendar e.g. "Friday for 45 minutes starting at 5pm"
Tools Needed:	Smartphone, iPad, Laptop, Power drill, Ladder, Supercomputer
Traffic Conditions:	High, Medium, Low
Waiting for a Trigger to Start:	Yes, No

Take a moment to discover which attributes feel most valuable to you by rank-ordering the ones that correspond to your areas of greatest scarcity.

Many (but by no means all) professionals immediately gravitate to Temporal Tagging because, like Rebecca, they are time-constrained. This comes as no surprise to executives and a number of college students: time is their scarcest resource. Both groups have a large number of time demands to execute against sharp deadlines, and represent what happens when the number of time demands increases: time quickly becomes the scarcest commodity. Here's how Rebecca made that particular transition.

How to Become a Time-Starved Professional

The final transition Rebecca made, with the help of her dad, was probably the most challenging of all. When she made the switch from multiple to-do lists to a single calendar, she needed to learn a tremendous number of new habits and unlearn old practices.

Curiously, given her penchant for high performance, she might be like many students who actually deprecate their skills upon graduation. I noticed this phenomenon after a conversation with Mark Horstman. I happened to be watching a training video I use in my live training. (Visit http://goo.gl/aqlS18 for the "Student Time Management Video.")

This clip shows a college student who puts together a regular weekly schedule that takes up at least 80% of her waking hours (and some of her sleeping hours). Most of my program participants react in terror – they can't imagine living their lives that way. However, a tiny handful quietly show me their schedules, which look exactly like those of the student.

There are, therefore, professionals who use a schedule as a kind of control center for their time demands. Instead of to-do lists, they use a schedule or calendar to plan each and every day. It makes sense: their scarce resource is time.

Mark Horstman's podcasts on Manager-Tools.com helped me make the link to CEOs, who also use the same technique. Prior to interviewing him for my podcast, I heard him belaboring the point in multiple broadcasts: the best executives put a lot of stuff in their calendars. Derek Dean and Caroline Webb echoed the sentiment in their McKinsey Quarterly article, "Recovering from Information Overload": "The calendars of CEOs and other senior executives are often booked back-to-back all day, sometimes in 15-minute increments."

Mark's experience working in the White House also helps make the case. He shared the fact that President Bush used a schedule with 15-minute increments to plan each day. It took me back to the television series "The West Wing," in which the fictional President Jed Bartlett would, after every meeting or activity, turn to his secretary and ask, "What's next?" A little more research showed that Presidents Obama and Clinton also used tight schedules.

As I watched the video, it hit me: college students managed their time like CEOs. The best students are often just as time-starved, and they put their calendar/schedule at the center rather than a to-do list. It appears that they are also driven by high stakes (the possibility of failure) to craft improved skills. However, upon graduation, research by Dezhi Wu shows that they lose the skill of managing their time using a calendar as they transition into entry-level jobs that, for the most part, are less demanding than their years as students. For links to content on the stress top college students are under, see my Lab Notes.[11]

What Time-Starved Professionals Do

Further research revealed that these students and executives are not alone. Select professions like project management, surgery and teaching stand out: these require the management of scarce time. In other fields, high performers do the same: they push the limits of how much they can do by creating lots of time demands, even when there aren't enough hours in the day to get everything done. Unlike their colleagues, they possess hyper-ambitions and aren't happy hitting the plateaus that satisfy others.

The research is clear: time-starved professionals belong to a special group. They manage the greatest number of time demands and are clear about their scarcest resource: it's time. They are the few among us who find themselves:

- Struggling to allocate the last few hours of every week.
- Devoting huge chunks of time to their job.
- Running the risk of not doing the basics, such as sleeping enough hours, bathing every day and eating properly.
- Fighting to retain some semblance of a balanced life, often failing.
- Always thinking about work, even when they shouldn't be.
- Using smartphones to be available 24 hours per day.
- Sometimes losing the bigger picture because they are so busy on a daily basis.
- Engaging in high-stake activities that bring a great deal of pressure, such as marathons.
- Constantly checking the time.
- Regularly falling short of their plans for the day due to naturally occurring interruptions.
- Feeling "the pressure of time on all occasions and during all activities, whether work, recreation or leisure," according to

Jan Francis-Smythe's article entitled "Time Management" in the publication *Timing the Future*. They experience time as running faster than it actually does.

Francis-Smythe reports time-starvation to be "an important predictor of both negative health … outcomes" such as "coronary heart-disease, hypertension, sleep, respiratory and digestive problems." It also predicts "positive performance outcomes" such as "higher classroom performance, better work-related attitudes and punctuality at work."

To others, those who are time-starved appear superhuman, and even crazy at times... perhaps obsessed. If this sounds like typical Type-A behavior, don't be surprised. It is.

However, my research shows that while there's a strong tendency for Type As to be time-starved, not all professionals who are time-starved have Type A personalities. Time-starvation is a pure capacity problem, solved only by the right habits, practices and rituals. From this point of view, personality is not immediately relevant.

As such, time-starvation can be a temporary condition that disappears once certain commitments have been fulfilled. For example, parents whose children leave the nest sometimes go from being time-starved to feeling as if they have too much time on their hands.

What these people need is not the perfect personality type (which may well be impossible to develop), but a way to learn the appropriate methods for a time-starved life. For most, cutting back on commitments (as I mentioned before) is not an option, even though some professionals do make the mistake of suppressing their natural drive to succeed in order to fit in with the crowd.

The time-starved also may try hard to get their memory or to-do-list-based systems to work using the advice of friends or gurus. This strategy simply doesn't work. Substantial research shows that as time becomes more of a scarce resource, the best way to manage all of it is with a calendar-centric system. To access research about professionals who are also known as experiencing "time-urgency" or "time-famine," see my Lab Notes.[12]

While it may seem that "time-starvation" and "time-famine" are bad things to avoid, I'll use these terms in a neutral way to describe the natural fallout of high ambition. In other words, it's the price a highly committed professional pays for setting challenging goals and having the energy to attempt to reach them.

Understanding What a Schedule Really Is

These high-flyers are actually following the same practices described earlier: tagging, searching and viewing. For them, time is by far their scarcest resource, so it becomes the primary attribute they use to explicitly tag time demands, which they would tag in the following way:

Complete the report: 9-11:30 AM
Stop by the gym for an hour: 6-7 AM
Eat lunch with new employee: 12-1 PM
Pick up milk on the way home: 6 PM
Attend monthly meeting: 4-5 PM
Send Vic new financials: 330-4 PM
Plan for Katie's birthday party: 8-9 PM
Watch Big Bang Theory: 9-930 PM

Here's what a calendar of these time demands looks like.

Figure 12-3

4:00 AM	
5:00 AM	
6:00 AM	stop by the gym
7:00 AM	
8:00 AM	
9:00 AM	complete the report
10:00 AM	
11:00 AM	
12:00 PM	
1:00 PM	
2:00 PM	
3:00 PM	send Vic new financials
4:00 PM	Attend monthly meeting
5:00 PM	
6:00 PM	Pick up milk on the way home
7:00 PM	
8:00 PM	Plan for Katie's Birthday Party
9:00 PM	Watch Bag Bang Theory
10:00 PM	
11:00 PM	

At a glance, for even this small number of time demands, a visual display is far easier to understand and manipulate than a list. By design, a calendar provides the following additional information:
- The relationship between time demands
- The time available to schedule new time demands
- Whether or not time demands are scheduled too close together
- Whether or not adequate time is being committed to a particular time demand
- Where plans may go awry
- Key dependencies between time demands

For time-starved people, this information is critical. Seeing and using it allows them to perform the juggling act that's so important in their quest for productivity and Peace of Mind.

To create this kind of detailed calendar, these

professionals do things differently. When they Empty, they place most of their time demands in a calendar after removing them from Capture Points. In other words, there's no need for a to-do list of any kind: their calendar acts as a full, complete replacement. This allows them to use their calendar as their single point of control: a calendar-centric life.

As a result, the other attributes that could be used to tag time demands are less important, so they often leave them as implicit.

Once the centrality of their calendar becomes a fact of life, they face a challenge that other professionals may not: "How do I keep my schedule current and viable?"

1. Keeping a Schedule Current: Time-starved individuals must become skilled at juggling their schedules on a daily basis. They need to be unattached to their plans and change them on a whim in order to keep them up to date. As a result, they should anticipate emergencies and surprises, developing ways to bounce around them effectively and treating their calendar as if it's infinitely flexible.

The truth is, as we discussed before, most people have mental calendars of what they plan to do each day, so this juggling act isn't altogether new. The difference is in the method. Many professionals can get away with manipulating mental calendars, while time-starved people can be effective only when they use external aids such as portable, electronic schedules and/or administrative assistants. There simply is no way to stay on top of so many time demands.

2. Keeping a Schedule Viable: In this context, a viable calendar is one that's feasible. It doesn't have overlapping tasks or stacks of items scheduled back-to-back without breaks. Time-starved professionals must learn how to space out tasks to account for unscheduled activity, even as they improve their skill at estimating how long tasks really take. These skills represent a steep initial learning curve for most.

In the chapter on Scheduling, we'll look at the finer techniques to be mastered. You will also hear from researchers such as Dezhi Wu, Christine Bartholomew, and others who show how effective a schedule can be for a large number of time demands.

How Scheduling Tools Have Evolved

Many years ago, when only paper desk calendars were available, maintaining the detailed schedule of a time-starved professional required an executive assistant. The unfortunate knowledge workers who lacked an assistant had to struggle with a pencil and eraser. The advent of portable planners in the form of DayTimers, FiloFaxes and Franklin Planners made the job much easier, because calendars were now liberated desks and could be carried at all times. In the early 1990s, having one of these was a sure sign of professional commitment.

However, juggling the items on a paper calendar is still difficult, if not impossible. Imagine trying to make even a few changes to the calendar depicted above on paper.

Today, we carry mobile electronic calendars in our smartphones. Coupled with bigger, sharper touch screens, juggling time demands on the fly has become much easier. Voice-recognition tools like Siri are also making it possible to place items in a schedule without even using fingers.

For time-starved professionals, these are life-saving innovations that have helped them increase their capacity to manage time demands in their schedules. They allow professionals, time-starved or not, to use the best of lists and schedules.

Combining Scheduling and Listing

At the start of the chapter, I mentioned the gurus, writers and trainers who advocate one of two extremes. Some argue that a to-do list or multiple lists should be central, while others argue for calendars. Most go an extra step to warn learners to avoid the alternatives.

These experts appear to have overlooked the following facts:

1. Managing different numbers of time demands requires different, custom blends of to-do lists and schedules.

2. Improved technology allows us to do things that were impossible just a few years ago. For example, it's much easier to juggle an electronic schedule than it once was.

3. You don't need to upgrade your system if both Goal #1 (increasing your capacity) and Goal #2 (reducing the incidence of lost time demands) are being met.

4. Sometimes, a necessary upgrade isn't possible, because the individual can't learn the new habits required. At other times, a new technology is just too hard to pick up – the fact is, we're only human. Some companies don't hire administrative assistants. In these cases, an upgrade might not be possible.

While some experts paint the picture of a simple, one-size-fits-all world, the reality of what we do every day suggests something different. My research shows that a time-starved professional makes the following transition between the use of memory, lists and schedules.

Figure 12-4

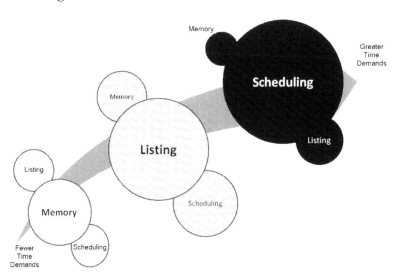

As the number of time demands they confront each day increases, they make a series of jumps or upgrades in order to cope. Rebecca's story illustrates what we do to solve "the problem of doing stuff later": we change our skills, mostly in ways we can't clearly articulate.

While the above diagram makes the transition seem neat and logical, it is anything but that. The fact is, we didn't teach ourselves how to manage time demands in a uniform way, and so at any point in time, a snapshot of our system looks idiosyncratic and overly complex. Few of us are aware of the overall trajectory our skills are taking, so we lurch from one suggestion to another.

The central premise of this book is that effective upgrades start with an understanding of your current method for creating time demands with implicit tags. Once you know and accept the process you use today, you can make targeted, surgical changes that require less effort. In this case, ignorance is expensive.

In the next two chapters, you'll learn that the fundamentals, Listing and Scheduling, go together.

Remember and Share

Managing time demands is a matter of matching the right technique to the right volume.

It's OK to manage your time demands using memory – if you're just a kid.

A list is easier than a schedule, but only for small numbers.

Overwhelmed with time demands? Try upgrading from a list to a calendar.

Look for turning points that indicate the time is right for an upgrade.

When you form a time demand, you implicitly tag it with certain attributes.

Why tag a time demand? It's a way of focusing your attention on the ones that matter.

Avoid the Zeigarnik Effect by managing all your time demands in lists and schedules.

The professionals who manage the most time demands progress through four major skill turning points.

What's your scarcest resource? Use it to tag and manage your time demands.

Time-starved professionals care most about temporal tags.

Implicit tags are the ones you add to time demands automatically – you can't stop yourself.

Explicit tags are the ones you use as handles in the digital world to sort and review time demands.

"The human being is the only animal that thinks about the future." — Daniel Gilbert

Chapter 13. Listing – A powerful technique for all professionals

(In which you learn that there's more to making a list than meets the eye).

Delta Flight 1141 was slated to travel from Dallas Fort-Worth to Salt Lake City on August 31, 1988. The Boeing 727 crashed, killing 14 passengers and injuring 76 when the pilots, in a lapse of what the National Transportation Safety Board (NTSB) called "cockpit discipline," forgot to extend the wing flaps to the right position for takeoff. They were distracted, according to the voice recordings, by flirtatious conversations with the flight attendants.

20% of major aviation accidents happen because of failure to "complete delayed intentions." So far in this book, we have been looking at fairly mundane examples, such as remembering to pick up the milk, but Key Dismukes reminds us that much more is at stake in our discussion about preserving time demands.

Key recently retired from a long and distinguished career at the NASA-Ames Research Center. Before he officially left to become a consultant, he spent almost ten years as the Chief Scientist of the Human Systems Integration Division at the center in Mountain View, California. He's more than a trained scientist, however. He's also a US Army veteran who served during the Vietnam War.

As a certified airline transport pilot, he holds glider instruction ratings and has, as recently as 2010, entered and won soaring championships as a member of the Skyline Soaring Club.

This combination of experiences makes him unique. He's not just a scientist with a detached interest in what happens in the cockpit. He's always thinking about ways to help pilots make better decisions, especially when they are under stress. In particular, one of the questions he's explored over the years is: "How can pilots be helped to remember to do what they need to do?" His studies of prospective memory in the airline industry have saved lives. He's not the guy who shows up at crashes: he helps prevent them, which is why he's a household name among insiders who know how many errors he has helped pilots avoid.

In 2009, he teamed up with Jon Holbrook for a study entitled "Prospective Memory in Everyday Tasks." They aimed to discover "ways individuals can improve performance in everyday prospective memory tasks." As you may recall, you can think of time demands as a particular kind of prospective memory.

In an experiment sponsored by the NASA Aviation Safety Program, they rated the effectiveness of techniques used by an experimental group of psychology students to remember to perform a series of tasks. 29 students succeeded and 40 failed. They interviewed both groups of students to find out what techniques they'd used.

They found that the students employed distinct techniques with varying results. As you can see from the chart below, their success or failure varied widely depending on the actions they took.

Figure 13-1

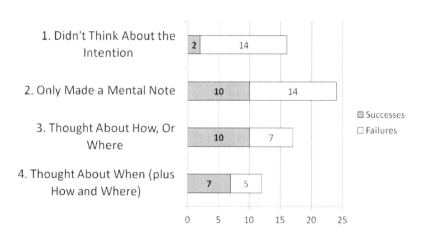

Experimental Results

If Rebecca had been included in the experiment as a subject, she'd fall into one of four groups, depending on the skills she possessed at different phases of her life.

Group #1 - Rebecca as a pre-teen, before she started creating time demands.

Group #2 - Rebecca after she began using her memory to store time demands.

Group #3 - Rebecca after beginning to use to-do lists.

Group #4 - Rebecca after beginning to use a calendar-centric approach.

In my Lab Notes at the end of the book,[13] I detail my assumptions and conclusions about this study, but here's a synopsis of the overall message it communicates about our skills as professionals:

1. Professionals undergo an evolution of time-based productivity skills in which each step leads to greater success.

2. Most of us try to get by using mental notes, i.e. we store time demands in prospective memory. In this study, 34.8% of the test population used Group #2 techniques. As expected, it remained an ineffective technique and had a failure rate of 58.3%.

3. In each phase or group, the cues we use to prompt action differ. Although we tend to use the same cultural excuse each time we fail ("I didn't remember"), we are actually over-generalizing the cause of a Phase 2 error.

4. Failing to create a time demand in the first place is the worst error to make (87.5% failure rate).

Remember, Dismuke's work is meant to improve the way pilots undertake time demands while they are in the cockpit, so its findings are directly related to saving lives. While our jobs might not involve these high stakes, we are still subject to distractions. For example, participants in my training have shared times when they pulled into their driveways after a hard day at work, only to realize that the kids weren't in the car – they had been forgotten at school.

Fact: In the United States, up to 50 children die each year from being left inside overheated cars.

According to Lyn Balfour, a 13-year veteran of the US Army whose son Bryce died after being left in the car on March 30, 2007: "How can I forget my kid? I can manage $47 million for the US military with every penny accounted for, and I was awarded a Bronze Star for those efforts, but how can I forget my kid? How can a loving, responsible, detail-oriented parent forget him, something so precious, so valuable?"

***

In the last chapter, we considered the idea that people jump from one level of skill to another at crucial moments. We called these "Turning Points." Arguably, when the number of time demands increases in our lives but we don't make this switch, tragedies occur, such as cockpit errors and the sad reality of babies left in hot cars. Letting time demands slip comes at a cost.

The story of Rebecca, however, demonstrates a series of positive responses to escalating time demands. At different moments during her career, she decided to change her habits, practices and rituals in ways that turn out to be quite predictable. These Turning Points are enumerated below and displayed in the diagram that follows.

Turning Point #1 - We discover time and, shortly after, start managing time demands using memory.

Turning Point #2 - We shift from memory to a single to-do list.

Turning Point #3 - We shift from a single to-do list to multiple to-do lists.

Turning Point #4 - We shift from multiple to-do lists to a single schedule/calendar.

Here's a diagram that illustrates each Turning Point.

Figure 13-2

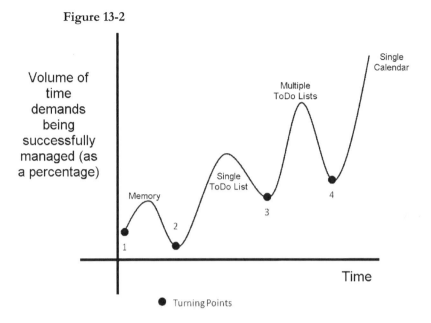

(The Holbrook and Dismukes study describes three of these Turning Points: 1, 2 and 4).

For most people, these four turning points are invisible. Depending on the work we do, moving past these moments and improving our skills can prevent tragedies and ensure our Peace of Mind.

However, you don't have to transform your behavior at these Turning Points to lead a successful life. Don't assume that this is a new version of one-size-fits-all thinking in which never reaching the fourth point is a sign of failure.

It's not.

Consider the analogy of foreign language proficiency. The only languages I speak are English, Jamaican Patois and a little Spanish. While I did some work in Latin America over 15 years ago, I doubt that I ever reached the Spanish proficiency of a five-year-old. Now, I am sure there are three-year-olds with better skills in conversational Spanish.

Is this a problem for me? Should it be?

The short answer to the first question is "No." However, it could be a problem in the future... if I get another offer to do work in Latin America. For the moment, however, I don't require greater Spanish proficiency. Likewise, many people have no immediate need to conquer all four Turning Points. People can achieve peace of mind at any level, depending on the number of time demands they must deal with each day. This is a matter of finding a match between your skills and the volume of time demands you process.

Also, moving through each point is not a trivial rite of passage for most people. At each one, they must learn and unlearn habits, practices and rituals, which we'll talk more about in later chapters. Rebecca had the support of her father as well as Graham Riley and a time management coach. You'll also need support of different kinds to help make each transition successfully: in the chapter on building an environment that supports new habits, we'll look at your individual needs.

Definition

A list is "a number of connected items or names written or printed consecutively, one below the other," according to Wikipedia. Listing is defined as safekeeping of time demands in a collection for later action. This definition implies that Listing doesn't cover every kind of list – some of the examples provided in the chapter on Storing, for example, don't consist of time demands at all (e.g. lists made up of phone numbers or passwords).

Wally White often uses only a mental list. As the NASA researchers showed, he may not even have the habit of using memory. He leaves the accomplishment of time demands to chance.

What kinds of lists do professionals like Greta Green use? In her calendar-centric life, Greta uses her schedule or calendar as her "control tower" for time demands, pushing her lists into a subordinate role.

Many people misunderstand the idea of managing time demands through her schedule. It doesn't mean that when she visits the grocery store, she makes a plan to "pick up the cheese" from 7:00-7:02 PM and the milk from 7:02-7:05 PM. Instead she uses a routine grocery list to support her scheduled shopping trip: "Visit grocery store - 7:00 PM to 8:00 PM."

Greta uses lists in a supportive role to help execute time demands effectively and to avoid cluttering her schedule with too many activities. Here are some examples:
- A list of items to discuss with someone in a conversation
- A Christmas list for use at the mall
- An agenda for an upcoming meeting
- A list of musical numbers for a rehearsal
- A Project List
- A Gantt chart
- A written plan to upgrade certain habits
- A prayer list

As you can see, all of these lists are collections of short time demands. Fortunately, most modern calendar programs and apps allow users to embed lists like these directly in a given activity. In the example we gave above, the grocery list can be slotted directly in the scheduled activity. This makes both the list and the activity easier to manage as a single combined entity.

An Alternate Approach

Time-starved individuals sometimes start the transition from using multiple lists to a single schedule by using broad temporal tags such as the following:
- Tomorrow
- Next Week
- Next Month
- Someday

Mark Forster, a productivity author, advocates outlining items to be done tomorrow, for example.

There is a drawback to this approach. When you build a list using these tags, you have no idea whether or not the plan you have made is feasible. In other words, you can easily schedule 35 hours of activity into a 24-hour day because you aren't accounting for each activity's duration.

The fact is, time-starved professionals are always being confronted by the last few hours in the day, which remain unscheduled. They are constantly asking themselves how to best use this time, deciding whether to leave it free for emergencies, add in some reading time, use it to bring a project forward, or plan to take a nap. These choices are harder to make when lists are used as the primary "control tower," even when they offer some temporal information. For time-starved professionals, this technique might not work.

Once again, however, please remember that the choice is yours. While I am pointing out the benefits of being like Greta in all respects, I need to reiterate that the fact that she has a Green Belt doesn't mean that you need to have one also. In other words, Turning Point #4 may not be for you.

A reminder: we are using a heutagogical approach where you are both the trainer and the trainee, so you need to guide your own development in a way that ensures success.

Views and Threads as a Substitute for Multiple Lists

When you reach Turning Point #3 and need to convert a single to-do list into multiple ones, consider the following three tactics:

Tactic #1 - Store all similar time demands in the same folder (electronic or paper). For email management, this is a useful practice, especially when each message only includes a single kind of time demand.

Tactic #2 - Use threading, or project grouping, to collapse (and hide) time demands you wish to ignore for the moment. (e.g. Gantt Chart software, which manipulates views of tasks and sub-tasks).

Tactic #3 - Create explicit tags for each time demand, and use software to hide the ones you don't want to see. Evernote has powerful tagging capabilities, and some people use it to manage tasks. Regrettably, it has no native calendar function; no software I am aware of performs this function.

For each of these tactics, it's possible to go further and store all your time demands in the cloud, including those that are Captured, Listed and Scheduled. In this way, you can manage your attention by viewing a few at a time.

Also, you can explore these options further by researching articles on email management. Here are a couple:

"Better to Organize Personal Information By Folders Or by Tags? The Devil is in the Details" by A. Civan *et al* and "Am I wasting my time organizing email? A study of email refinding" by S. Whittaker et al. (Visit the References to find the full citations for this and all other articles).

Not all software supports these features, unfortunately, so you'll have to do some hunting. Hopefully, in the near future, new innovations will close these gaps.

Evaluating Your Skills

Before we move on to the next chapter, take this opportunity to rank your own skills in this important area. Notice that in keeping with our discoveries in this chapter, as professionals improve their practices, they transition from using no lists to using a single to-do list, then to using multiple lists, and finally to using very few lists. In other words, they move from being memory-centric to list-centric and then to calendar-centric.

The second line of the chart below illustrates this idea: both White Belts and Green Belts "Never" use to-do Lists. It's not an error. A to-do list is the perfect tool for a certain number of time demands, but eventually, it's not good enough. Once again, use Peace of Mind to decide whether or not you are using the best methods for now and for the future.

Figure 13-3

Listing Cheat-Sheet

Behavior	White	Yellow	Orange	Green
Mental Lists	Often ☐	Sometimes ☐	Rarely ☐	Never ☐
ToDo Lists / Task Lists	Never or Rarely ☐	Always ☐	Never ☐	Never ☐
Portable lists	Never or Hardly ☐	Sometimes ☐	Often ☐	Always ☐
Lists that serve psychological purposes	Never or Hardly ☐	Sometimes ☐	Often ☐	Always ☐
Maintain lists that support scheduled items	Never or Hardly ☐	Sometimes ☐	Often ☐	Always ☐

Current Belt ☐   ☐   ☐   ☐

What's the best method for you right now?
- Mental lists
- A single to-do list
- Multiple lists
- Mobile lists
- Lists that support scheduled activities

Once you have finished, give yourself an overall Belt in this skill. Then, use the Planning Sheet to draft an improvement plan.

In the next chapter, we'll examine the other side of the equation: your Scheduling skills. As you may recall, in the last chapter, we established the fact that Listing and Scheduling should work together in a careful balance.

Remember and Share

It's possible to transition from using no lists whatsoever, to using a single list, to using lots of lists, to using only a few lists while becoming more productive along the way.

Time-starved people who use detailed schedules still need lists.

There's a limit to the number of time demands that can be managed using lists. Be wary.

Lists play a subordinate role for professionals who are time-starved. Their schedules take center stage.

Using a paper to-do list has its dangers – there's no backup.

If you store your time demands in a cloud, you can use all kinds of apps to view them in different ways.

Chapter 14. Scheduling – Mastering a Complex Skill with Awesome Benefits

(In which you learn that advanced Scheduling skills are easy to understand but challenging to develop).

In the Introduction, I shared some difficulties I faced after moving to Jamaica, which drove me to look for solutions. Here's what it was like to flounder without having a clue about the source of the problem.

***

September 2005: Kingston, Jamaica

My wife and I had just filled the tank and were driving through the edge of Grants Pen, a volatile community. "I don't know why this traffic isn't moving," I said.

"Honey," she replied, "do you think it has something to do with the increase in gas prices?"

I hoped not. After all, she had only been in Jamaica for a few weeks, and had arrived a month after me. I knew what "gas demonstrations" could mean – a possible riot.

With that in mind, I pulled a sharp U-Turn. We drove up the hill and took the long route back home, a 20-minute detour from our usual path. We settled in and turned on the television and radio.

We were lucky, we discovered. Grants Pen was later acknowledged as one of the flashpoints of a day that brought Kingston to a standstill. Ahead of us that morning was a group of demonstrators who had just started burning tires in order to block the road.

Days later, an edgy wariness remained in the air. Was this what life in Jamaica would be like? Needless to say, our plans for the week were dashed.

A few months later, I had a realization. As I flipped over pages of books and clicked through websites, it slowly dawned on me: *I'm doing this all wrong.*

Now, several months after the demonstrations that September morning, I was struggling to be as effective as I knew I could be in this new environment. I just wanted to feel as productive as I had felt in Florida, New York, New Jersey, South America, the Caribbean, and while traveling around the States. Back then, my life felt steady. I got stuff done at a rate that made me feel fulfilled. Now, entire days could pass in which all I did was chase my tail, expending lots of effort with little to show for it.

With a slight edge of desperation, I kept reading and came to a new thought: What if my commitments are falling apart because I have been putting all of my stuff in calendars instead of lists?

After all, I reasoned, "No one else is writing about this technique you have been using." As I read and listened, it seemed as if every guru had the same stern advice: "Don't use your calendar that way - you'll fail." None of the credible ones said anything different.

So, believing I had obviously done something wrong and needed to take things up a notch, I took their advice and switched. Instead of using my calendar to track all my stuff, I started using a combination of lists and tags.

It took me a few months to establish that I had only made things worse. Much worse.

Now, instead of having a clear plan for each day, I had only a vague idea. Without a detailed calendar, I felt stressed trying to remember what I had to do and when. Plus, I hated returning to my list over and over again to establish what I should work on next. I was forced to do this several times per day, because I couldn't make a mental plan that would last more than a few hours.

So, I made a U-Turn, deciding: *I need an upgrade… to go back to whatever I was doing before.* I shook my head and converted the tasks in my lists back into events in my schedule, but this time, I made a change. The Jamaican environment was more hectic, so I had to assume that every task involving other people or organizations needed to start earlier. It was also crazy to expect life to flow smoothly. There would be twists and turns and I had to create more slack time in my schedule to account for unplanned interruptions, like demonstrations or even riots.

***

Based on our discussion in the last chapter, I can now describe what I tried to do specifically. Faced with an inability to manage a new volume of time demands in an unreliable environment, I went back to Turning Point #3 from Turning Point #4, hoping it would help. I didn't realize I was turning back the clock. Floundering, I just needed to try something different.

Today, most gurus tell you to do what I did: stick to Turning Point #2 or #3, but don't consider Turning Point #4. A few say the opposite: you *must* reach Turning Point #4, regardless.

But the average professional who looks over Greta Green's shoulder to view her calendar-schedule recoils in terror. He/she might see something looking like this:

Figure 14-1

	Monday	Tuesday	Wednesday	Thursday	Friday
5:00 AM	Fitness run				
6:00 AM					
7:00 AM					
8:00 AM	Time to plan the week	Time to plan the day	Time to plan the day	Time to plan the day	Time to plan the day
9:00 AM	Check email and respond	Check email and respond	Check email and respond	Check email and respond	Check email and respond
10:00 AM			Prepare for CEO pre-briefing		
11:00 AM	Morning morning team meeting		CEO pre-briefing		Prepare for Monday meeting
12:00 PM	Lunch	Lunch	Lunch	Lunch	Lunch
1:00 PM					
2:00 PM					
3:00 PM					
4:00 PM					

To the casual viewer, having a detailed schedule of activity is the epitome of anal obsession. He feels nauseous and cannot imagine how she does it. The idea of planning almost every minute of almost every day appears ludicrous.

Fortunately for Greta, research performed in 2010 shows a positive relationship between free time management and quality of life. Contrary to expectations, "increasing free time does not itself contribute to quality of life; rather the way people use their free time does so." (Wang, et al.)

At the same time, someone like Wally can't avoid the fact that Greta appears to get more done than he could imagine. She has a family and kids, yet finds the time to complete two marathons a year while holding down an executive position. She ran six miles this morning while he was still asleep. *Is 'Leaning In' the secret of her success?* he wonders. *Or does it reside in her calendar?*

Let's explore Turning Point #4, the switch to a single calendar from multiple lists, by looking at the research around it.

What Recent Research Says About Detailed Scheduling

It's not hard to conclude from academic studies that maintaining a detailed calendar works for many professionals, and it's not hard to see why.

Earlier, while introducing the idea of time demands, I mentioned the work of Peter Gollwitzer on the effectiveness of planning "implementation intentions." As you may recall, it showed that in a group of women who agreed to do a breast self-exam during a period of 30 days, 100% of those who said where and when they were going to do it completed the exam. Only 53% of the others did.

In summary, you are more likely to complete time demands successfully if they are tagged with specific information outlining when, where and how the action will take place. Most of us implicitly create this information when a time demand is born, but like Wally, we keep it in our minds. The Greta Greens of the world use this information in an explicit way to plan a schedule of activity.

Also, a lot of data shows that complex time demands are easier to execute when they are broken down into small steps. A study by Justin Kruger and Matt Evans from the University of Illinois at Urbana-Champaign showed that people underestimate how long it takes to complete tasks: a phenomenon we discovered earlier called the planning fallacy. "Unpacking" a task into its components helps prevent this problem.

Siegried Dewitte, Tom Verguts and Willy Lens supported this finding in 2003. They discovered that complex goals don't benefit from definitions of where, when and how they'll be accomplished. Instead, they need to be broken down into small steps, each of which has its own definition of where, when and how it will be accomplished.

These scientists have echoed the timeless words of Mark Twain: "The secret of getting ahead is getting started. The secret of getting started is breaking your complex, overwhelming tasks into small, manageable tasks and then starting on the first one."

In summary: when you translate a time demand into its components and place them on your calendar, you increase the odds that you'll get the item done because you are making better estimates.

Another field of research is related to the power of a daily plan or schedule. Someone who makes such a plan can, according to David Rock, take advantage of the natural ebbs and flows of their attention each day. He says: "It's helpful to become aware of your own mental energy needs and schedule accordingly [...] One technique is to break work up into blocks of time based on type of brain use, rather than topic [...] divide your day into blocks of time when you do deep thinking such as creative writing, other blocks for having meetings, and other blocks for routine tasks such as responding to emails."

He also shows that when you make a schedule for the day, you have more energy to deal with interruptions and emergencies that may cause you to change your plans. You therefore make better decisions than you would otherwise. Kathryn Welds echoes his research in her blog post, "Time of

Day Affects Problem Solving Abilities," where she outlines the work of a number of scientists.

These aren't the only benefits to be derived from using a schedule to optimize your allocation of time. Cal Newport, an MIT-trained scientist and productivity author, recently described the benefit of planning a day that ends at a particular time on the blog "Barking Up the Wrong Tree." He writes: "Assume You're Going Home at 5:30, Then Plan Your Day Backwards." It echoes a brilliant insight from Mark Horstman: when you limit the time to do a particular task, like Emptying, your mind finds a way to get it done in the time allotted.

Oriana Bandiera from the National Bureau of Economic Research revealed another benefit in the Wall Street Journal. Extensive time-use studies revealed a correlation between CEO time use and corporate productivity, driven entirely by the number of hours the CEOs spent in planned activities.

There's also a benefit from having a visual calendar, which, according to Rock, takes less energy to manage. He starts off by comparing a mental list with a physical one: "If Emily gets a piece of paper and writes down the four big projects for the day, she saves her brain for comparing the elements instead of using energy to hold each one."

The transition at Turning Point #4 to displaying time demands in a calendar rather than a list can also allow you to use less energy:

"Creating visuals for complex ideas is one way to maximize limited energy resources [...] reducing the load on the prefrontal cortex whenever possible." He adds, "Picturing a concept activates the visual cortex in the occipital lobe, at the back of the brain. This region can be activated through actual pictures, or through metaphors, and storytelling, anything that generates an image in the mind." In the chapter on doing stuff "later," we compared a list of time demands with its counterpart in order to underline this point.

Having a visual calendar probably makes it easier to plan not only our work time but also our free time. In fact, a study from the I-Shou University in Taiwan showed that *managing* your free time affects your quality of life directly, but the *amount* of free time you have doesn't.

Lastly, Dan Ariely, the Duke University scientist who has also addressed these issues in his 2002 paper "Psychological Science, Procrastination, Deadlines and Performance", has discovered that self-imposed deadlines work better than no deadlines at all (but not as well as externally imposed deadlines). In a series of carefully controlled experiments, he points to the reason why having a detailed schedule works so well for some people: setting themselves a series of deadlines focuses the mind, preventing the kind of last-minute rush that can be so detrimental.

He also makes note of our tendency to make "hyperbolic discounts" and how it can be moderated with good plans. Julie Dirksen discussed the phenomenon in a recent podcast, in which she defined hyperbolic discounting as our tendency to prefer rewards that come quickly over those that come later. Ariely defines it as a "time-inconsistent taste for immediate gratification."

Apparently, when we do our planning, that time-inconsistent taste rears its ugly head, causing us to cram activities into short time frames, making today extremely busy, next week relatively light and next month appear as if we are on vacation. It's a mistake – the fact is, today is hardly likely to be more action-packed than tomorrow or any day next month. The result is that we end up having to juggle and reschedule our plans too often, creating unnecessary churn. Unfortunately, it takes great self-control to put together a schedule that isn't biased in this way.

It's not hard to see that it's easier to escape the clutches of hyperbolic discounting and the planning fallacy by using a visual calendar. In particular, Project Managers know this from their use of Gantt Charts (a form of task calendar), which proves far superior to an equivalent list of tasks. They know that visual tools make it easier to see the information (such as the interconnection between tasks) that a list either hides or forces the user keep in mind.

These researchers from different fields make it clear that people are more successful when they are able to manage time frames not implicitly (in their minds) but explicitly, in the form of visual schedules.

However, their findings are theoretical in nature and point to general benefits. Some might still argue that in day-to-day life, there are no practical ways to manage a schedule as well as we should: we should still avoid Turning Point #4 because it's too hard a transition to make. Let's take a look at the research that's been done on individuals who actually use a calendar each day.

Research on Calendar Usage

Dezhi Wu is a relatively new Associate Professor at Southern Utah University. She received her PhD in 2005 from the New Jersey Institute of Technology, but she's not in the psychology department, like most of the other experts cited in this book. She's actually a computer scientist. In her seminal book, *Temporal Structures in Individual Time Management: Practices to Enhance Calendar Tool Design,* Wu makes it clear that subjects in her study who use calendars and schedules are more productive than those who don't.

Her research is confirmed by Christine Bartholomew, who published a 2013 paper entitled "Time: An Empirical Analysis of Law Student Time Management Deficiencies." I outline their findings with those of others, such as Dan Ariely and researchers at McKinsey & Co., in my Lab Notes.[14]

The research is unequivocal. Some professionals have found a way to manage their lives using the same scheduling tools we all have in our smartphones and on our computers. They experience sustained, empirical advantages, even though they lack well-designed software and hardware. The only question is, what do they do to be effective, and how do they do it?

Knowing When to Upgrade

Once again, it's a mistake to conclude that everyone should have a calendar that looks like Greta's. If they don't, it does not mean they aren't optimizing their productivity. As I showed in the last chapter, she made changes in response to a high volume of time demands. She didn't make them because she's better or smarter.

Therefore, if your life doesn't involve a high volume (and you don't anticipate an increase), then you may not need to change a thing. Earlier, I used the analogy of speaking a foreign language to emphasize that it's not necessary to learn skills that you don't need. In other words, no one *needs* to move through a Turning Point unless they experience some level of time stress and can't handle the volume of time demands they are creating.

Furthermore, if you haven't experienced and don't expect an impact on your Peace of Mind, you may not be nearing a particular Turning Point, and you don't need to effect an upgrade.

These aren't strict rules by any means, and it's unfortunate that there isn't more empirical research to provide some clearer indications. We need them.

Once you have decided that you need an upgrade, how do you make the switch?

Preventing Failure

First, remember that many people who try to make the transition through this Turning Point #4 end up failing. Their expectations for immediate results are confounded by what they actually experience as they attempt to change old habits and learn new practices. Someone mentioned in an online group conversation: "I gave up after a day," having concluded that the turning point was impossible. (At least he/she tried – some gurus don't even experiment, while others use their experience of paper calendars as a definitive baseline.)

With the right expectations in mind, you also need the right tools and supports.

Perhaps the best support to have isn't technological at all, but human: a competent administrative assistant. If you have one, all you need is an open channel of communication to work out kinks, resolve conflicts and juggle commitments. This particular finding was reiterated in the McKinsey & Co. study mentioned earlier by Bevins and De Smet.

If you don't have an administrative assistant or secretary, then you must choose between paper and electronic devices. It's much harder to use paper as we explained in the chapter on Storing. Here is some more evidence, as it relates to calendar use.

Before digital calendars became widely available, professionals without administrative support used handwritten schedules on paper desk calendars and appointment books. Those who tried to go further than scheduling simple appointments quickly experienced the difficulty of tracking a changing schedule on paper. Their response to the massive friction caused by writing, crossing out, erasing and rewriting events was to:

a) Insist on following a schedule once it was made, thereby limiting the burden of juggling their schedule on paper.

b) Give up trying to schedule all their activities in their calendars, write in only those commitments that involved other people. These were deemed the most important and therefore most difficult to change.

These were natural, commonsense responses to the limitations of using paper.

Now, with the advent of electronic calendars, we realize that paper acts as a limit. It prevents users from easily doing the following, which electronic users now take for granted:

- Putting in repetitive events, such as a visit to the gym every Monday, Wednesday and Friday.
- Adding information to a particular event, such as a grocery list that's added to a scheduled trip to Kroughers Supermarket.
- Making backups, as we noted in the chapter on Storing. ("Backing up" a paper calendar is hard, but it's better than losing it).
- Sharing calendars with colleagues or family members.
- Importing pre-scheduled events such as meetings and holidays.
- Linking a sequence of time demands that together make up a project.
- Maintaining a cloud-based calendar that's displayed and updated on a device of our choosing.
- Juggling a calendar as needed using touch-screens.
- Overlaying multiple views of a single calendar, each of

which emphasizes a particular kind of time demand, such as meeting time, free time or family time.

- Inserting audible, visual and tactile reminders that an appointment is about to start.

It's hard to cling to paper calendars when the benefit of these features is so evident. Nevertheless many use paper for a number of reasons, working around some of its limitations, but not all.

However, as cool as the new technology might be, there are still lots of glaring gaps in the electronic tools we have available, as I'll explain in the chapter on New Tools.

Case Study: In her book, *Temporal Structures in Individual Time Management: Practices to Enhance Calendar Tool Design,* Dezhi Wu shares a five-month study in which two subjects are asked to adopt advanced scheduling skills. Before the study, they used a combination of memory, lists and paper calendars, just as our model predicts. In a three-hour session, they were taught how to use a Yahoo! online calendar instead. Interviews at the conclusion of the study suggested that the subjects perceived "great improvements" in their personal time management quality, recommending that their team members also adopt the tool. They were "more productive and more organized." They added the following comments, as noted in Wu's book.

Before the Transition:

- "Most of the time (my wall calendar) was used only for short-term planning, like a week ahead or so."

- "Most of the time depending on my memory to memorize important deadlines or events."

- "A lot of my time management was between everything on top of my head or using my cell phone."

- "The biggest problem was trying to remember the tasks in my head… Overall, the problem with having everything in your head is one of 'trying to remember.'"

After the Transition:

- "I was able to sync my calendar between my PDA and MS Outlook™ and hence always be updated and have more control of my time."

- "I became more productive by using the calendar-sharing feature with teammates."

- "The advantage was that I gained more time by only using one tool instead of many tools."

- "Yahoo! calendar has everything in front of you."

- "The changes […] improved my organization skills and increased my efficiency, quality of work, set my priorities straight, arriving on [sic] meetings and appointments on time."

While this particular portion of her overall study compared only two students' experiences, it broadly reflects my experience of training professionals to make the transition. This was a five-month study that required at least 14 meetings with the experimenter, underlining the point that these skills don't come easily.

Assuring Success

Making the transition effectively, however, isn't primarily a matter of having the "right" electronic tools. It has to do with habits, practices, rituals and routines. For example, the use of technology requires the development of certain routines. That surprises many users, who discover that they must devote time in new ways to needs they never anticipated.

Almost everyone who transitions to using a smartphone discovers they need to develop new "battery-life" habits, such as:

- Plugging in the device at night.
- Keeping charging devices in several locations.
- Monitoring the battery level periodically.
- Managing the number and nature of apps that are always running.
- Looking for opportunities to recharge wherever possible while travelling.
- Finding a suitable battery alarm or monitoring system.

These are simple but inescapable habits. Old practices, such as recharging on an ad-hoc basis, no longer work and have to be unlearned.

Notice, however, that you probably had no idea you'd be learning these habits until you owned a smartphone. Also, there are no classes to teach them. Finally, even if someone gave you a list of their habits in battery-charge management, you probably wouldn't just copy them. As you scan the list, you can probably see ways in which you would do things differently, probably for good reason.

These are useful principles to keep in mind as we address the transition to highly skilled Scheduling. Here are the steps that someone like Wally might take as he tackles Turning Point #4.

Step 1: Place all future time demands in his calendar while continuing to complete those that currently reside on lists.

Step 2: Be conservative by allocating more time than he thinks he needs (avoiding the planning fallacy).

Step 3: Separate time demands with enough slack time to account for unexpected variations, emergencies and surprises.

Step 4: Consider blocking out time for personal activities.

Step 5: Use specific language in time demands that makes it more likely that you'll actually do it.

Step 6: Practice checking your schedule before saying "Yes" or "No" to new time demands.

Blocking Time for Personal Activities

Most professionals who use Greta's scheduling skills come to realize the truth discovered by David Neal and other researchers at Duke University: some 45% of what we do each day is the stuff we do every day, in the same location, by habit. To save time, Greta has set up a "standard" week made up of these recurrent activities that acts as a starting point for her schedule. Here's an example of her "standard" week, before one-off items have been added. This technique relieves her of the burden of starting each week with an empty schedule that must be made up from scratch.

Figure 14-2

	Monday	Tuesday	Wednesday	Thursday	Friday
5:00 AM	Fitness run		Cycling		Go to Gym
6:00 AM					
7:00 AM					
8:00 AM	Time to plan the week	Time to plan the day	Time to plan the day	Time to plan the day	Time to plan the day
9:00 AM					
10:00 AM	Check email and respond	Check email and respond	Check email and respond	Check email and respond	Check email and respond
11:00 AM	Morning morning team meeting		Prepare for CEO pre-briefing CEO pre-briefing		Prepare for Monday meeting
12:00 PM	Lunch	Lunch	Lunch	Lunch	Lunch
1:00 PM					
2:00 PM					
3:00 PM					
4:00 PM					

This technique aligns with the idea of an "Unschedule," defined by Neal Fiore as a schedule that starts by blocking out time for sleep, leisure, family time, idle time – all the things that you choose to do, rather than have to do because of work obligations. The end result might appear to be the same, although there's something positive about taking care of yourself and your loved ones via your schedule before you even consider the first action item from work.

It's easy to set up your own schedule using the recurring appointments function in your digital calendar.

Employing Specific Language

Research performed by Edwin Locke and Gary Latham shows that the language used to describe a time demand influences whether or not we actually do the task. Highly skilled Schedulers have become quite sophisticated in the language they use, choosing words that are designed to increase the odds that they'll execute, rather than ignore, each activity. For example, take a look at the following changes they'd make:

- "Choir practice: 6:00 PM - 8:00 PM" could be changed to "fulfill my potential as a singer by attending practice: 6:00 PM - 8:00 PM"

- "Do taxes: 4:00 PM - 5:00 PM" could be changed to "avoid penalties from IRS by completing 1040 on time: 4:00 PM - 5:00 PM."

They take care to express actions in a way that pulls them towards their commitments, especially if there's some resistance or reluctance to completing the action.

One easy way, for example, to increase the odds of implementing a strategic plan at the individual level is to create time demands using language that links back to the long-term plan.

Not only do we seem to respond to the way a task is expressed in words; we are also influenced by the timing of the task. In one 2014 study, Yanping Tu and Dilip Soman showed that subjects were more likely to complete a six-month task scheduled to end in December rather than January. Apparently, we categorize tasks into chunks such as "this year" and "next year." We are more apt to start and complete tasks that fall within the current category than within others.

Saying "No" and Other Unexpected Benefits

Here is a list of other benefits that professionals like Greta derive from leading a calendar-centric life.

1. Greta often has a black-and-white reason to say "No" to meeting requests. Why? It's right there on her calendar: something is already scheduled in that time slot. Contrast her schedule with Wally's, which has lots of empty space and gives the illusion that he has a lot of free time. In Greta's schedule, she has actually incorporated the "standard" week described in the diagram above. Having a schedule arranged in this way means, for example, that she can negotiate in good faith with anyone who wants to schedule some of her time.

Also, Greta recovers more easily on those days when she has to erase everything she had planned due to an unplanned emergency. In this situation, a standard schedule is a huge benefit: Greta simply moves time demands around with a few clicks or swipes. By contrast, Wally has only a vague idea of what he wants to accomplish. When the emergency hits, he cancels his thoughts and promptly forgets about the time demands he'd originally planned for that day. That's why he gets to the end of a month and realizes, for example, that he hasn't made it to the gym even once.

2. The key to being reliable is to follow Greta's example in the use of her calendar. Someone who commits to an activity, project or deliverable and manages his time like Wally is likely to fail, just because the other stuff that he must do has not been accounted for in his schedule – it's only in his mind. This produces time-stress and miscues. Colleagues learn that his "Yes" actually means "Maybe." Greta, on the other hand, is far more reliable and less likely to over-commit herself. Her life is also more balanced when it comes to her family, health and wellbeing.

3. If you ever decide to take Peter Drucker's sage advice from The Effective Executive and analyze your actual, historical time use, it's much easier to do with advanced

scheduling skills. In essence, the best analysis is a comparison between your planned and actual time use. Only then can you properly explore the causes for major discrepancies. The McKinsey study by Bevins and De Smet also includes time use data from the best time managers and recommends that executives perform periodic audits. I have tracked my time for as long as I can remember and have found it a useful practice.

4. Following Mark Horstman's and others' advice to schedule lots of time alone is easier said than done. Meetings scheduled by other people can be all but impossible to decline, even if nothing of value is likely to be accomplished. On the other hand, time set aside to work alone is easy to ignore or delay. It's hard to make the transition to being the kind of professional who treats meetings with suspicion and time alone as sacred. Unfortunately, without the advanced skills that Greta uses each day, it's easier to go with the flow and show up at meetings because "you're expected to."

This particular weakness has far-reaching consequences. After a strategic planning retreat, for example, there's a tremendous need for attendees to spend time alone to absorb the decisions made. Unfortunately, I have seen the opposite happen. Lacking advanced scheduling skills, executives don't set time aside to work on strategic priorities by themselves, even as they continue to attend pre-scheduled meetings with other people. In other words, a professional with Wally's skills often gets buried in day-to-day concerns, ignoring the big picture – a dangerous combination of habits if he happens to be the CEO.

5. In Chapter 15, we'll look at the power of using cues and reminders to interrupt our daily activities and start important ones. These are much easier to set up if you're already using an electronic schedule with a reminder attached to it, thereby increasing the probability of completing a time demand.

Evaluating Your Skills

Use the following Cheat-Sheet to assess your skills.

Figure 14-3

Scheduling Cheat-Sheet

Behavior	White	Yellow	Orange	Green
Over-scheduled days	Often ☐	Sometimes ☐	Rarely ☐	Never ☐
Electronic schedule	Rarely or haphazardly ☐	Sometimes ☐	Often ☐	Always ☐
Portable schedule	Never or Hardly ☐	Sometimes ☐	Often ☐	Always ☐
Carefully worded items in the schedule	Never or Hardly ☐	Sometimes ☐	Often ☐	Always ☐

Current Belt ☐   ☐   ☐   ☐

Use the Planning Sheet to create a plan to guide your improvement skills.

In the chapter on Flowing, you'll look at one of the reasons why pre-planning your time allows you to operate at your very best. Rock gives us a hint of what's possible: "One final insight about prioritizing involves getting disciplined about what you don't put on the stage (of your mind). This means not thinking when you don't have to, becoming disciplined about not paying attention to non-urgent tasks unless, or until, it's truly essential that you do." He concludes, "The bottom line to all this is one simple message: your ability to make great decisions is a limited resource. Conserve this resource at every opportunity."

In our next chapter, we'll pull together the seven Planning Sheets you have crafted from the chapters covering the 7 Essential Fundamentals. Our goal will be to create a single realistic, easy-to-implement Master Plan. If you're going to skip chapters in this book, don't skip this one!

Remember and Share

Not everyone needs to use advanced Scheduling skills.

The learning curve for adopting advanced scheduling skills is steep.

Managing a paper calendar is becoming far less efficient than managing an electronic one.

Beware of scheduling with the planning fallacy – underestimating how long things take.

Avoid hyperbolic discounting – working on stuff that you like right away just to get a dopamine rush. It can wait.

Not everyone would be better off using techniques that allow them to handle the maximum number of time demands.

An implicit tag is one that we keep in mind to tag a time demand. We can make them explicit by writing or typing them out.

Managing your free time is positively related to your quality of life.

Adding to your free time doesn't help if you don't manage it well.

Chapter 15. Putting Your Master Plan Together

(In which you learn how to create a single improvement plan starting with seven separate plans).

Of all the chapters in this book, this is perhaps the one that requires the most attention. Why? It speaks to the moment where most people's improvement plans fail: during the transition from planning to implementation.

As I mentioned in the Introduction, the single most important deliverable from this book is not the information in the research or the background of the 11 Fundamentals. What's most important is your plan to make changes.

If you are feeling overwhelmed by all the plans you have made in the last few chapters, you are right to be concerned. There's no way to make all those changes in the next few months. At some point, you may have had the thought, "This is crazy!"

You are not crazy: the seven plans you put together are a recipe for failure if you attempt to make all those changes at the same time. However, this chapter is about your success. We'll look at ways to create a single realistic Master Plan that has much higher odds of success. To do so, we'll have to overcome the planning fallacy – our strong tendency to be over-optimistic.

***

Nobel Laureate and psychologist Daniel Kahneman had the same problem, as he shares in his book *Thinking Fast and Slow*. A team of experts he assembled in order to put together a curriculum for teaching judgment and decision making for the Ministry of Education in Israel had reached the end of its design process. Now, it turned its attention to making an implementation plan.

They began by trying to estimate how long it would take to complete a finished draft of the textbook they had promised. After doing a short brainstorming exercise, they wrote the results up on a blackboard. The median estimate appeared to be about two years, and most clustered around one and a half and two and a half years.

The team was wrong. The project didn't take two years – it took eight. By then, the Ministry of Education had lost interest in the project, and the text was never used.

How could they have been so wrong? Given their expertise, commitment and long history of working on similar projects, you'd expect that they might make an error of perhaps a few months, not years. And certainly not a four-fold error.

Kahneman describes the steps the team took to improve its estimate. He asked for some details about team members' prior experience. After gathering them, it appeared that a team of similar experience had never completed the job in fewer than seven years. That seemed so unrealistic that the team never used the seven-year estimate, to its detriment. If they had, they might have stopped the effort immediately.

If you can't relate at all to the experience that Kahneman describes, conduct a few experiments of your own. In my classes, I use an example that afflicts my wife and me when we take the drive from Kingston to Montego Bay. On Jamaican roads, the 150-mile trip "should" take a little under four hours to complete.

The fact is, it never does. It's always longer. If you ask me how long it takes, however, I'll predict the best-case result every time.

More recently, the planned launch of The Affordable Care Act website ("ObamaCare") on October 1, 2013 was spectacularly botched. Even when the deadline was clearly flying by them, top managers continued to push over-optimistic estimates, pressuring their employees to perform miracles. They couldn't, and the site failed.

If this phenomenon sounds familiar, it should. We discussed it briefly in the chapter on Scheduling, in which I described the problems professionals like Greta have when they first start using a schedule as their main point of reference.

They discover the "planning fallacy." With it, they learn that they have been using illusory, over-optimistic estimates for years.

***

The planning fallacy, as we mentioned before, is the tendency to assume that ideal conditions will prevail in the future, even when firsthand experience tells us that something always goes wrong. Kahneman and Amos Tversky first introduced the term in a 1979 paper.

In a fascinating 1994 follow-up article entitled "Exploring the Planning Fallacy: Why People Underestimate Their Task Completion Times," Roger Buehler, Dale Griffin and Michael Ross went a few steps further to discover why we are better estimators of other people's time than our own. My parents would never take fewer than four hours to make the Montego Bay trip, in my estimation, but it's not because I consider myself a faster driver. It's because I can see their obstacles more clearly than I can see my own. Also, I use information about their past trips far better than I do my own. I diminish my own mishaps, attributing them to individual cases of bad luck rather than a pattern of errors that are each likely to occur next time I make the trip.

What does all this have to do with pulling together a plan for implementing changes in the 7 Essential Fundamentals?

If you have guessed that I'm about to pour some cold water on the plans you have developed so far, you're right. To leave you alone to implement seven plans developed independently of each other would be criminal, now that we know a bit about the planning fallacy!

If I were to do that, you'd probably respond by setting some sky-high expectations. You might argue that the concepts are simple enough to understand, so implementation should be easy. Big mistake... as Werner Erhard said, "Understanding is the booby prize." In other words, understanding something says little about how well you can make it real.

Quickly glance at the seven plans you assembled. If looking at them combined for the first time makes you laugh at your optimism, then you're on the right track.

While they're an improvement over the alternative (i.e. having no plan at all), when you see them all together, you realize that it would take a superhuman effort to implement them all in the same time frame.

What we need is a plan that's more suited to Clark Kent than to his alter ego.

In the last chapter, we mentioned research conducted on the planning fallacy and the need to unpack a task into its components. Working with these components reduces the effect of the planning fallacy, leading to more realistic estimates. This would help ensure your success in our next step – assembling a Master Plan.

Crafting Your Master Plan

Let's return for a moment to the idea of taking small steps and use it to create a feasible Master Plan.

Here are the steps I recommend:

Step 1: Bring together all seven planning sheets.

Step 2: Make a master list on a piece of paper of all the changes planned for the next three months, without dates.

Step 3: Make a single new plan for this time frame, pushing to the future all items that no longer fit. Don't try to change more than a few (two or three) habits at a time.

Step 4: Continue planning for as long as you can maintain your energy, in three-month increments. You may end up with just one three-month plan, or you might construct one that runs for as long as 24 months.

Step 5: Pause, stand back and ask yourself honestly: "Is this doable?"

To borrow a term from statisticians, your plan should appear to you to be "unbiased." That is, the milestones and activities you set should give you an equal chance of success and failure. I like to call these 50-50 estimates: you have a 50% chance of meeting your deadlines (and therefore a 50% chance of being late).

Here are some more useful hints to use as you forge your Master Plan. Remember, your goal is to create long-term, low-maintenance habits that take place without much conscious effort. While you have to start with new, high-energy behaviors that you attempt for the first time, that's not where you want to end up.

- Look to convert behaviors into habits in your planning. (There is more on this topic in the chapter on "Habiting").

- Plan conservatively.

- Combine low-hanging fruit (i.e. easy changes) with more difficult changes.
- Pay attention to which Fundamentals are weak, and use that information to decide which ones to work on first.
- Don't be daunted by a long planning horizon. These behavior changes take time to become habits.
Some may take several years. When I spoke with behavior design expert B.J. Fogg, I learned that regular cycles (such as 30-day periods) help focus the mind on short-term improvements.
- Focus on working with tiny habits, another Fogg principle that helps prevent the planning fallacy.
- Don't worry about how you'll keep the momentum going - we'll also address that in the chapter on Habiting. For now, focus on putting together the best possible plan.
- Use lots of reminders on available tools (smartphones, laptops, tablets, etc.) as cues to learn habits until you don't need them anymore.

Here's an excerpt from a simplified Master Plan.

Figure 15-1

Habit Change	Start Date	Due Date
Carry Capture Tool with me everywhere	May 1	June 30
Empty once per day	May 15	July 15
Use Outlook Calendar at Yellow Belt level daily	August 1	September 30
Do Daily Content review	July 1	July 31

As you put your plan together, notice any inner resistance as your ego goads you to inflate estimates of your abilities. "Surely," it argues, "you can do better than that! C'mon now!"

If it kicks in with full force, take note. This is the same dopamine rush that fuels the planning fallacy, ruining projects like the curriculum effort Kahneman led. See this as an opportunity to engage the rational part of your mind that's *not* excited or inspired by the idea of making upgrades as soon as possible.

Case Study

As I mentioned before, your overall belt at any point in time is simply the lowest belt you happen to possess in any of the 7 Essential Fundamentals. Like many participants in my programs, your Master Plan may also include a timetable showing your intended future progression from your current belt to other, higher belts. These targets can be quite motivating if they're realistic.

Here's a 27-minute interview with Michael Zajac, a participant who attended my pilot program in 2008. His initial evaluation ranked him as a White Belt, but his plan allowed him to successfully attain a Yellow Belt and then an Orange Belt 18 months later. Follow this link to hear his interview online: http://goo.gl/6AAeOv

Allow yourself to be inspired by his example as you finish up your own Master Plan.

At the end of this chapter, I'll describe some ways to make the most of the remaining chapters in this book. But before we move on, take a moment to compare your profile with that of the average participant in my live programs.

Comparing Your Profile

Earlier in this book, I mentioned that you'd have an opportunity to measure your progress against the average attendee of one of my recent programs. Here is what the average profile looks like, derived from the median score of profiles reported by a mixed population of 72 participants in 7 training sessions. The numeric score at the right is the median on a scale of 1-100.

Figure 15-2

	White	Yellow	Orange	Green	
Capturing	☐	☐	X	☐	51.6
Emptying	☐	X	☐	☐	44.9
Tossing	☐	X	☐	☐	44.7
Acting Now	☐	X	☐	☐	47.9
Storing	☐	X	☐	☐	44.2
Scheduling	☐	X	☐	☐	41.8
Listing	☐	X	☐	☐	40.6
	1-25	26-50	51-75	76-100	

I was genuinely surprised to discover that the median score for each of the 7 Essential Fundamentals clustered so tightly around the Yellow Belt ranking. While each participant's scores were all over the map, the medians appeared to cluster.

Who were these participants, and exactly and where did the data come from?

Facts

- The majority was female (I estimate a 60-40% split).
- They were all employed by Jamaican companies, and only a handful are citizens of other countries.
- Each evaluation was performed within minutes of being taught the distinctions that underlie the particular fundamental.
- The setting was a class called NewHabits Foundations – a one-day crash course that covers the 7 Essential Fundamentals. The 4 Advanced Fundamentals are mentioned only in passing.
- The course materials used to train the groups that yielded

this data underwent only minor changes.

- I was the instructor for each group, which never exceeded 25 individuals.

Assumptions

- Most participants have had some tertiary education.
- Most participants have been with their respective companies for at least five years.
- The evaluations were performed by participants who were instructed in the same way. In other words, my technique changed little during the 15-month period of data collection.
- People who have been trained to do their self-evaluations do so quite differently than untrained people. As I indicated earlier in my discussion with Jeremy Burrus, more inside knowledge leads to lower self-evaluation. This phenomenon is known as the Dunning–Kruger effect. According to Wikipedia, it's a cognitive bias whereby unskilled individuals suffer from illusory superiority, mistakenly rating their ability much higher than is accurate. This bias is attributed to a metacognitive inability of the unskilled to recognize their ineptitude.

How to Use the Data

I make a general recommendation to class participants: focus on the weakest fundamental, and examine whether it should be your first area of improvement. You can compare your own profile against the average and determine where the biggest improvement gaps are and why.

Ultimately, you can use this information to influence your Master Plan and help make sure it meets your needs.

Future Research

If you'd like to join in and share your own profile data, visit my website's data entry page at the following address: http://perfect.mytimedesign.com/dataentry. I plan to share the cumulative data I collect from readers of *Perfect Time-Based Productivity* on this page.

If you are a statistician or researcher, you may see a number of technical issues with the approach I have taken to gathering the data in this fashion, e.g. at the moment, I am the only one who can rigorously administer the instrument as it's presented during a day of live training. Therefore, I could be biasing the data, yielding systematic errors. For example, is the relative ranking of Capturing high because of the way it's presented?

I welcome questions and discussion, and if you visit my website's forums, you can join or initiate an open discussion with other readers and with me.

Corporate Data Comparisons

Recently, I shared some new data collected from a single corporate client with Andrew Staroscik. He's an expert in data visualization who graciously volunteered his time to help me look at the data I collected. So far, he's come up with two charts, which I'm sharing on a page I set up at http://2time-sys.com/profile-analysis. This page will evolve over time, but for now, it includes two charts he created that can help you compare your profile against that of my sample.

One diagram looks like a heat map of different skills that you can use to precisely compare your profile along each of the 7 skills. The second allows you to compare your entire profile against that of other people. For example, if you received a White Belt Level 3 in Capturing, it reveals the profiles of all the other people who also received a White Belt Level 3 in Capturing.

These comparisons can give you an idea of how your skills have developed over the years compared to other people.

Your Next Step in This Book

This brings us to the end of Part Two. It's a natural point to pause and evaluate your progress so far as well as where you'd like to go next. Here are the remaining chapters in Part Three - Advanced Topics.

First of all, congratulations! You are among the very few professionals who have completed a self-evaluation of the behaviors you use to manage time demands. Your current profile will help you build on some sophisticated understanding and give you interesting insights into the behaviors you have used for several years, perhaps without thinking too much about them. Your habits, practices, rituals and routines have left the dark shrouds of the past and are up on a well-lit stage for your active consideration.

Also, you have completed a Master Plan for upgrading your self-taught behaviors and will no longer rely on teenage knowledge to run an adult life (unless you're still a teenager!) Your plan gives you a future that's consciously designed for a particular intention. It's all yours – a custom pathway to achieve your goals.

What's next for you? I can see three options.

1. **Pause to Reload** - You may be interested in taking a

break from this book after the work you have done. If so, I invite you to skip Part Three for now and read the Summary at the end of the book. It discusses a number of interactive resources and communities related to what you have just read.

2. **Complete Your Profile** - If you're keen on completing your evaluation of the four remaining Advanced Fundamentals, you can continue on to the next few chapters, which will address a key behavior, Flowing, then take you right to Interrupting, Switching, Reviewing and Warning. After doing these self-evaluations of all 11 Fundamentals, I'll invite you to adjust your Master Plan accordingly. At the end, you'll have a simple but complete plan. You can then skip to the Summary, returning to pick up the other chapters whenever you like.

3. **Go with the Flow** - This path involves reading the book all the way to the end. While your evaluations will come to a close in just a few chapters, you may value the following chapters as a professional with an interest in time-based productivity. We'll look at what it takes to become an expert in creating new habits, practices and rituals, plus some of the challenges of living in the modern world with its ever-changing technology. To help you cope, I'll show you how to set up your own ladders of improvement using the approach I used to build the 11 Fundamentals. Finally, we'll examine some of the obstacles to being productive that are hard-wired into corporate environments.

So, take a deep breath and choose. Whichever choice you make, enjoy your next step.

In the next chapter, we will discover why we must pay attention to moments of high productivity so that we can produce and experience them on demand.

Remember and Share

It's better to try to change one habit at a time.
The main output of *Perfect Time-Based Productivity* is a simple plan for immediate implementation.
It's best to break down a complex new practice into small steps.
A plan for changing habits should be based on small changes

taken gradually, one step at a time.

Tune in to hear a time-management trainee improve his skills from White to Yellow to Orange Belt in 18 months. http://goo.gl/6AAeOv

Part Three

Advanced Topics

I wouldn't give a fig for simplicity on this side of complexity, but I'd give my right arm for simplicity on the other side of complexity.
Justice Oliver Wendell Holmes, Jr.

Chapter 16. Flowing – The Art and Science of High-Performance Moments

(In which you learn that it's hard to maintain high productivity in today's typical office environment).

I'm writing these lines at 3:25 AM, which isn't unusual. Most of this book was written very early in the morning, before 8 AM, when most people are making their way to work.

Early bird writing is the solution I found to a problem that all authors have – finding uninterrupted time to focus on doing a challenging task. In my case, I know that when I can't carve out this kind of quality time, writing the book takes longer (or becomes simply impossible).

Of course, it's not the early hour that creates the environment needed to produce superior results. Instead, it's the window of opportunity for uninterrupted, focused activity which for me, being awake this early allows.

But that's not enough. I have also noticed that when I'm distracted by poorly-managed time demands, I'm also unable to focus, regardless of how early I rise. Instead, the Zeigarnik effect I mentioned earlier weighs in, as I mentioned earlier, and my subconscious mind starts a nagging, pinging routine designed to continuously remind me that something important remains incomplete. Storage in memory alone means that it could slip through the cracks and disappear.

As your professional life picks up momentum, resulting in greater numbers of time demands, you must become more skillful at managing them, especially if you want to enter periods of high productivity. Highly focused problem-solving and creative endeavors become a function, in part, of being well organized.

***

When you're young, it's easy to stay focused. When you have a small number of time demands to manage, you are relatively free from the Zeigarnik effect, in which unmanaged time demands are a continuous source of distraction.

However, as you grow older and your number of

obligations increases, your ability to maintain the same number of focused hours suffers. Not only is there more competition for your time; there's also more competition for your attention. For athletes, for example, off-field distractions grow with age, making it increasingly difficult to stay focused on training, competition and recovery.

Maintaining world-class performance in the latter stages of an athletic career become, in part, a matter of managing off-field time demands. The same applies to knowledge workers, but unfortunately, we aren't trained to make the distinction. In this chapter, we'll look at what it takes to be our very best and why the art of managing time demands is so important.

Knowledge Workers vs. Sprinters

"I have noticed that ever since I got promoted, I never have time to do focused work by myself."

We were in the corporate boardroom of a financial institution, high above the hustle and bustle of the streets below. Bert, the General Manager, was speaking in a soft voice that most of us had to strain to hear. "I only get time to really think when I come in on weekends or leave late, which I simply have to do in order to get in uninterrupted thinking time."

For employees, it was a rare peek into his world, and the room was silent for a few seconds after he spoke.

He was reflecting what I hear often: the modern workplace makes it increasingly difficult for employees like Bert to do their best work, and it's not anyone's fault in particular.

As he explained, numerous obstacles prevented him from accessing the single tool he needed most: quiet, uninterrupted time. Instead, he had to use weekends, late nights and holidays to carve out time alone: time that was originally meant for his kids, the gym and his favorite hobby, cooking.

"I remember when I was a student," he continued. "Doing this kind of work was easy!"

He was right. College campuses are designed to provide lots of quiet locations. When a knowledge worker graduates and gets that first job, all of a sudden, this resource becomes scarce.

***

One big difference between knowledge work and the daily commitments of high performing athletes is that there's a clear differentiation between time spent competing, when high performance is required, and all the other times spent in preparation. Athletes engage in warm-ups, focused practice, drills, weightlifting and other activities to get themselves ready for competition. By contrast, knowledge workers have a tough time separating the two.

Thanks to the work of Mihaly Csziksentmihalyi, they can also determine when peak performance is required. In his book, *Flow: Psychology of Optimal Experience*, he observes that high performance happens in a particular context, which he calls *the flow state*. He defines *the flow state* as moments of intense concentration in which we produce our best results.

It's hard to miss his message, as his work has been popularized in his books, on blogs and via Ted Talks and YouTube videos. Professionals have become well acquainted with the idea that top-quality work comes from:
- Quiet, uninterrupted focus on a single task.
- A blend of challenge and required skill that makes the task possible but not boring.

During this state, time seems to float past, and you feel one with the activity, which feels near euphoric. These are the moments when you are able to achieve an outstanding outcome: the corporate equivalent of running at the Olympics.

Notwithstanding Csziksentmihalyi's groundbreaking work, corporations aren't set up to take advantage of his findings. While his book was written in 1990, corporations have allowed email, mobile technologies and open floor plans to create environments that hamper employee productivity daily. These office obstacles will be discussed in depth in the chapter on corporations near the end of this book.

In this chapter I have defined the ability to mindfully enter, maintain and exit *the flow state* as "The Skill of Flowing."

Key Dismukes, the NASA scientist we met in earlier chapters, has found evidence that employees operate in only three states when executing time demands:

1. The flow state: our optimal, peak state of high performance.

2. Habit execution: our neuro-muscular memories have taken over, requiring minimal effort while engaging the region of our brain called the basal ganglia.

3. Somewhere in between: we aren't focused enough to achieve the flow state and also haven't developed sufficient habits. Our performance in these moments is mediocre and unconscious, based on an effort that barely keeps things going.

By these definitions, high performance in day-to-day corporate life is the exception, and the vast majority of workers have no idea what the flow state entails. In fact, those who try too hard to achieve the flow state are sometimes branded as misfits who lack social skills.

In spite of these obstacles, what are the strategies the most effective professionals employ to consistently achieve these periods of high performance?

What's Required to Master "Flowing"?

1. Conscious Awareness

The most productive professionals don't merely fall into the flow state as a matter of coincidence. They ask themselves the following questions:

- When do I require the flow state to get a job done?
- What conditions will help me move into this state?
- When am I in the flow state? How do I know?
- How do I know when I have left it unwillingly or unwittingly?
- How do I return to it?

On one level, Csziksentmihalyi's book gives some general answers that are meant to apply to everyone. On another, more specific level, we must answer these questions for ourselves if we hope to be productive. Without this awareness, it's impossible to carve out the right kind of physical, visual and auditory environment we need.

The book *Flow* describes a euphoria that comes from the flow state in which feelings of happiness, spontaneous joy and ecstasy are not uncommon. However, professionals should go past these heightened feelings, argues author Cal Newport. In his Study Hacks blog, he writes, "Flow is the Opiate of the Mediocre": it's not enough to focus on these feelings. When the task at hand becomes quite difficult, there may be a feeling of strain or even struggle.

Deliberate practice, in which we focus on our weakest areas for long periods of time, is essential to improvements. Newport performed a three-month experiment to boost his ability to master hard concepts in his field of computer science. In the beginning, there was no ecstasy or euphoria, but over time, he got better. He argues that deliberate practice does not put you in the flow state, but perhaps he's being literal: high performance may not require happy feelings as it's being mastered, but focused, non-interrupted effort is required for both the flow state and deliberate practice. For the purpose of our discussion in this book, let us assume that the term "Flowing" refers to either the flow state or deliberate practice – a highly focused state that may or may not be euphoric.

Given this finding, it may be important for some professionals to know what kind of flow is required in order to prepare accordingly. Cal Newport appears to know the difference, and he prepares his mind accordingly.

2. Peace of Mind Around Time Demands

According to the Zeigarnik Effect and the research of Baumeister and Masicampo mentioned in earlier chapters, when time demands aren't being managed well, they intrude on our thoughts.

That makes it difficult to enter the flow state – our minds won't let us. It's the opposite of having what David Allen calls a "mind like water," which comes from having what he calls a "trusted system."

Why is our subconscious so insistent? Remember that time demands arise from our commitments, and the more important they are, the harder our mind tries to make sure we don't forget them. It's a continuous inner struggle between what we want and what we think we can handle. When we achieve perfect time-based productivity, we have a system that always matches the number of time demands we need to handle. This often means continuously upgrading it to handle new commitments.

3. Turning the Flow State On and Off

You can use the flow state to accomplish a wide range of objectives, but most of us don't know when to turn it on or off.

For example, now, it's 4:19 AM, and I am "using" the flow state to write this chapter, which for me qualifies as an intense creative activity. When I'm done, I'll switch over to a different, unrelated task: editing a newspaper column, which also requires the flow state, although it has a different quality. Before I finish, my wife will wake up, and I'll start interacting with her a bit while I make my edits. It's not enough to interrupt the flow state, as long as our interactions are brief: light edits don't require the same level of intensity as purely creative work.

Generating creative output and editing prose are just two possible uses of the flow state. Others include working to meet a deadline, conducting "deliberate practice" a la Malcolm Gladwell / Cal Newport, studying a difficult topic, sharpening your memory for a test, or climbing a challenging hill on a bicycle. Those are just a few examples, but my point here is to have you reflect: what activities do you need to accomplish within the next week that require the flow state? Use your diary to write them down, anticipating and planning these moments of peak performance.

4. Limiting Random Human Interruptions

The flow state is much easier to accomplish when other people aren't around, which is why staying home to "get some work done" is often a good idea. Bert would have enjoyed that particular luxury. However, the people closest to us are often the most likely to interrupt us – our kids, spouse, boss, colleague, etc. These are the ones who are most likely to create a sustained interruption.

Staying in the flow state in today's world requires some negotiating skills just to get time away from those with whom we are close. It may call for lengthy explanations. Some may

insist that they need to get our attention regardless of what
we're trying to do. Our job is to describe the consequences of
their interruptions while being firm about the need to be left
alone. There's no need to be rude – explain yourself
professionally and calmly, and use facts. Sometimes, it's smart
to rehearse these conversations so they have the right tone.

According to Csziksentmihalyi and other researchers, it
takes between 20 and 25 minutes to return to the flow state
once it's interrupted. In the context of an 8-hour day, there
simply aren't many opportunities to spend 20 minutes
"warming up" for peak performance. After an interruption,
the cost of recovery is high as we try to recapture the state
that was lost.

While I have focused on the flow state for individuals
in this chapter, I believe it's also possible to attain this state
when working with other people. For example, a quartet
singing in harmony might also be in the flow state. If
sufficiently interrupted, the group may not return to the state
immediately: it may take some time to get back into the
groove.

5. Scheduling Time

In the last chapter, I dispelled the notion that you
should never use your calendar to set aside time for solo
activity. Unfortunately, there's another downside to using
calendars only for appointments with other people – if you
follow that rule, you'll never set time aside to enter the flow
state on your own.

Professionals like Greta Green, who demonstrate
higher skills in Scheduling, know the truth. The flow state
requires pre-planned, sometimes extensive arrangements. At
the very least, it often requires blocked-out calendar time. If
tomorrow, for example, is Sunday, and I schedule 3:00 AM-
6:00 AM as the time to write the next chapter, that helps me
not only to remember to set an alarm but also to go to bed
early enough. Also, I'd make sure to have coffee close by,
plus a few snacks to eat – all of which require some
coordination with my wife.

While it is possible to fall into the flow state as a matter
of luck, I doubt I'd be up at this hour just by chance. It's

more reliable and easier, from my experience, to pre-plan the times when I intend to enter the flow state.

For time-starved executives or college students, scheduling time to enter the flow state is a must. Professionals who share calendars with colleagues are also better off blocking out time to be in this state each week, rather than trying to slip it in between other appointments.

If it's important for you to spend quality time working alone, then you need to schedule it, preferably where others can see it.

6. Mobile Alerts

I once heard a story that may be apocryphal: Blackberry, which used to ship units with all its alerts turned on, had a change of heart and started shipping them with all the alerts turned off, with the exception of the phone's ringer.

Why the switch, according to this tale?

Simple: they were driving people crazy!

Unintentionally, Blackberry had initiated a worldwide behavior change. Millions of users, rather than turn off the alerts, simply learned to check their BBs to see what the alert meant. Even while they were driving. Or having sex. Or giving a speech. Or crossing a busy road. Or, for our purposes, while they were in the flow state.

It means that, for example, someone who receives 100 email messages each day checks to see what each message has to say when it pops up, pings, vibrates or flashes a light. That translates to maybe 10 alert-driven responses per hour.

If you intend to access the flow state, the remedy is easy. Before entering it, turn off your mobile, tablet and PC alerts. If you are expecting an urgent call or want to be available for emergencies, set up a unique method to receive interruptions that's distinct from everyday, ordinary channels, e.g. via an administrative assistant or a text message.

The fact is, software designers don't care that you're trying to maintain the flow state. They aren't productivity experts; we'll discuss this more in the chapter on new tools. For now, consider adopting this rule: *Don't allow your flow state to be interrupted by software developers' arbitrary design decisions.*

7. Not Managing Random Noise and Visual Distractions

Tuning into talk radio, watching television, viewing YouTube videos, listening to a podcast, working in a bustling office in an open environment... we often fool ourselves into thinking that we can manage these intrusions and maintain the flow state. While the research is unequivocal on this point (it says you can't), you need to experiment to find what you can or cannot tolerate.

For some people, the white noise of classical music, traffic or waves crashing actually helps them achieve the flow state by blocking out other sharp or sudden sounds.

Some go further and use apps on their browsers to prevent themselves from logging into Facebook or other distracting sites. For example, as I edit, I turn off Internet access, which allows me to resist the temptation to leave the flow state by browsing. Others use countdown timers such as the 25-minute clock used in the Pomodoro Technique. The idea is to work for a set amount of time in the flow state and take a short break when the timer goes off.

This time frame is too short for me: I can stay in the flow state for hours without needing a formal break. Also, if the planned break is too long, or too disruptive, then the technique needs to be adjusted.

You can use all of these approaches to reduce the chance of being distracted. You are an individual, and you need to adjust them so that they work for you.

8. Resisting the Temptation to Multitask

By now, you may have concluded that multitasking – sharing your cognitive attention between tasks – ruins the flow state, which relies on mono-tasking. I won't belabor that topic here, given Rock's statement: "The idea that conscious processes need to be done one at a time has been studied in hundreds of experiments since the 1980's." This is probably old news for you, too.

What's new is a phenomenon called "continuous partial attention," a phrase coined by Linda Stone, a former executive at Microsoft. As she puts it: "To pay continuous partial attention is to keep a top-level item in focus and constantly scan the periphery in case something more important emerges." This is a more subtle form of multi-tasking that's fuelled by smartphone use. It can be just as unproductive.

The discovery of this behavior helps us understand professionals' propensity to engage in bad habits during meetings, conversations, or conference calls. Their bodies are present, even as they look for something more urgent to switch their attention to. An understanding of brain science helps to explain this: "The brain is easily distracted," writes David Rock, and "distractions have a big energy cost (because they exhaust the prefrontal cortex). Staying focused requires learning not just to switch off your cell phone. The harder part is learning to inhibit impulses as they arise."

The good news is that if you can put new words to the phenomenon of being distracted, it can help you stay focused. Rock describes experiments in which knowing that you have a particular habit can help you interrupt it by noticing its subtle beginning, an activity also undertaken by your prefrontal cortex. This finding is woven into all aspects of this book. If you can give words to the time-based productivity methods that we all use, you may be able to change them at will. In this case, knowledge can help you resist the temptation of applying continuous partial attention.

9. Making Skillful Interruptions

The flow state is compelling and can become positively addictive. However, the fact that it involves losing track of time means that it carries a danger: you can make a mess of your other commitments. Artists and writers have been known to make this mistake for centuries, sometimes forgetting to sleep, bathe or eat for several days because they are engrossed in the task at hand.

Obviously, this might be a bad thing – most professionals don't have studios in the attic. Instead, they have kids who need to be fed.

One tactic is watching the clock. This might work, but it resembles the "continuous partial attention" that Linda Stone warns against. A few people go to the other extreme, making sure they never go into the flow state at all. They don't want to devote too much attention to one thing for fear that they might drop the ball on other things that are also important.

The solution to this dilemma lies in mastering "Interrupting," one of the Advanced Fundamentals we'll address in the next chapter. There, we'll talk about how to use notifications of different kinds to allow the deepest possible flow state.

Where are the Cheat-Sheets?

You may be a bit disappointed if you have gotten used to the idea of seeing a Cheat-Sheet at the end of each chapter. There isn't one here. While I have assembled a rudimentary draft of the diagram, it has not been tried and tested by several hundred people, like the other Cheat-Sheets in this book.

Instead, I have opened up a thread in the forums on my website http://perfect.mytimedesign.com/forums. If you have a suggestion for a Cheat-Sheet for Flowing, or a modification of any form in this book, please post a comment for us to discuss.

Remember and Share

Your best work is done in the flow state, which doesn't happen by accident. It must be planned.

Schedule time to enter the flow state and take advantage of peak moments of productivity.

Don't allow the flow state to be something you enter by luck. Use your schedule.

Negotiate time with other colleagues and family to enter the flow state.

Lead cultural change in your company by educating your colleagues about the flow state.

Manage your mobile technology so it doesn't interrupt your flow state.

Turn off all the notifications you aren't actively using so that your flow state isn't randomly interrupted.

Avoid continuous partial attention – always scanning the horizon for something better or more important to focus on.

White noise (or some kinds of music) may help you stay in the flow state.

"Deliberate practice" can help you develop critical skills rapidly – focus your improvements on developing difficult new skills.

Chapter 17. Interrupting and Switching – Executing the Next Task

(In which you discover one of the actions needed to maintain the flow state.)

This chapter focuses on two Advanced Fundamentals required to maintain the flow state. Just like the 7 Essential Fundamentals already presented, you may be surprised to discover that you already practice these specific habits, practices and rituals on a daily basis. What you learn may confirm your ability to self-create, even as you explore opportunities for improvement.

Interrupting

In 1991, a tower controller at Los Angeles Airport, engrossed in the task of clearing several aircraft to cross the end of a runway, forgot to give takeoff clearance to a commuter aircraft she had been directing minutes earlier. Another aircraft received permission to land, hitting the commuter plane. 34 people died.

In a hospital, a doctor entering information about a patient's treatment on her smartphone in 2011 stopped what she was doing to return a text message about an upcoming party. Unfortunately, she forgot to return to the task of entering the treatment, and four days later, the patient needed emergency heart surgery.

From the last chapter on being in the flow state, you understand that giving all your attention to the task at hand can be wonderful. It's such a positive experience that when you enter it fully, you do your best to remain immersed in it, even though you do lose track of time.

I also mentioned that the answer to losing our temporal bearings is not to devote partial attention to the clock - this takes away from the full attention required by the flow state, making us far less efficient. What must we do to prevent a problem from cropping up in somewhere else because we ran over the allotted time? On a larger scale, how do we know when to pop out of our routine in order to undertake a pre-planned task at just the right moment?

The first answer that comes to mind for many business-people would be to hire the perfect administrative assistant – someone who forcefully alerts us when we need to stop what we're doing and start something new. This imaginary assistant would also be great to have in cockpits and operating theaters, making sure that pilots and surgeons return to incomplete tasks.

As I mentioned before, most of us don't have the luxury of administrative assistants.

Instead, we attempt to split our attention in two, using one part to attend to the task at hand and the other to watch the clock. Brain scientists refer to the part that watches the clock as the "the executive function": our built-in, self-trained administrative assistant. Fortunately, they already know what happens when we try to split our attention and multitask in this way: it lowers our performance.

In fact, studies show that when both roles are highly activated, we play them both badly. It's a dual performance that further degrades under stress. Also, research by Francis-Smythe and Robertson shows that people who self-report as great time managers do poorly when asked to report how much time has passed at different stages. That may be related to their skill at Flowing, which causes them to lose track of time.

Fortunately, there is a solution, and it lies in our knowledge of brain science. Our parietal lobes are the parts of the brain that respond to visual and spatial cues, such as a flashing light on your car's dashboard or bright red light on your coffee makers. When we recruit this sub-region of the brain to prompt us to start a task, our performance improves dramatically.

To use its power, we need to set up what are called event-based cues. These are visual, audible or kinesthetic hints in our environment that tell us when to start a particular task. Thanks to our parietal lobes, we are much more likely to respond to these cues than to purely time-based ones. It's the reason why the following cues work so well:
- The whistling of your kettle when the water is boiling
- A vibrating phone that tells you, silently, that an urgent call

is coming in during a meeting
- The sight of people joining a line in the departure hall at an
airport, indicating that the time is right to head over to the
gate

The key is to carefully embed these event-based cues in
our environment, not relying on time-based cues which, by
definition, are invisible, intangible and inaudible.

The same applies to other everyday activities that don't
even require the flow state. Many people, such as Wally
White, rush around each day from one task to another, never
spending enough time on a single activity to enter the flow
state. Their daily firefighting also needs to be interrupted to
do important tasks. It's just that people like Wally only use
time-based cues which are haphazardly recalled by their
executive functions. The result? Frequent failures, as they are
rarely interrupted at the right time. (In my Lab Notes, I
explore some of the research focused on people who improve
their performance by converting time-based cues into event-
based cues[15]).

***

I started the chapter by explaining that it's impossible
to enter the flow state completely if we have to watch the
clock at the same time. Research led by Timo Mantyla in
Sweden backs this up: as a deadline approaches, our clock-
checking increases, further eroding our performance.

The answer? Eliminating this activity altogether with
the use of electronic devices that already exist in our
environment. The key is to use them to boost our overall
executive function, boosting our ability to enter the flow
state.

It's the reason why the Pomodoro Technique,
discussed in the prior chapter, works so well. The alarm that
sets itself off after 25 minutes allows us to forget that it's even
there. By forgetting and focusing, we allow ourselves to be
more productive.

However, once again, it's important to remember that
you need a system that works for you. There's no magic in
working for 25 minutes and resting for 5. There's also no

magic in allowing yourself to be interrupted by every beep, buzz, ping, flashing light and vibration set using whatever standard your smartphone manufacturer happens to prefer.

Like Greta Green, you must manage reminders carefully, asking yourself which ones are critical and which audible, visual or kinesthetic cues you should use. Then, you must ruthlessly disable the rest.

The same applies to other platforms: PC, tablet, smart watch... whatever. Consider them a potential orchestra of cues and reminders that you need to assemble to make sure your needs are truly served. You may think this is painful, but it's the price you pay for being a professional who is skillful at Flowing.

Fortunately, modern calendar programs have their own cues and reminders built in, as do task management programs. I use cues on both my laptop and smartphone, and I recently had to reshape them when I switched from a Blackberry to an Android platform. It's been a difficult upgrade, but I don't have a better option.

As you may imagine, this tactic may seem like a terrible idea to people like Wally, who have never heard of the flow state. To them, it may be more evidence of anal retention and some of the worst aspects of Type-A behavior. They believe that such attention to time detail would drive them crazy, and they are probably right.

I have concluded that most people aren't like Greta – they don't handle enough time demands to require this kind of precision. They aren't time-starved.

Special Interruptions

Now and then, I entertain the notion that there should be a way to set up a special channel for interruptions – like a personal 911 line from the outside world. Obviously, the best person to have on the other end of such an emergency line would be an administrative assistant.

A few years ago, a participant in one of my classes gave strict instructions to her department: "Do not call me unless there's an emergency with my kids, as I'll be in training." Unfortunately, just before lunch, she received a message to call her administrative assistant because something had happened to one of her children. She ran out of the room in a panic, only to hear her administrative assistant say, "There's no emergency; I just used that excuse to get you to the phone." It turned out that the real reason for the call was a routine query. Her livid response said everything about the wisdom of that particular strategy.

Even a personal 911 channel may become corrupted. It happens in much the same way that these numbers are abused by citizens in every country. Keeping one functional requires the disciplined cooperation of others in your life.

However, even if you have a special channel for interruptions, it's still important to limit time spent away from the original task. Setting a loud, intrusive timer like the bright, red tomato-shaped one used by some users of the Pomodoro Technique can help.

Another recommended practice for interruptions is to have a system for picking up a disrupted task where you left off. For example, if you're in a meeting and have to leave before it's done, you need someone to capture the minutes and any time demands that were generated while you were gone. The same applies when you're alone and experience an interruption that forces you to exit the flow state. In some cases, the use of a checklist as described in *The Checklist Manifesto* by Atul Gawande can help anyone resume a lengthy task successfully.

***

High-performing professionals like Greta use these techniques routinely, connecting their ability to interrupt effectively to high levels of effectiveness. They'll admit that it's not an easy skill to master, but it's essential. However, does it become so important that they become slaves to a beeping device? When it goes off, do they drop what they are doing in order to immediately start the next task? Is this a new level of unwelcome, slavish automation?

We'll answer these questions in the following section on Switching, but before we move to that topic, let's spend a few minutes to evaluate your Interrupting skills.

Evaluation

Figure 17-1

Interrupting Cheat-Sheet

Behavior	White	Yellow	Orange	Green
Outsources the task of stopping to external mechanisms ☐	Never or Hardly	Sometimes ☐	Often ☐	Always ☐
Responds to auto-reminders in the midst of flowing ☐	Never or Hardly	Sometimes ☐	Often ☐	Always ☐
Appointments run over ☐	Often	Sometimes ☐	Rarely ☐	Never ☐

Current Belt ☐   ☐   ☐   ☐

Switching

Have you ever fallen into a lull right after completing an intense project? It may have happened right after you completed a task that required the flow state. The task is behind you, but you're not sure what to work on next.

Logically, you know that the world kept on going while you were completing the activity, and any number of emergencies could have broken out while your head was down. Also, stuff that you planned to complete that day may remain unfinished.

Consider the following for example: what do you plan to do when you complete this chapter of *Perfect Time-Based Productivity*? Do you have another time demand lined up? Will you check email right away? Should you stick to your original plan for the day? How about taking a break to visit Facebook? Are there any missed calls? Is this a good time to pay bills? Do you simply search for the most urgent issue and

work on that, perhaps based on your boss's instructions?
Should you go and check the References of this book to look
for interesting source documents you haven't read before?

Deciding what to do next isn't trivial – the choice you
make has consequences. It will delay every other task you
could complete.

When we make lots of bad decisions each and every
day, their costs add up over time, perhaps to a failed career.
Perhaps the cause is simple: the way you habitually decided
what to work on or do next was flawed.

Switching is the act of deciding what to work on next.
It ends only when the new task begins. Wally White makes
his choices unconsciously. He's not aware of what he does –
he just reacts. Greta Green, however, Switches skillfully and
always seems to make the right choices.

***

Healthcare workers are among the most studied
professionals, due in part to the high cost of even the smallest
errors and the fact that their workplace is full of
interruptions. For example, a group of Australian scientists
reported in 2008 that one of the most common and critical
tasks in healthcare is blood transfusion. Unfortunately, using
the wrong blood accounts for about 37% of all transfusion-
related errors.

This research revealed that when a specialist
undertaking a transfusion was interrupted by a series of tasks,
he or she was likely to forget to fulfill the original intention to
review the patient's records. The patient would get the wrong
blood because the caretaker forgot to complete the necessary
check. The missing link was one simple step.

Researchers Dismukes and Nowinski discovered that
pilots were able to improve their performance by simply
pausing at the end of each task to consider which one to
complete next; maybe the same solution would work in
healthcare.

This pause is more than just an opportunity to take a
mental break before moving on. It's a great example of

Switching.

How Do We Switch?

When we switch, choosing what information to consider isn't easy: the more data we have, the harder it is. Before smartphones and other mobile devices, people didn't read books and check their email at the end of each chapter. You also couldn't hunt down research papers by jumping from one app to another.

Constant access to information tempts us to pick up peculiar habits. A year ago, after a meeting, Nancy had an anxious premonition: something was wrong. She checked her email inbox (her main Capture Point) and discovered that her daughter had broken a leg during soccer practice. Now, whenever she feels nervous, she checks all her Capture Points at the end of every activity, just to make sure. Eventually, she won't need the premonition to check: she'll have the habit of looking for emergencies after every task.

Is Nancy doing the right thing? Is this an acceptable practice?

There's no easy answer. More than likely, one size doesn't fit all, so it's not as simple as laying down some rules for everyone to follow. Instead, consider the following principles.

Given our knowledge of the flow state, we know that continuous Switching is a source of very low productivity. When we interrupt tasks repeatedly, we simply can't be productive. The same applies, of course, to multitasking. Wally, for example, is always cutting one activity short to start another – his Switching is haphazard and often driven by his perception of what the most urgent item is. He spends little or no time pausing to consider whether or not he should chase down the next emergency. Like a dog chasing a car, he just reacts.

When Greta is in the flow state, she's aware of it. She's reluctant to interrupt herself, doing so only in exceptional circumstances. Therefore, while we all experience anxious thoughts that encourage us to switch, highly skilled time managers typically resist the temptation.

At the end of a task, Greta is likely to consult her most

important source of time demands – her calendar. At the start
of each day, she makes a schedule of activity, and her
intention, unless an emergency erupts, is to follow her plan.

Her reasoning is simple: as we saw in earlier chapters, it
takes a lot of cognitive energy to construct a plan for the day,
which is why she does it only once. She tries not to second-
guess herself, following David Rock's advice: decision-making
depletes our mental resources. As a time-starved professional,
her best strategy is to follow her predetermined priorities and
save energy for execution, rather than for repeated rounds of
deliberation.

However, earlier in her career when she had to deal
with a smaller number of time demands, Greta didn't have
advanced scheduling skills: she used lists and a calendar of
appointments typical of a Yellow Belt. When she Switched, it
meant checking her list and maybe glancing at the next
appointment. These habits made sense, given her then list-
centric profile.

When she got promoted, however, she made the
upgrade to Orange and then Green Belt skills, simplifying her
Switching to a calendar review: an appropriate change, given
her need to be calendar-centric.

Greta is also an expert at closing down tasks. She
knows how to make sure to Capture all the new, follow-on
time demands that are created when a prior one has been
completed. For example, completing a meeting that reviews
the feasibility of a project is the end of one time demand and
the start of many others. She faithfully enters a new one in
her smartphone to cover them all: "Plan steps in new launch."

When she's in the middle of a task and receives a pre-
programmed interruption, she doesn't just drop everything
and vault herself into the first step it dictates. Following
Dismukes and Nowinski's advice, she pauses to reflect: is
taking that step now the best course of action? Sometimes it's
not. Instead, it is better to finish what she was already doing,
and delay the new task.

***

Some gurus argue otherwise. They say that she needs to

follow her calendar without question, and a deviation from her plan reflects a lack of discipline. They view her original plan as sacred. This point of view supports an error that many people make when their plans go awry – they feel guilty or ashamed.

As a result, in an effort to avoid these negative feelings, many simply do no planning whatsoever. For them, Switching does not involve a free, flexible choice. Instead, it's all about being rigid and self-punishing, so avoiding the practice of planning altogether seems to be a way to prevent unwanted feelings.

In the absence of research data, it's hard to say whether this harsh approach is correct. It's safe to assume that it doesn't work for everyone, which puts the ball back in your court. Switching effectively is all about consciously seeking a balance at the moment when you have to make a choice about what to do next. If you are enjoying a Caribbean beach with your kids on your first vacation in years and you're expecting an important email, do you check your messages before eating lunch, while they are taking a nap, or when you receive a notification on your smartphone? There's no one-size-fits-all answer, but a lack of awareness can lead you to act in a way that ruins your experiences and those of your family members.

Let's analyze your Switching skills. After running a few of your own experiments, you'll need to decide what changes you should make to your current methods. Spend a few moments to evaluate your skills in this particular fundamental. Use the Cheat-Sheet below as a guide and create a plan to improve your skills in Switching.

Figure 17-2

Switching Cheat-Sheet

Behavior	White	Yellow	Orange	Green
Always refer to the time management system before deciding what to do next	Never or Hardly ☐	Sometimes ☐	Often ☐	Always ☐
Drop activities in mid-stream based on what's most pressing	Often ☐	Sometimes ☐	Rarely ☐	Almost Never ☐
Assess prior activity for follow-on time demands	Never or Hardly ☐	Sometimes ☐	Often ☐	Always ☐

Current Belt ☐ ☐ ☐ ☐

In the next chapter, we'll take a look at your system as a whole: a dynamic collection of habits, practices and rituals that you use to manage time demands each day. But first, make sure that your Master Plan includes the results of the planning activity for both Interrupting and Switching.

Remember and Share

The executive function in our minds tries to keep track of all the stuff we have to do, but when there's too much, it often fails.

Don't trust your executive function to remember – use visual, audible and kinesthetic reminders instead.

Programmed interruptions are an important counterpart to the flow state.

Deciding what to do next is an important next step in managing your time.

Switching to the most urgent item at any point in time is a recipe for stress and kills your productivity.

A task is never complete until the tasks that result from it are safely accounted for.

While you are working on a task, don't watch the clock – use a mechanism other than memory.

Switching tasks is an easier activity if you use your schedule to manage most of your time demands.

End an activity by carefully Capturing all the new time demands it creates.

To maintain high performance, pause after completing each time demand to decide what to do next.

Chapter 18. Reviewing and Warning – Taking Care of Your System

(In which you discover commonsense methods for managing your time management system).

Like any man-made mechanism, your time-based productivity system needs maintenance. The two fundamentals described in this chapter help prevent this natural decay. However, they differ from maintenance activities performed in the physical world, because the processes they support deal with psychological objects.

Reviewing

You might not know it, but if you're reading this book while completing the forms, you are performing a Review: a proactive examination of your time-based productivity system. It's your way to ensure it's working as planned: a method to identify improvement opportunities.

At the start of this book I identified two possible ways to read this book: as Julie or as Michael. As you may recall, Julie needs to solve a problem urgently, while Michael is satisfying his curiosity for new ideas. In both cases, however, they aim for real-life improvements.

For both, reading *Perfect Time-Based Productivity* is a way to understand their current skills. They hope that new insights gained from a prolonged look in the mirror will give them a way to improve. Perhaps they know that the better they get, the more difficult it is to get better. After a while, the "low-hanging fruits" disappear, and it takes superior insight to make even small gains.

This book is hardly the last word on the matter: new books and programs will emerge to help us get better, superseding the ideas presented here. More science and less "anecdata" will emerge to help professionals make better decisions. Innovators will develop new training built on interactive technologies that help make learning fun and fast. Also, new technologies, devices and gadgets will allow us to improve the way we manage time demands.

As professionals, we review these innovations in order to include them in our repertoire as part of our time-based productivity systems.

However, as we choose between these new offerings, we are on our own. There is little academic research to help us decide between one choice and another. As I mentioned previously, things are changing too quickly for scientists to keep up.

For example, it took half a decade between the year when mobile phone subscribers hit the 50% of the population in developed countries and the year when the first influential texting-while-driving study was performed.

Working professionals just can't wait that long. We need to do our own experiments to determine whether or not a particular technology or improvement idea will boost our productivity.

Beyond the possibilities that lie in the future, another important reason to conduct Reviews is to ensure that our system is working now as intended. This may be far less exciting than searching for cool new stuff: most of us hate reviews of our workplace performance, our physical health and our automobiles. But Reviews are important – even if you don't see symptoms every time, you need them to head off trouble. The way to do a good Review, therefore, is to be like a detective who is willing to go below the surface to discover cracks invisible to the naked eye.

We can undertake two kinds of preemptive Reviews. The first involves your execution of the fundamentals, while the second involves the nature and quality of the time demands you are tracking.

1. Reviewing Your Process: Habits, Practices and Rituals

We perform each of the 11 Fundamentals in order to produce a particular result. With the help of the 11 Cheat-Sheets (including the two described in this chapter), we should ask ourselves:

- Is this fundamental functioning as intended? Have I been experiencing any problems with it?
- Are there signs that my overall improvement plan isn't working?

- Where kinds of time demands are most likely to fall through the cracks?
- What's taking too long?
- What's costing too much?
- Are other people in my life unhappy with my execution of time demands? Why?
- Do I need to upgrade any of the 11 Fundamentals faster than planned?
- Do I have sufficient support in making my upgrades?
- Where am I experiencing a loss of Peace of Mind?

In a review of the 11 Fundamentals, you can discover performance problems that aren't readily apparent. As an author and teacher, I regularly examine my system, looking for improvements. I have used specialized techniques, such as Issue Trees, Hypothesis Testing and Mind Maps, to get to the root of some of my own issues. (These techniques are described in the Chapter on Habiting).

The better your method for reviewing your system, the faster you'll gain insights about its limits. The content in the Cheat-Sheets is just a start. Expect to add new behaviors in each of the 11 Fundamentals as you fine-tune your performance to higher levels.

Regrettably, I don't have a solid recommendation for how frequently to do this review – I simply don't have enough data. My reviews happen weekly (on a Monday morning or Sunday night), but I'm hardly the best role model. Once a month? Twice a month? For one hour? Ten minutes? As with most of the key decisions necessary for a "perfect" system, only you can make the call.

2. Reviewing the Content

In addition to examining your own habits, practices and rituals, you also need to look at the quality of time demands being tracked in your system. The goal is simple: make sure that none of them are superfluous and that each one includes the correct information while being "saved" in the right place, such as your schedule, list or memory.

In this activity, which you can do alongside your Process Reviews, you amend or remove time demands that are dead, completed, duplicated, ill-defined or misplaced. You may also look for missing time demands.

Once again, I can't give specific advice about the frequency or duration of this activity. I review the time demands in my schedule for the day in the morning, starting with any items that remain incomplete. Every Sunday night or Monday morning, I do the same when I set my weekly goals.

During these reviews, I focus on time demands that are at risk because they aren't being well managed. I also reschedule or toss those items I didn't complete the previous day. During awfully hectic days filled with morning emergencies, I may end up with many incomplete items because I treat my schedule as a flexible plan, rather than a rigid requirement. I feel no guilt whatsoever in abandoning my schedule for a day, or even several days. Sometimes, that's what life requires. I just have to make sure to carefully manage the consequences of going "off-schedule."

I represent a sample of one. But even if there were multiple studies available, you would still need to define a review method that fits your personality, style and habits.

***

Unfortunately, an un-reviewed system often tends to become progressively worse over time. (Some mistakenly explain this phenomenon as the Second Law of Thermodynamics or the Law of Entropy). It's not that you become worse at a chosen activity; instead, the world is changing so rapidly that some habits, like making a paper copy of each email message you receive, don't make sense, given all the changes that are happening. Yesterday's solution becomes tomorrow's problem.

When you aren't Reviewing your system's performance, it's easy to become comfortable with practices that are obsolete or unsuitable. For example, a good Review might anticipate the birth of your next child or your upcoming promotion, leading you to proactively instigate the next Turning Point. You could decide to make the switch slowly and gently, rather than in haste, when it's more difficult to execute properly.

Also, without good reviews, unwanted behaviors may slip in without notice, dropping your standards. Your Review is a way to give yourself the feedback you need to make the best corrections.

Your system should meet your needs now and in the future. This "perfect" fit between your needs and your system is a balance; you can maintain it only with a lot of hard work. It means looking for early and unwanted symptoms and analyzing them to see if they are part of larger trends. It also means deliberately keeping your number of time demands to a minimum so that your system remains lean.

Take a moment to evaluate your skills in Reviewing. Compared to prior Cheat-Sheets, you may notice that the two mentioned in this chapter are relatively undeveloped: both of these areas still need a lot of further research and development.

Figure 18-1

Reviewing Cheat-Sheet

Behavior	White	Yellow	Orange	Green
Performs Content Reviews	Never ☐	Sometimes ☐	Often ☐	Always ☐
Performs System Reviews	Never ☐	Never ☐	Often ☐	Always ☐

Current Belt ☐	☐	☐	☐

Warning

When you're driving on the highway and a light on your dashboard starts flashing, you should be grateful – it's alerting you of the early signs of malfunction. Your computer's antivirus does the same.

Both signals take place automatically, without your active involvement. They prevent disasters from happening.

In time-based productivity, with its combination of human and technological elements, you also need that kind of information. Warning, therefore, is all about receiving an alert from your system that something is not working.

For example, imagine receiving an email that analyzes your calendar and reports that you missed 75% of your recent appointments. Or maybe it's a text message indicating that you have overloaded one of your Capture Points.

In my prior book, *Bill's Im-Perfect Time Management* Adventure the protagonist's company used a program called "Tzinbox" that provided him (and his boss) with a score that reflected how well he was managing email. Unfortunately, it's only a piece of science fiction at this point – there is no time management system dashboard to flash a bright red icon just before you get overloaded. In other words, these tools just don't exist.

Sadly, there's little evidence that developers or researchers are working with these ideas. As a result, I have made a future projection in the Cheat-Sheets that might take you by surprise.

Self Evaluation

In order to understand this particular fundamental, let's do things a bit differently. Take a look at the following Cheat-Sheet.

Figure 18-2

Warning Cheat-Sheet

Behavior	White	Yellow	Orange	Green
An automatic warning system is maintained	■	Unaware ☐	In progress ☐	In use ☐
A manual warning system is maintained	■	Sometimes ☐	Often ☐	Always ☐

Current Belt ☐   ☐   ☐   ☐

You may notice something a bit strange: In the absence of the automatic tools we need, there's no way to achieve a Green Belt because the software required doesn't, as yet, exist. The reason is simple – I crafted this range of skills six years ago, believing (perhaps naively) that it was just a short matter of time before software to perform the Warning function would become widely available.

I was wrong: it just didn't happen.

Unfortunately, apart from a few software programs like Clear Context, which provide some statistics on overall email inbox health, this gap is yet to be filled with technological advances.

So, until it is filled, I decided to keep the scorecard the same, observing that it serves useful purposes:

1. It is a reminder that there are future belt levels to accomplish, for all of us. The only limit is the human imagination. For this reason, I haven't defined a Black Belt or any other belts beyond Green. In time-based productivity, even in a book that claims to provide a "perfect" solution, there is no final destination. "Perfection" means committing to a personal, moving target.

2. Selfishly, I wanted to give myself a stretch goal I couldn't easily reach. Having an Orange Belt in this fundamental (and therefore an Orange Belt overall as we discussed in a prior chapters) keeps me honest and makes things interesting. Like you, I have to keep looking for the

next level.

3. The belt levels are not meant to be personal prizes. They are intended to reflect external standards that have nothing to do with individual self-esteem or effort.

4. I want the Cheat-Sheets to represent a standard that no one can fudge. While it's possible to self-score yourself as a Green Belt in every other discipline, the definition of this fundamental should stop people from easily giving themselves the highest rank just because they think they deserve it.

A participant in one of my workshops arrived several hours late, left the room for long stretches of time and multi-tasked his way to complete distraction. At the end of the day, I noticed that he awarded himself a Green Belt in each fundamental, confirming my hunch that people can use assessments to evaluate their skills according to their preconceptions. Needless to say, I excluded his evaluation in my data. Recently, I started experimenting with 360-degree evaluations of the fundamentals in order to bring more objective data to the attention of the individual doing the self-assessment.

This decision to prevent everyone from getting a Green Belt until someone invents a solution might not sit well with you. There are some good reasons to change the scale, but I'd prefer not to spend too much time debating. Instead, let's lobby software developers to give us the Warning software we need, a discussion we will continue in the chapter on New Tools. (You can however, discuss this topic and any other in my book's forums at http://perfect.mytimedesign.com).

Until these new tools are invented, you can start by building a manual warning system. Start by making a list of the indicators that your system is in trouble. If you don't have an idea what these might be, observe yourself operating for a week or two and notice the early warning signs of system malfunction.

Here are some suggestions. The blank space is for you to insert a number that would represent a threshold alert. Here's an example.

"My system might be in trouble if there are more than 25 time demands waiting to be processed in Capture Points for more than 12 hours."

I am using Google Keep — https://keep.google.com/ — as my primary Capture Point, and if the magic number hits approximately 10 items, I know that my next session for Emptying is way overdue. Here are some early indicators that you can use for your system.

1. _____ total time demands sitting in Capture Points for more than 12 hours.

2. _____ Capture Points with time demands waiting to be Emptied.

3. _____ time demands incomplete from yesterday's schedule.

4. _____ stale time demands on a list.

5. _____ days since the last review of your system.

6. _____ days since your last round of Emptying.

7. _____ paper stacks of un-stored information.

8. _____ times an activity was missed due to a poor cue.

9. _____ times late in the last week.

10. _____ missed due dates in the last month.

As you may imagine, you need your own indicators. Set these up in your diary, and start to monitor a handful of them regularly. As you become skillful at keeping them in view, add new ones that better reflect the state of your system. You may want to schedule Warning activities in your calendar to keep things fresh.

The good news is that you probably already have been using an informal Warning system. Just before you engage in a Kamikaze Weekend, for example, there's something in your environment that lets you know you need one. This chapter is about making these unconscious indicators part of your explicit Warning system.

***

Take a moment to complete your evaluations and create the appropriate plans for both Reviewing and Warning. Congratulations on completing all 11 Cheat-Sheets, along with their plans! While the forms are important, take a moment to reflect on the knowledge that you need to complete each evaluation.

Return to your Master Plan and update it with the plans you have developed in this chapter.

In the next chapter, you'll learn two things at once: how to craft your own Cheat-Sheet for new behaviors you wish to improve and how to build a strong habit-change support system that makes implementation easier.

Remember and Share

Your time management system needs to be maintained and managed: it won't just take care of itself.

You need to maintain your time management system so that it performs its intended function.

Look out for signs that your time management system needs improvements.

Build a Warning system that indicates whether or not your time management system is about to break.

Let's lobby software makers to develop an early Warning sign for our digital productivity systems.

In *Perfect Time-Based Productivity*, there is no Black Belt – it remains to be defined.

"Perfection" in time-based productivity means committing to a personal, moving target.

Chapter 19. Habiting – A Way to Increase Your Odds of Success

(In which you learn that most people fail when they try to implement new habits).

It's late October, and the fourth-place finisher in the Bay State Marathon, Angie (I've changed her name), is just crossing the line. She looks strong to those around her, who know that this race is not only a qualifier for the Boston Marathon but also the fastest 26.2 mile race held in Massachusetts each year.

But inside, she feels differently. The last few miles felt slow, and Angie's convinced herself that she has barely been moving at a 10-minute-mile pace. Her finishing time tells the truth, however: she'd not only set a personal record, beating her previous personal best by over four minutes. In the past week she also had to nurse her husband and two daughters back to health after a bout of the flu, even as she got her paper accepted at a national electrical engineering conference. Angie is not only a marathon runner, but also a Mom and a full-time engineer.

As others cross the finish line, she ambles over to her family, leaning up against the barricades. They had been cheering, but now, the moment has passed, the excitement has worn off, and it's time to go back to being Mommy. As they slip back into familiar roles, Angie's mind goes back to her schedule of events. She scans her memory to see what's next for the day. A few minutes later, before she reaches the car, she checks the schedule in her iPhone to be sure. Even as she continues her cool-down routine, she remembers that there are errands to be run.

Her Mom texts words of congratulations, as do her friends. Those who run make insider comments and ask detailed questions about her pace, while those who don't seem to stand back a bit, in awe. Only a tiny handful of her acquaintances ever volunteer to join her at the gym or on the road, even though they can recite the benefits almost as well as she can.

They just give the same excuse over and over again: "I just don't have the time for anything like that."

To which she always answers silently, to herself, "And I do?"

They're partially right: there is something she has that they don't, but it's not more time. What delivered her to the finish line in a personal record at age 39 is not what friends usually think it is – willpower, talent or discipline.

Angie will explain it to anyone who listens: she knows how to change her habits.

In the future she plans something even more ambitious – an Ironman Triathlon – even though her swimming skills are weak and a 2.4-mile open-water swim is the first leg. She's confident that she knows how to convert a fleeting moment of inspiration into solid habits that deliver her to the finish line of her races. This invisible ability also kept her going through the 10 months it took to write her conference paper.

Her friends don't see this skill at work, and she has never quite put it into words. She just knows that she's different.

***

Imagine what happens when 100 people sit in the average time-based productivity program, mandated by an executive who just came back from Germany and wants a touch of uber-efficiency. At the end of the program, which seems to most people to be little more than common sense, those who are deeply motivated to change their behavior leave with a list of actions to start doing differently.

Visit them a year after the fact, and the result is predictable. By then, the fact that the ideas were easy to understand doesn't matter. Most people will have implemented little or nothing at all, even if they could pass an exam based on the program's contents.

Why does this happen?

Doing what Angie does so well isn't easy. Translating inspiration into sustainable action that last months and years is a learned skill, that's hard to teach yourself as an adult. In this chapter, we'll refer to this skill as "Habiting," a term I coined writing this book.

Habiting is the ability to unlearn old habits and learn new ones at will. In time-based productivity, as in many areas of learning, Habiting is essential – no Habiting, no long-term improvement.

The good news is that a number of great books can help you transform a single behavior change into a habit. We don't have to become experts in this area in order to implement our Master Plan.

But the bad news is that none of those books offer "The Final Answer." At best, they offer partial solutions that help in their own way.

They miss the mark because they fall into the same one-size-fits-all trap we distinguished in Chapter 2. You need your own special way of Habiting that works for you. That also explains why you may have shaken your head if others have suggested their own methods of changing habits to you.

Perhaps you could clearly see the results they produced, understanding how Habiting helped them. At the same time, you could never use their method. For example, some people swear by support groups and the power of being in a small community focused on a single improvement (e.g. 12-Step Programs). Many, however, can't imagine doing that, even if research supports the effectiveness of these groups.

Therefore, you won't find a list of "must-use-or-else" supports in the pages of this book, although I will give lots of recommendations. Instead, it's better to deepen our Habiting skills. Let's start with some tools that will help us understand our current methods.

Going Meta on the Skill of Habiting

In earlier chapters, we described the fact that habitual behavior differs from intentional behavior that results from the creation of time demands. Habitual behavior, like brushing your teeth each day, requires little energy to initiate. All you need is a trigger – you require no deliberation or overt intention, according to Benjamin Sood from the Human Behavior Research Centre at the University of Central London. When you form a habit, routines are pushed down into the region of the brain called the basal ganglia – it's where sequences of cues and actions are stored permanently.

The newly-defined Self-Reported Behavior Automaticity Index defines a habit as an action that passes four tests:

- Is it something I do automatically?
- Is it something I do without having to consciously remember?
- Is it something I do without thinking?
- Is it something I start doing before I realize I'm doing it?

The Master Plan you defined in prior chapters to improve your skill at time-based productivity would be a cinch if you could translate new, hard-to-learn behaviors into new habits. How can we make that happen?

Before we delve into the method I recommend, let's make something clear: This chapter isn't about specific habits. Instead, I'm interested in boosting your ability to change, which is far more important for long-term success. It's what adult learning experts call meta-learning: looking in the mirror at the way you learn with a view to making lasting improvements.

Of course, we're not looking at everything that happens within learning, just a single aspect: how to turn insights into habits that have an effortless quality.

Given the above definition, how do we consciously create habits in the first place?

***

Let's start with a well-researched fact: we tend to overestimate our ability to change habits. While new behaviors are easy to understand, we give little thought to the true nature of the challenge.

The following four-phase model of habit development is based, in part, on the work of Dr. Jason Selk, who, in turn, credits a coach named Tom Bartow for defining the first three phases.

Phase 1: The Honeymoon Phase

When you complete a productivity program or book, your motivation in the hours that follow is at an emotional and intellectual peak. Inspired by what is possible, you make the mistake of setting aggressive goals, as if you'll remain this highly motivated forever. In prior chapters, we noted the tendency to commit the planning fallacy in these moments of inspiration.

Phase 2: The Fight Thru

Unfortunately, the peak never lasts; when reality hits, so does failure. In his book "The Power of Habit," Charles Duhigg speaks to the combination of cues, behaviors and rewards that reinforce habits. As you exit the sterility and safety of the training environment, and re-enter real life, these abundant, old cues assert themselves as they always have, causing you to repeat the old habits while forgetting to execute the new activities. Also, your neuromuscular memory hasn't changed one bit – your body unconsciously performs the actions it used to, regardless of the intentions you developed during the training.

As a result, you find yourself still responding to habits like the "Smartphone Itch" – the tendency to pick up your smartphone while undertaking other more important tasks, even though you may have vowed to stop multitasking. Guilt can set in as you fail to meet your post-training expectation, and the aggressive goals you created turn into burdens that threaten your Peace of Mind.

In a *Wall Street Journal* article, Cal Newport, whom we met in our discussions on Scheduling and Flowing, says that this phase is part of what is called "deliberate practice" – a focused effort to intentionally improve our performance. This practice requires clarity and feedback and may feel unpleasant at times.

Phase 3: Second Nature

Once you get past the awful second stage, new habits start to emerge, and so do different neuromuscular memories. Bartow calls this "getting in the groove." You can still fall back to old habits after a severe disruption – and you could stay there forever – but you're over a hump.

Phase 4: Permanence

At this point, you hardly remember your state before the habit change. For example, as a child, I used to suck my thumb, until one day, encouraged by my parents, I decided to stop. Now, just the thought of giving my thumb a suck is odious. I can't imagine an emotional or physical benefit that would make me give it a try.

On the positive side, exercising each morning is now as automatic for me as brushing my teeth. In this moment, I sit at my computer, mentally preparing to go to the gym in a few minutes. I notice that I didn't have to consciously decide to work out: everything in my body is prepared for the effort as soon as I wake up. Not that this happens magically – it's slowly developed after almost 20 years of continuous triathlon training.

By contrast, there are lots of behaviors I have tried to turn into habits, but my skills at Habiting just weren't sufficient. For example, I know that whenever I move homes, taking out the garbage each night is usually one of the first habits to disappear. When the environment changes, old cues disappear, and the habit falls apart. The research of Dr. Mark Bouton shows that behaviors decay over time, even after they are "learned."

What can you do to increase the odds that you'll get to Phase 4 each time you try to change a habit? Your success depends on the answer to this question, as your Master Plan is nothing more than a list of new habits, practices and rituals.

The Skill of Habiting

My research shows that Habiting involves mastering the following skills (in no particular order):

Skill #1 - Setting up a habit change support system.

Skill #2 - Establishing a process for getting back on track.

Skill #3 - Mitigating your weakest moments.

Skill #4 - Creating plans made up of small steps.

Skill #5 - Using feedback tracking to determine whether the habit you are trying to learn/unlearn is actually changing.

My hypothesis is simple. If you practice these skills, you should be able to navigate Phases 1-4 mentioned earlier with greater ease. In other words, the better you become at Habiting, the easier it is to implement positive changes that require a long-term commitment.

I've found research to support the helpfulness of these individual skills, but I haven't found much that focuses on developing the skill of Habiting, which includes all five.

Hopefully, the topic will enjoy more research attention soon.

***

Let's break each of these five skills into some specific activities I've observed. These are just examples, not a comprehensive list.

Skill #1 - Setting up a habit change support system.

Example (i) - Create independent reminders that don't require involvement or memory.

Good reminders to engage in habits and practices work automatically and don't need your attention. They may use software, mobile apps, gadgets, etc. Other humans can also play this role: a disciplined administrative assistant, accountability partner or coach can help you remember to act to build certain habits. Just be careful: even the most carefully planned reminders can fail. For example, software upgrades can ruin your reminders. You might also develop the habit of ignoring a digital reminder. People often hit "snooze" three, four, or five times before paying attention to their alarms. Other reminders can be just as hard to attend to.

Example (ii) - Find an accountability partner.

An accountability partner is willing to confront you if you fail to follow through on your commitment to new behaviors. He or she can also act as a backup, as we discussed in Skill #3, and help you with reminders, as discussed in Skill #2. Your partner may be a group of people or an individual whose opinions you value. Here, you are leveraging your connection with the person to keep your progress on track. Websites like http://www.stickK.com take this concept to a new level, attaching actual dollars to commitments.

Example (iii) - Reward yourself.

Plan rewards that you can unlock only after you achieve certain milestones. If aim to move up to the next belt within six months, set up a celebration when you do.

Skill #2 - Establishing a process for getting back on track.

Example (i) - Write down a backup plan.

You probably won't be able to maintain a perfect record as you implement new behaviors. What will you do to make sure that if a habit falls away, it won't simply disappear? Keeping a diary is one way to make sure you won't lose sight of your commitment.

Example (ii) - Become Resilient to Stressful Thoughts and Feelings

In the chapter on Capturing, I made reference to the work of Byron Katie and her bestselling book, *Loving What Is*. The steps I described in her process provide a simple, effective way to deal with stressful thoughts. The fact is, any plan can be disrupted and undermined by unwanted thoughts that drain your energy, but you can use her approach to become immune to your own negative judgments.

Example (iii) - Avoiding the "What-the-Hell" Effect

Researchers have discovered that when we fail to achieve a goal, such as eating in a healthy manner, we tend to release all inhibitions. Instead of eating a little bit more, we binge, dramatically surpassing our initial intentions in a moment of madness. With knowledge of this "what-the-hell effect," we can rein in our excesses and return to the original habit.

Skill #3 - Mitigating your weakest moments.

Example (i) - Schedule difficult-to-learn new habits for times when you have the most energy.

If, for example, you need a lot of energy to Empty Capture Points such as email, schedule that activity for the times of the day when you have the most energy.

Skill #4 - Creating plans made up of small steps.

Example (i) - Your Master Plan, created in prior chapters, is a plan made up of small steps. One way to prevent the planning fallacy is to ask yourself, "How long would this take my friend to do?" Consider this question for three of your friends. If your predicted performance far exceeds theirs, you might be inflating your own abilities, perhaps unconsciously.

Another way to think about taking small steps is called habit stacking. According to blogger James Clear, "The quickest way to build a new habit into your life is to stack it on top of a current habit." "Stacking" involves initiating a new habit right after the completion of a strong, current habit. For example, you may decide to start flossing your

teeth (a new habit) in the moment after you finish brushing
your teeth (an already existing habit).

Skill #5 - Using feedback tracking to determine
whether the habit you want to learn/unlearn is actually
changing.
Example (i) - Track your progress using a tool like the
Practice Tracking Template. It's easy to update your original
profile to reflect your progress over time.

***

B.J. Fogg, the behavior change specialist we met in
earlier chapter, explained to me that it's essential to define the
triggers for a new habit. If Habiting is ever to become a
routine of its own, what might be some of its cues? Here are
some possible examples:
- In a Review, you discover that your Bucket List is
stale – you need a new habit of refreshing it every month.
- As part of your Warning system, you receive a
message that your saved folders are over-loaded. You need to
run an archive every week, instead of every month – a fresh
routine.
- You haven't Zeroed your Inbox in weeks (or months)
and need to develop a daily habit of doing so. This means
breaking the habit of skimming your inbox.
You may recognize that I have used a familiar
technique – implementation intention – to set up these cues.
They each follow the "if_____ then_____" construct. For
example: "If I discover that I need to develop a new habit or
break an old one, then I'll kick off a new round of Habiting."
A *Harvard Business Review* article from the May 2014 edition
entitled "Get Your Team to Do What it Says It's Going to
Do" offers a great explanation of implementation intentions
that can drive behavior in the corporate world. Setting the
intentions up ahead of time allows you to prepare for future
mishaps.

***

The next steps to take are all yours. Consider your

current skill at Habiting carefully, and put together a plan to develop one or more of the five skills.

Then, ask yourself what your Master Plan requires so that the behavior changes you want can turn into permanent habits. Use your newly discovered skill at Habiting to make a plan that has too much support to fail easily. Take out your diary and start to write down some possibilities.

As James Clear implies in his blog post "This Coach Improved Every Tiny Thing by 1 Percent and Here's What Happened," you don't need to construct the perfect support system the first time you set one up. Instead, create the best plan you can at the moment, with the understanding that you'll improve your Habiting as time goes on.

There are no shortcuts – only accumulated improvements. Unfortunately, even if you repeat a habit for 30 days, it might not become permanent. That's actually an urban myth, which UK-based researchers later examined. They showed that 97 volunteers who attempted to change a variety of health habits took an average of 66 days, ranging from 18 to 254. The good news is that missing one day here or there didn't have much of an effect. That corrects some outdated research from 1890, which asserted that missing even one day would cause failure.

The researchers also found that early repetitions of the chosen behavior produced the best results. After a while, increasing the repetitions had no effect. This indicates that we need to spend some extra effort to repeat the habit in its early days so that it sticks.

So, take a moment now to craft a support system for your Master Plan for the next three months. Make sure to use a blend of supports that, taken together, work for you. To help you start, here are some questions you could answer.

- Who could be your accountability partner or buddy? Your boss? A mentor?

- Is there a support group you could join?

- Should you keep track of your progress in a diary?

- Is there a structured activity you could follow to make implementation easy?

- Would putting some money at risk help you focus, a la http://stickK.com?

- Does it help you when other people know your goals?
- Where are you most likely to fail, and why?
- Who will check in on you every few weeks to make sure you're on track?

In the next chapter, we'll look at how the world around us, including our gadgets and tools, leads us into different habit patterns without our knowledge.

Remember and Share

Habiting is the skill of unlearning an old habit and/or learning a new one, and it's the foundation of learning new behaviors.

Willpower is overrated as a mechanism for changing habits.

Habits change more easily in the right environment.

Knowing when it's time to implement a habit versus a single change in behavior is a key to long-term success.

Time-based productivity is all about knowing and then changing your system of habits, practices and rituals.

New time-based productivity habits are hard to learn because the ones you have in place are hard to change.

Good habits become bad habits when the environment changes – it's up to you to see this coming.

Seeing which of your habits currently makes you unproductive is a sign of mastery.

Change a complex habit by breaking it down into small behaviors; then, change them one at a time.

Upgrading your time-based productivity is about retiring old habits and learning new ones, which isn't easy!

Chapter 20. What's the Best Way to React to New Technology and Fresh Thinking?

(In which you learn how to react to the promise of new gadgets and fresh ideas).

Spanish Town, Jamaica, 2012

What makes someone text and drive?

I sat in the passenger seat as we sped along the highway, trying to beat the rush-hour traffic back into the city. It wasn't quite dark, and the driver, a physician in his early sixties, was taking us home from a meeting we had attended as volunteers. We both valued the cause – it could save lives, and we were both proud to be part of it.

He still had his smartphone in hand, fingers paused over the keypad. But now, instead of checking email, he was talking to me. He couldn't drive, text and talk at the same time. So, I kept talking and talking, asking him one open-ended question after another, just to keep him from using his phone.

Truth be told, I would have preferred silence, because I was quite tired. But I couldn't stop thinking about the statistics I had repeated so often in my workshops: "Texting while driving is 23 times more dangerous than regular driving and five times more dangerous than drunk driving."

I didn't know him well enough to tell him to cut it out; plus, I told myself that the trip was short. So, I chickened out and just kept him talking. And talking. I watched as he eventually put down his smartphone after I kept the conversation flowing for almost an hour. Then, I was safe.

***

What makes someone who should know better text and drive?

Apparently, we don't know the full answer to this question. Unlike other kinds of risky behavior like smoking and drinking, there are no obvious physical benefits.

However, recent discoveries show that subtle changes in brain chemistry occur when we check for new messages via email, Twitter and Facebook.

A *Psychology Today* article by Susan Weinschecnk sheds some light. In the chapter on Emptying, we looked at the role that dopamine plays in the brain, but she highlights the fact that it's believed to cause "seeking behavior" – feelings of wanting, desiring, seeking out and searching. We need dopamine to feed what's called the opioid system, which makes us feel pleasure or "liking." These two powerful impulses, seeking and liking, exist in a balance. We tend to do a lot of seeking for comparatively little liking – an evolutionary habit that keeps us continually on the move.

Thanks to dopamine, we use our smartphones as modern-day hunting tools, employing their far-reaching capabilities to seek and find stimulation for the brain's pleasure center. In fact, the brain shows more activity when it's anticipating a reward than when one actually arrives; just checking Facebook, Twitter, email and Instagram gives us the hunting sensation we crave. Also, when a cue such as a ping, buzz, beep or flashing light interrupts us to indicate that a new message has arrived, it's intoxicating: our hunger for satisfaction – hunting and finding – is heightened, and we struggle to stop ourselves from responding by "just taking a peek."

Would the dopamine-opioid loop explain why my driver was texting and driving?

***

Research shows that teens engage in distracted behavior while driving more often than adults. However, recent studies indicate that the gap is steadily closing, but it's not because teens are learning safer habits. Instead, adults are learning more dangerous ones.

We don't precisely know why this happens among the mature, better-educated population, but I have a hypothesis derived from related research. I see three reasons:

1. We are anxious.

Our generation is afraid that it's missing out on something important and possibly urgent. When the phone beeps, buzzes or rings, our mind forms an impression of the worst case: "What if the kids are calling because Grandpa has fallen and hurt himself?" Under heightened anxiety, we don't even need the phone to send a signal; we create our own in advance. "What if the kids have NOT called because Grandpa has fallen and hurt himself?" In either case, the result is the same. Our anxiety drives us to multi-task, making us pick up the phone.

2. We are bored or lonely.

While driving, the thrill that comes from exchanging messages with other people beats listening to the radio or staring at the road. Reaching out is better than falling asleep, the mind reasons – it's safer to stay awake and also more fun. Interactions with others help push away unwanted feelings.

3. We want to save time.

By multi-tasking, we feel that we can be more productive, saving precious minutes. After all, we think, we are in the car, doing nothing, so we might as well turn our attention to something useful.

In the language of time-based productivity, we'd say that the driver is creating new time demands. In the moments after their creation, he has an urge to Capture them right away without relying on memory.

He may experience a strong impulse to Act Now to free himself from the Zeigarnik effect mentioned earlier. Taking either course of action (Capturing or Acting Now) would stop the incessant pinging that starts when a time demand is created, but neither Captured nor completed. The truth is, if he takes either action, he experiences the immediate sense of relief I described in earlier chapters.

These three impulses aren't new to use as human beings, but mobile devices change everything. When an action such as texting while driving is successfully repeated often enough, it turns into a habit.

While I can't know the exact thoughts that were going through my driver's head, he did talk about how much stuff he had to do and how much email he received. His complaints made me think that his dangerous multi-tasking was in line with the third reason I mentioned: he was trying to save time.

In other words, he had developed the habit of texting and driving as a way to boost his time-based productivity.

***

There are other ways in which technology is being used badly.

Recently, Randstad of North America completed a study on employees' use of new technology.

According to CEO Linda Galipeau: "As enhanced technologies and increased access to information continue to blur the lines between our professional and personal lives, many workers mistake being busy for being productive. These are two very different concepts that, when looked at from an organizational standpoint, could have serious implications for a company's bottom line."

The study discovered that 68 percent of women say technologies have not made them any more productive. People reported that the increasing prevalence of mobile technology, such as smartphones and tablets, made it harder to balance work and life. The reason? Work simply took over their private lives, with 42 percent of women reporting that new technologies made it harder to disconnect from the office.

In the short term, mobile technology has benefited companies, but in the long term, it may harm workers who respond to time pressure by living in a semi-permanent state of smartphone-induced imbalance.

It's not difficult to see why this happens. Smartphone users get more stressed because they get more email. Only 12 percent of Americans who do not use smartphones to receive work-related emails experience email overload, a figure which rises to 37 percent among those who do. At the same time, 43 percent of mobile email users check email four or more times per day, compared to 29 percent of those who do not use mobile email, according to Merkle's "View From the Digital Inbox 2011."

Mobile email also affects our day-to-day productivity. In a study at the University of Washington, Professor Christopher Barnes' team found that "using a smartphone to cram more work into a given evening results in less work done the next day." A digital hangover, perhaps?

Furthermore, in our rush to keep up with time demands, we aren't doing other things that would keep us safe: in a study by the London School of Hygiene & Tropical Medicine, some 16 percent of cell phones were found to have traces of fecal bacteria on them.

Now, there's even a word for the fear of losing or being without our mobile phones: "Nomophobia," where "nomo" is short for "no mobile phone."

It's hard to imagine that Apple's Steve Jobs or Blackberry's Mike Lizardis had this in mind when they released their products to an unsuspecting, tech-hungry public. It's not as if they were creating an inherently dangerous product or a new drug.

Yet, here we are – using a technology that's supposed to boost productivity in ways that don't. How did we get here? How do we make sure that we don't arrive at this point when the next new technology is invented?

The Big Picture

To answer this question, let's look at the example of email. It's probably the number-one corporate culture changer of the last 20 years. Only a tiny handful of companies around the world do not use email.

When the technology was introduced in the mid-1990s, workplace transformation specialists didn't recognize it as a culture changer. In retrospect, it's clear that email made an unpredictable and irreversible change to our lives. It had a combined positive and negative effect on our productivity.

With such mixed results, what should professionals do? Hide from new technology? Chase after every new thing that Amazon.com has to sell? From the point of view of time-based productivity, what's the best approach?

The answer is that instead of blindly following the crowd, we need to be critical of new technology while we decide whether or not it closes or widens real-life productivity gaps.

Technology that Fills the Gaps

When I lived in Florida (through 2005), I never thought about how I could acquire new technology. Ordering anything new was as easy as visiting eBay or stopping by Best Buy. I never needed to wait, unless it was for a sale, and reasonable prices could almost always be found.

Fast forward to life in Jamaica, where acquiring new technology comes at a price. Not only is there an additional cost to buying locally, a purchase from Amazon involves a delay of at least two weeks.

I delayed purchasing a smartphone until much later than most, preferring to watch and wait. At the time, I saw only a marginal benefit from jumping into the fray. Plus, I could see lots of ineffective smartphone habits spreading like an epidemic to the hands of new users, and I became wary of the lower productivity that seemed to come with the choice to upgrade. I didn't want to become yet another guy pretending to be in a conversation while replying to email or posting an update to Twitter.

While I deliberated, I decided to go public, putting out blog posts, newspaper articles, YouTube videos and a webinar on the topic of making the smartphone choice. I determined that when I made the switch, it would be for the right reasons, and if I did it well, I could avoid the worst tendencies.

What I learned from waiting until 2011 to get a Blackberry was that it's hard to make good technology choices, because there's a great deal of confusion between convenience and productivity.

The Confusion of Greater Convenience

As I queried those who owned smartphones, I noticed a similarity in their responses: "I am more productive now because I can [perform particular function] in [an unusual place or time]." Examples include:

"I'm more productive now because...

...I can now text while I'm driving my car."

...I can read my email on the train."

...I can get work done in boring meetings."

...I always have my camera with me, so I can take a picture

whenever I want."

…I can always update my Facebook page, even when I'm on vacation."

These simplistic advantages have driven millions of dollars of sales of mobile products, while confusing many. Why? It feels good to gain even a tiny bit of convenience.

But are these the kind of time-based productivity improvements you should be going after? Are they enough to justify the side effects?

While I considered the switch from a feature phone to smartphone, I performed a thought experiment shared on my website: is there any advantage to replacing a knapsack filled with electronic gadgets with a single smartphone? (The knapsack might include my feature phone, a laptop, a camera, an mp3 player, a GPS device, and whatever else might fit).

Obviously there's a weight and size advantage. But that's just a matter of convenience, not productivity. At first, I couldn't see any benefit. It wasn't until I got my first smartphone that I could see a clear advantage.

A big plus built into all mobile operating systems is the ability to benefit from the interaction between apps. For example, now I can Capture everywhere using voice-recognition technology and upload the file to the cloud in a moment, where the file is not only instantly safe, but it's also backed up. Before, that would take several long, difficult steps. Further, it improves the way I do my Capturing.

I recognize these new advantages as elements of greater productivity. They are true innovations because they allow us to execute the 11 Fundamentals in profoundly better ways.

On the downside, now that I use a smartphone, the temptation to multi-task has grown considerably. It's easy to see how these losses can wipe away minimal productivity gains. Certainly, someone who loses his life on a highway due to texting while driving has made a bad investment by any measure and would have been better off without mobile technology.

In terms of time-based productivity, how can you tell whether a new technology adds a net benefit?

There's still very little research on how to make this

determination, so once again, we're on our own. Lots of researchers study the after-effects of bad mobile habits, but few ask the ultimate question: how can we determine beforehand whether a new technology will help or hinder? Must we incur painful, high costs before we wake up to the latest unproductive habit?

Given the multi-billion dollar nature of the mobile industry, why is this question not being asked?

It's the same reason that Dezhi Wu's work stands out, as I mentioned in the chapter on Reviewing. She is one of the few researchers who is effectively studying the question of technology that's supposed to improve productivity, but doesn't. As a computer scientist by training, she's become conversant in a number of other disciplines in order to do her work.

Most academics, as I mentioned, shun multidisciplinary studies. As a result, simple questions like "Has email made us more productive?" go unanswered.

Or perhaps we're also being lazy. It's much easier to buy and then discard the latest gadget than it is to ask hard questions. Never mind the cost.

Real Productivity

Perhaps real productivity improvement needs to come from somewhere other than the manufacturer or retail store du jour. I suggest that a better place to start is the mirror – with your current profile of your skills in the 11 Fundamentals. Your Master plan is an excellent place to start.

Whenever you review the forms you have completed while reading this book, you can create a picture that tells you a story: it reveals where the biggest gaps in your personal productivity might be. Like a surgeon, you can focus on the handful of changes required to produce the greatest improvements.

Rather than slick advertising, the latest buzz or peer pressure, you can make your plans based on informed, skillful self-knowledge of your habits, practices and rituals.

Your Master Plan can also tell you what to do when new technology emerges, and how to proactively search for new advances.

1. When New Technology Becomes Available

In 2014, Samsung, Google and Apple all announced what appeared to be the first commercially viable smartwatches. As other manufacturers get into the game, I predict that you'll be making a choice within the next few years: "Should I get one?"

A better set of questions to ask, based on your Master Plan, are the following:
- What are my current time-based productivity gaps?
- Which fundamentals am I trying to improve at the moment?
- Which improvements need to be made next in my plan?
- Will this new device move me closer to my productivity goals?
- What new habits will I have to learn to maintain this technology?

In a single room of working professionals, I'd expect a variety of answers. No one-size-fits-all solution exists.

A great reason to be vigilant, and ask tough questions, is that companies are pouring more resources than ever before into understanding your habits, practices and rituals. Their objective is to engage you without educating you, perhaps intending to disengage your conscious mind. You can find great proof of this in the work of Nir Eyal at www.nirandfar.com.

In his introductory video, Nir says, "[...] I [...] study how technology persuades people. [...] Facebook and Twitter [...] (the fact that) these companies manage to get people to do behaviors they've never done before fascinates me." His goal is to help entrepreneurs build products that tie right into people's habit patterns, as explained in his book: "Hooked: A Guide to Building Habit-Forming Products."

I suspect he's getting lots of calls.

While it's a bit of a chore to ask yourself the kind of questions I listed before, consider the downside of ignoring them: giving in to product designers who are keen to build habit-forming products. Here's a case study to consider regarding a technology that's just about to be introduced to the general public.

Smartwatches are predicted to be a big Christmas gift this year. While many are excited by the prospect, a few see it as a new, unavoidable source of 24-hour-a-day, seven-day-a-week distractions. I'm sure it will be extremely convenient, but what impact will it have on the average professional's productivity?

If you don't ask these questions, you're likely to be wearing one soon – just wait for the first wave of catchy advertisements backed by market-researched graphics and soundtracks. The manufacturer fully intends to use the kind of research Nir specializes in to get you to "do behaviors (you have) never done before."

Therefore, from a time-based productivity point of view, the launch of a new technology is mostly just noise. To find the signal, if it exists, we must pay attention to the questions I listed above, even though we might struggle to answer them.

2. How to Search for New Technology

A better approach than waiting for the optimal innovation to appear is to start defining, in your mind, the technologies you need. The best way to define them is to study your Master Plan. When you do so with some rigor, you can discover gaps that call for new software or hardware. For example, earlier, I described a gap that must be closed for all of us to achieve a Green Belt in Warning.

Most gaps, however, will be determined by your individual needs. When you realize you have a gap that might be closed with technology, start with a Google search. Sometimes, you can already find what you need.

If what you want doesn't exist, you may join me in lobbying developers to create the tools you need. Ultimately, if you happen to be a software or hardware creator, you could even lead the creation of these tools, perhaps becoming the Steve Jobs of productivity!

Long before your fame reaches that point, however, I recommend that you become an expert at improving your own methods, starting with a change in your habits, practices and rituals. This can help you remain focused on the shortest path to improvement, even when everyone around you is rushing to buy the latest device.

Using New Thinking and Avoiding Snake Oil

Experience tells me that the most important, high-priority changes won't need new technology at all. The data suggests that most people gain the most from behavior changes they convert into new habits.

However, the 11 Fundamentals are hardly the last word on the subject. New ideas constantly suggest additional fundamentals and new technologies. Ultimately, someone smarter than I am will revamp the ideas in *Perfect Time-Based Productivity* and replace them with something better.

You need to be open to those ideas, but where can you find them?

New books, programs, blogs and podcasts are everywhere, revealing the results of new research or insights based on personal experience. In the References and in my Lab Notes, I have quoted a wide range of peer-reviewed journals; they represent a subset of the academic articles I used to write this book.

At the same time, here's a word of caution: authors, gurus and thought-leaders in productivity can sidetrack you. They might have something valuable to say, but they often over-reach by claiming that their habit-patterns are one-size-fits-all answers.

Some also over-promise, and claim that:
- Their system will double or triple your productivity while providing no proof of the standard of measurement.
- Their approach will never require further improvement.
- Their method is perfect and will be unaffected by new technology.
- You must totally accept their suggested behaviors – or fail.

As I mentioned earlier, a recent *Harvard Business Review* blog article warned against the use of "anecdata" in building broad theories: be wary of ideas that are based on only one or two stories, even if they happen to be intriguing.

But you're armed. With the specialized knowledge you possess from the development of your profile and Master Plan, you need not be distracted. Instead, you can pick new ideas apart, looking for nuggets of gold. When you figure out the specific fundamental hidden inside a new, suggested behavior, you can evaluate it from the point of view of your plan and use it accordingly. Needless to say, don't waste time improving behaviors that are already strong at the expense of weak ones.

For example, recall the story of Marsha (with the multiple steno pads) from the chapter on Emptying. If you are also strong at Capturing but weak at Emptying, you won't improve much by acquiring the nicest $30 Moleskin notebook. It might be easy and familiar, but it's better to plan some deliberate practice on the sub-skills that make up Emptying.

Sometimes, however, you may want to implement a new practice distinct from the 11 Fundamentals. In the next Chapter on Creating Your Own Ladders, I'll show you how to dissect a brand-new behavior, regardless of its source, so that you can take the small steps needed to implement new behaviors.

Also, if you have suggestions to improve the 11 Fundamentals discussed in this book, check out the forums on my website. Look for the topic title "Improvements" at http://perfect.mytimedesign.com/forums.

Remember and Share

Before adopting new technology, figure out where your real productivity gaps lie, and try to fill those gaps first.

Don't be the first to buy a new gadget – be the first to understand the gap it fills in your system.

Should we become trapped by new technology, or should we drive the changes we make from intelligent diagnoses?

Avoid the Zeigarnik Effect by putting your time demands in order.

Don't focus on managing time – that's futile. Instead, here's something you are already managing: a time demand.

Keep your commitments alive by creating and managing time demands.

Don't fall into the trap of thinking that greater convenience is the same as greater productivity.

Greater convenience can bring lesser productivity (e.g. texting
and driving).

Chapter 21. Creating Your Own Ladders of Improvement

(In which you learn how to pick any improvement goal and create a step-by-step process to achieve it).

If you have followed the steps laid out in the previous chapters, you should have 11 completed Cheat-Sheets – one for each fundamental. Each represents your current level of skill in a single time management fundamental. As you know by now, each of these Cheat-Sheets includes a description of sub-skills that together make up a more complex behavior.

Along the way, you may have wondered, "How did he come up with these sub-skills? What if I want to define my own?

In this chapter, I'll show you the process I used to define (and refine) each fundamental, sharing how I took vaguely-defined practices and used them to develop Cheat-Sheets, or ladders of skills. By the end, you should be able to create your own Cheat-Sheets and ladders, starting with just an idea. While some paths, such as learning the piano or becoming a mathematician, are well defined, many others aren't. In my opinion, life is just too short to wait for someone else to figure out the pathway to high accomplishment. You can do it yourself and find tremendous satisfaction at the same time.

More specifically, I'll show you the process I used to develop the Fundamentals and their definitions. We'll revisit the behavior of "Habiting" – a skill I talked about for years but never actually named until I started writing this book.

At the moment, there are no "official" Cheat-Sheets for this skill, so I invite you to read this chapter and then contribute to its development in the forums on my website - http://perfect.mytimedesign.com/forums. Furthermore, I'd also love to hear your suggestions on what cheat sheets might look like for "Flowing," another behavior that I've only just started to define. Far from an academic exercise, this is a real opportunity to jointly create content that we can all use.

A Process for Crafting a New Ladder

I often begin with only a vague idea of the new behavior I have in mind. Even a notion is enough to get started. First, I decide if it's a behavior I already engage in. Usually, I discover that I have already been performing it at some level.

As you worked through the Fundamentals, you may have noticed that I described them as behaviors that you probably already use without really thinking about them. It's far easier to start with first-hand knowledge. Without this kind of experience, it takes me longer to explore a skill fully.

Also, if I can, I observe other people who use the skill (or lack it completely). Jamaica is known more for the speed of its runners than its high productivity, so I often see what happens when a productivity skill is missing. My experience with top companies in the United States also gives me an idea of what the behavior looks like when it's done particularly well.

If you're lucky, you may find in your research that an expert has already detailed the sub-skills that make up your behavior. For example, it's better to learn the complexities of games like chess or Go from masters who are good teachers. If that kind of help is available, use it, but be careful to separate the findings of actual studies from anecdata. There's a big difference. If you can find research based on surveys or experiments, you're in luck, as it tends to be the most trustworthy. However, in the area of time-based productivity, I have found that both academic studies and self-help books are tricky to work with. Here's why.

- They're often fragmented: the information and answers you need might be available in multiple fields of study, which all use different jargon and background literature. They may even contradict each other, as their respective traditions might vary tremendously.
- They are rigid, as we discussed before: there's a tendency to go overboard and claim that one size fits all or "it's my way or the highway."
- They are technical. The layperson without a research background may have a hard time understanding the way academics write. Use Google to find other

authors or bloggers who refer to the original research
in plain English.

Once you have done some introductory reading, jump
right in to your initial design activity using your intuition and
the information you have gathered. Later on, there will be
time for more investigation, but for now, it's important to get
started quickly so that you can define the parameters of the
behavior.

***

I have boiled down my often-chaotic process into the
following five steps.

1. Clearly define the new behavior.

2. Outline specific sub-skills or practices.

3. For each sub-skill, define the extremes in
performance.

4. Fill in the gaps between the highest and lowest
performers.

5. Score yourself, setting new targets, creating plans to
fill gaps, and setting up a support system.

To truly understand them, select an actual habit,
practice, ritual or routine to work on while I show you the
examples. Pick any behavior you're interested in (e.g. flossing
your teeth) and write it down in your diary to start.

Step 1: Clearly define the new behavior.

I start out by making a mind map in order to place all
the information I know in a single place. It's a brain-dump
intended to free up my mind. For example, here's the one I
created for "Habiting." As you may recall, Habiting is defined
as the ability to unlearn old habits and learn new ones at will.

Figure 21-1

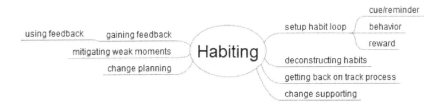

Once I complete the first draft of the map, I try to paint a picture in my mind of sub-skills that I have observed. Here, I draw on the research reading I've done. I keep adding new branches to the tree until my thoughts are exhausted.

Once I'm satisfied that my top-of-mind thoughts have been mapped and I can picture the desired behavior, I develop an issue tree that focuses on finding answers to questions like these:

Why does this skill fail to appear when it should? Why don't people exhibit the behavior when it's in their best interest to do so? Why isn't everyone Habiting with the highest skill possible?

In this example, I developed a basic issue tree based on the third question. At this point, I'm happy to be guessing – this is only the first draft, as you can see below.

Figure 21-2

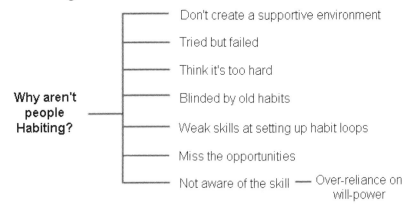

If you have a behavior in mind that you'd like to work on, spend a few minutes developing your own mind map and issue tree. If you need further training on these tools, check the References at the end for some useful links. Having a real example to work on is, I believe, the absolute best way to understand this method from the inside.

Step 2: Outline specific sub-skills or practices.

From your analysis above, define the handful of practices you need to execute the skill effectively. This is your first list, so it needn't be perfect. Attempt to make it what McKinsey consultants call "MECE" - Mutually Exclusive but Comprehensively Exhaustive. Try your best to be rigorous.

Note that the sub-skills you capture need to pass what I call the "Videotape Test." That is, they need to be observable to the naked eye – able to be captured on videotape. The corollary to this test (which is derived from Time and Motion Studies I learned as an industrial engineer) is what I call the "Fool Yourself Test": if you can honestly make the mistake of thinking that you're doing the practice when in fact you're not, then something is wrong with the definition. Go back to the drawing board and find better-defined sub-skills.

Here's the initial list of five sub-skills I came up with for Habiting.

Sub-skill #1 - Setting up a habit change support system.

Sub-skill #2 - Establishing a process for getting back on track.

Sub-skill #3 - Mitigating your weakest moments.

Sub-skill #4 - Creating plans made up of small steps.

Sub-skill #5 - Using feedback tracking to determine whether your habit is actually changing.

Step 3: For each sub-skill, define the extremes in performance.

Here's where the research you conducted prior to the first step comes in useful. What is it like for someone who doesn't use this sub-skill? What do they do instead? What are the consequences?

You also need to discover and outline the highest performance you can find for each sub-skill. What is it like for those who are great at this practice?

Here are the extreme cases of two sub-skills in Habiting: "Setting up a habit change support system" and

"Creating change plans made up of small steps."

Figure 21-3

	Lowest Level	Highest Level
Setting up a habit change support system	no system	a fool-proof system
Creating change plans made up of small steps	no planning	a full plan in place

Here's my reasoning.

In "Setting up a habit change support system" at the Lowest Level, the person would not be aware of the distinction and wouldn't understand the concept. The same applies to "Creating change plans made up of small steps."

Someone at the Highest Level would successfully set up a support system made up of multiple elements. It would be foolproof and almost perfect in helping the person to change habits. They'd have a keen understanding of what works well for them. (For a superb discussion on masterfully creating a support system for behavior change, see Eric Barker's blog entry: How To Get In Shape Using Psychology: 6 New Tricks From Research. http://www.bakadesuyo.com/2014/11/how-to-get-in-shape/.)

They may even use wearable technology such as Pavlok to help shape their habits. This device delivers a beep, buzz or electrical shock if a pre-determined habit pattern isn't followed. While it may be far-fetched based on today's norms, in the future, more sophisticated devices will probably be developed. (https://www.indiegogo.com/projects/pavlok-the-habit-changing-device-that-shocks-you)

Also, if that same, skillful person were setting up a plan, he or she would know how to convert a complex habit into small behaviors and focus on implementing them gradually, over time, according to a schedule.

Step 4: Fill in the gaps between the highest and lowest performers. As you know, I use the martial arts ladder, simply because it's universally understood, but any method would work.

Here is the full chart covering the four skill levels in Habiting.

Figure 21-4

	Lowest Level			Highest Level
Setting up a habit change support system	no system	tried one support	multiple supports	a fool-proof system
Creating change plans made up of small steps	no planning	drafted initial plan	tested and refined a plan	a full plan in place

Step 5: Follow the steps I suggested earlier in this book by scoring yourself, setting new targets, creating plans to fill gaps, and setting up a support system.

When I follow these steps to create a new ladder, I try to make sure to enjoy the process and have fun along the way as I create my own improvement plan. It's exciting to see what unfolds as I use my creativity and knowledge to forge a new pathway.

***

I have noticed when using this method that it's important to be a true scientist – to throw away all misconceptions and biases. With a clear mind, you can find examples of extreme practices wherever they may be found in the world.

One way to create better ladders is to do it with the intention of sharing them with other people as a contribution to their development. This frame of mind will push you to think from other people's point of view, improving the quality of your final product.

This echoes one of the messages in *A Course in Miracles*, a spiritual self-help book. In it, the self-described scribe Dr. Helen Schucman states that "real" things increase when they are given away. The book's primary example is love, but I happen to believe it's also true for teaching aids like ladders, especially when they're created in the right spirit.

For example, the term "Habiting" may never have been chosen and clarified if I hadn't started this book. The process of giving away ideas helps sharpen them. You may find the same to be true of the ladders that you develop. Be sure to share them in the forums if you'd like some friendly feedback.

Red Herrings

There are a few behaviors that I have found hard to define and almost impossible to convert into ladders and Cheat-Sheets. While the terms may be popular, they're based on poorly defined notions. I use the "Videotape Test" to weed them out. If a behavior can't be placed on video, then it can't be coached or taught. If it can't be taught, then it's beyond my ability to describe it well — a clear indicator I'm looking in the wrong direction. I recommend that you use the same test. The great thing about placing this restriction up front is that it forces clarity.

Here are a few of the terms used in time-based productivity that I have difficulty with because they fail the Videotape Test. Can you videotape someone as they are:
- Procrastinating?
- Prioritizing?
- Focusing?
- Managing their time? (vs. time demands)
- Managing their energy?

If you can't watch them do it, you should be suspicious — the behavior might not be a good candidate for this process. Let's look at the first example: procrastinating.

There are multiple definitions of the word, only a few of which pass our test:
- From Wikipedia: "Procrastination is the practice of carrying out less urgent tasks in preference to more urgent ones, or doing more pleasurable things in place of less pleasurable ones, and thus putting off impending tasks to a later time, sometimes to the 'last minute.'"
- From Dictionary.com: "The act or habit of procrastinating, or putting off or delaying, especially something requiring immediate attention."

- From the World English Dictionary: "To put off or defer action until a later time; delay."
- From the Free Dictionary: "To put off doing something, especially out of habitual carelessness or laziness. To postpone or delay needlessly."

"Putting off" is not an action you can videotape. Also, it's easy to think that you are not putting anything off when in fact you are, and vice versa. Instead, the term needs to be broken down into specific sub-skills that pass the test and can therefore be used in a ladder.

While procrastination is a popular topic of conversation and a frequent complaint in many workplaces, we use the word so imprecisely that no amount of change in behavior can ever make it go away. (I realize that there is an extreme, chronic version of this behavior, but most people don't have it).

Another red herring is the belief that our stressful thoughts are real. People who complain to themselves and others that, for example, they are "too lazy" might be caught up in negative thinking that, by itself, shapes their world and ruins their productivity. In this case, the shortcut involves working on the negative, stressful thought directly.

In a recent book, *Overwhelmed: Work, Love, and Play When No One Has the Time,* Brigid Schulte appears to arrive at the same conclusion. Her research, reported on the Business Insider website, shows that for some people, chronic busyness has become a mark of social status. "People are competing about being busy," she reports. The emphatic answer to this disease comes from sociologist John Robinson, who is known as "Father Time" because he collects time diaries. His empirical research shows that we are nowhere near as busy as we think we are. The answer is simple: stop believing the thoughts you tell yourself about how busy you are.

Negative thoughts have little to do with the 11 Fundamentals or with time-based productivity directly. This makes them red herrings, and you need to examine the behavior you have selected to ensure that it doesn't fall into this category.

The fact that red herrings are thought-based, however, doesn't mean they are harmless. They can have real psychological effects. Here are some of the remedies I have personally used: a good therapist, lifestyle coaching and self-help programs by Tony Robbins, Landmark Education, and Byron Katie. *Loving What Is,* Katie's book, is the one that I have found most useful.

So far in this book, I have bemoaned the fact that the right hardware and software tools are not available and in their absence we develop unproductive habits. In the next chapter, we'll take my complaints a step further and consider the tools that need to be developed to help us manage time demands effectively.

Remember and Share

Creating your own ladder for improving skills is sometimes the only way to achieve superior results.

When you are both the coach and coachee, step back and create a ladder of skills to carve a pathway to excellence.

The easiest skills to learn can be videotaped.

The hardest skills to learn can't be observed and therefore can't be measured.

Any new skill we encounter can be converted into a ladder of smaller skills, but we need to study it in depth.

A good system that supports your change in habits doesn't rely on your memory or anything internal.

Coaching yourself is sometimes the only option. If it is, use best practices to achieve superior results.

Chapter 22. The New Tools We All Need

(In which you explore the tools you need to manage time demands and why they don't exist).

At this point in Time-Based Productivity, you may agree with a key underlying premise: humans manage time demands in a common, but idiosyncratic way. You may also agree that it's never been an easy task, constrained as we are by the limits of physics, the design of our brains, the way the mind works, and the logic of process management.

So far, I have argued that this overall structure is inescapable. As humans, we share the same physical limitations and can't change any aspect of our essential nature. However, as I have mentioned, technology can extend our ability to manage time demands in remarkable ways.

Unfortunately, the time management tools at our disposal hardly live up to the promise of the best technology that exists in the world. Mankind has progressed in so many ways, yet colossal errors still occur each and every day as time demands are mismanaged.

Ask the project managers of the website for the Affordable Care Act, who were ordered, against their better judgment, to launch the site on October 1, 2013. The result? Millions who logged in when the site went public were met with impossibly slow responses or no access whatsoever.

Every day, professionals struggle to keep time demands alive with hardware and software that is supposed to meet their needs. The fact that they do so without understanding the definition of time demands, peace of mind and the 11 Fundamentals is testimony to their grit. Their achievements take place in spite of the fact that they are self-taught and lack suitable tools.

In other areas of life, we have awe-inspiring technologies; why is it that software and hardware seem to fall short here?

Recent Research in Time-Based Productivity Tools

Mona Haraty is a PhD student in Computer Science at the University of British Columbia. She's already broken ground by simply defining the challenge professionals face in this area accurately. Something interesting happens when you define a problem truthfully: solutions appear.

In 2013, she wrote a paper titled "Supporting Behavioral Differences and Changes in Personal Task Management." She's studying the way software tools need to be designed to accommodate users' needs, given that:

- "People have different needs and preferences when using software tools to (manage their) daily tasks."
- "People's behaviors change over time."
- People's "changing needs and desire to improve" lead to changed behaviors.
- "Without being given the right tools, people will be forced to live a '*default life*' dictated by their tools."
- "The design of (personalized tools) for accommodating behavioral differences is largely unexplored."

As she puts it, "In my PhD, I aim to fill this gap."

One of her goals is to explore how tools can be designed for users who want to customize them while also helping those who don't want to invest a lot of time fiddling with tricky features. She has also included a diagnostic step "aimed at helping users to find the underlying mismatch between their needs and their system." The results of this diagnosis will provide users with suggestions about how and where they can find and implement the solutions they need.

In the context of our discussion in this book, she's headed in an exciting direction. She has the potential to impact the way every single person manages time demands using software tools that reside on laptops, gadgets, tablets, smartphones, the cloud and more. The fact that so few researchers are focusing on this area is heartbreaking, but understandable. As we established before, it's tough to do interdisciplinary research.

Also, we badly need Haraty's research because "existing […] systems do not adequately accommodate the needs of a broad range of people." Part of her evidence lies in the fact that there are "e-systems that support adults in their work, where a small number of applications dominate the market, such as word processing, spreadsheets, and email clients. The same cannot be said for task management."

She argues that designers have focused on creating average software for the average user, and they fail to address people's individual differences. To illustrate, let's look at the results I shared regarding the mythical "average participant" in my live programs: she has a Yellow Belt in six of the seven Essential Fundamentals.

I also stated that while this profile represented an average, it didn't reflect the typical user, whose profile is far from following the uniform picture the chart suggested. Per user, the actual dataset shows a great deal of variation: an individual sometimes has both White and Green Belt skills. As a result, designing a system that meets individual needs is difficult, as Haraty suggests.

Dezhi Wu, the researcher we met in earlier chapters, also studied the tools used by the "better time managers." If you recall, her work showed that they use calendars heavily to track a large number of tasks and reminders.

Wu discovered that people usually need assistance to undertake activities such as "plan in advance," "prioritize tasks" and "communicate and coordinate time with others." They also experienced "difficulties with current time management tools." She notes that their complaints could be translated into a set of additional functions, such as:
1. "Lack of integration…with other task or project management tools and their organizational calendaring systems."
2. "Lack of flexibility to schedule group activities or a series of events easily, in particular it is hard to make any modifications with the current tools."
3. "Lack of convenient and proper synchronization features among different devices."
4. "Lack of user-friendly interfaces."
5. "Lack of true personal time management features (e.g. the ability to assess one person's time management practices) instead of being mainly used as a time recording tool."
6. "Lack of effective collaborative calendar features."
7. "Cost of getting a seamless calendar system."

In particular, she reports, "Almost all interviewees commented that their time management tools lacked support for developing time management strategies and assessing their time management efficiency."

Wu summarized these complaints into four basic needs for time management tools:
- Portability
- Ability to gain an overview
- Ability to better coordinate between multiple tools
- Collaborative scheduling

At the time (2004), she noted that only the first two needs were being met. One could argue that in the past ten years, there has been a great deal of progress in the third need and moderate progress in the fourth.

Near the end of her paper, "Knowledge Worker Adoption of Time Management Tools," Wu alludes to the same problem that Haraty notes: "Most of the users selected their time management method through random choice rather than assessing their time management needs. They then adopted [sic] the tool or combination of tools to their needs without much judgment". This fits with Haraty's observation: "without being given the right tools, people will be forced to live a '*default life*' dictated by their tools."

Their findings raise the question: how much individual lack of productivity is driven by inappropriate tool choice?

Wu adds more weight to the problem by observing: "…most of the features provided by the electronic tools were not used… and even when integration… existed, [it] …was not always exploited. Or, if it was, [it] did not work conveniently, because each tool was used differently."

Clearly, there's a long way to go to provide users with the tools they need to manage time demands in today's workplace. Let's try to understand why this situation exists by reviewing the history of popular tools.

Time-Based Productivity Tools: A History

Microsoft Outlook is one of the most popular email management programs. When the program was introduced in 1992 it had all the essential functions bundled into one: email client, task, calendar and contacts. However, people used it primarily to manage email, preferring to continue using paper diaries for functions more directly related to time-based productivity. The stated fear at the time was that the use of an electronic solution was risky: you could "lose everything," and many did just that when they made their first forays into replacing paper with electronic solutions. (Cloud and mobile computing were more than a decade away).

Most people stuck with paper for everything other than email, it seems, and it wasn't until the first Personal Digital Assistants (PDAs) were introduced that a clear advantage appeared. Now, with the right gadget, you could leave your desk and bring along important information related to your time demands. If you managed backups properly, you could also ensure that if the device failed, the impact wasn't catastrophic.

However, in terms of managing email, little changed. Most people who used Outlook or Lotus Notes did so to manage email, rather than as tools for managing time demands. When other programs, such as Gmail, Yahoo mail, AOL Mail and Mozilla's Thunderbird entered the space, users' main goal was to replace Outlook as the core email client. The calendar, to-do and contacts features were after-the-fact add-ons seen as nice-to-haves.

Google, for example, released GCal (Google Calendar) in 2006, a full two years after the splashy introduction of Gmail. By then, Google was clear they had a hit on their hands with Gmail.

Where are we today?

While many new apps have emerged on smartphones and tablets to replace these desktop programs, email applications remain the most popular and important. There are also more choices of calendar, to-do and contact systems, but fewer people use them and for shorter spans of time.

Here is a summary of some of the most recent trends:

- By January 2014, more email was being read via mobile than on desktops, according to Litmus' "Email Analytics." For services like Gmail and Yahoo!, that number has risen to 68%.

- Email clients on mobile devices have become standalone applications that are looking more and more alike. As we mentioned in the chapter on Capturing, we all feel the need to bring our Capture Points together into a single location. For many, having all email coming into one inbox or at least a single device serves that purpose well. Email, which used to be seen as information sitting in a program on your desktop, is now being seen as cloud-based.

- Calendar and to-do apps are also becoming standalone programs that rarely interact with email programs, reversing the trend from just a few years ago. Some mobile apps have blended both calendar and to-do functions, but the trend favors small, single-function apps rather than full, integrated suites.

- Calendar apps of all kinds are not designed to help you manage a full schedule of time demands: they are still designed around the concept of keeping track of appointments with other people. The interfaces still look like the appointment books of old, with a separate list of time-slots for each day, arrayed in the form of a list. So far, no application I have seen has strayed from that formulation, which constrains the user and makes it hard to juggle a moving set of daily time demands.

A Deeper Understanding

Most professionals have developed the practice of checking email first thing in the morning, before making a plan for the day, reviewing their schedule or consulting their to-do list. This habit is probably an outgrowth of the way Outlook and other email clients were developed – as email-centric programs that demoted the importance of other functions.

In terms of time-based productivity, that's perfectly understandable. We go looking for fresh time demands via email before doing anything else. While there has been popular talk of giving up email for social networks, it's not likely to happen anytime soon. There are simply too many time demands arriving in your inbox each day to give up using email.

Also, checking email (a form of Emptying) offers a dopamine rush as we hunt for new sensations that feed our pleasure centers. We can't say the same for checking a calendar or reviewing a to-do list. After all, the items on these lists aren't new: we put them there, so from the point of view of brain chemistry, they are routine activities.

However, managing already-existing time demands is more important than chasing after those that are only potential. In other words, looking over your calendar and to-do list should have a higher priority than checking email. To put it yet another way, achieving your goals is less a function of uncovering time demands that other people are trying to trigger than of fulfilling the ones you already have identified.

In the chapter on Acting Now, we looked at the mistake of dropping everything to complete new potential time demands that appear in messages from other people. We also talked about the unproductive way some professionals are drawn into chasing one crisis after another each day.

This temptation is compounded by the existence of multiple Capture Points: Facebook, Twitter, WhatsApp, etc. They are just as important as an email inbox for many professionals, deepening the challenge, and their existence on the same device instantly elevates the attention we give them.

Given this state of affairs, it's fair to say there's a gap between what people actually do and what they should do.

I can't tell whether or not Microsoft, Google and other software companies consider themselves to be in the "time-demand management business." It seems clear, however, that these companies' design choices have shaped people's habits, even if they were made many years ago.

Helping People Do Their Best Work

Beyond these major companies, hundreds of smaller firms spend considerable resources trying to replace Outlook, Gmail and Yahoo! Mail. Most have offered themselves as *de facto* task coordinators – a place to manage time demands transferred from Capture Points. (You can find an extensive list of some of these programs in the References). Some are modeled after to-do lists, while a few are based on schedules.

The reason you may not have heard of any of these programs is that they aren't very popular. Why?

Most people manage email in unproductive ways. Far from using the Zero Inbox strategy, they just use their receiving email Inbox as a single location to read, store, sort and manage messages. They don't move their messages into folders, because they are afraid they'll lose track of them.

According to Steve Whittaker (who we met earlier in the first chapter) "leaving the original message in the inbox as a reminder about that task [...] serves to manipulate attention. Users know that they will return to the inbox to access new messages [...] they hope that they will see the reminder and recall the outstanding task."

He continues by citing Gina Venolia, who found that this technique was "by far the most frequent reminding strategy [...] more common than [...] flags or classifying messages as "to-do" items."

Unfortunately, those who try to stop using their inboxes to manage tasks rarely succeed at first. Whittaker studied those who set up dedicated "to-do" folders as a replacement method. He reports that "the majority of users (95%) abandoned this strategy, on the grounds that it required an additional cognitive step."

Therefore, a new task management program that offers to help people manage time demands in a remote location is seen as dangerous, due to the additional "cognitive steps" required. Hiding cues in an app, program or website feels threatening for the majority of users who use their inboxes for this purpose.

Even those users who follow the Zero Inbox discipline and therefore use lots of folders (or tag-based filters) aren't willing to change programs or switch locations. Just like those who use their inbox as a place to manage time demands, they also have a habit they are unwilling to break unless there's a high payoff. So far, for both groups, the cost of adopting this new tactic, plus the inherent risk, have just seemed too high.

Recently, however, our ingrained habits have entered a state of flux because so many of us are switching over to the use of mobile devices. Email programs are now offered as standalone apps that don't include calendars, to-do lists or appointment books. This signals an opportunity for a new kind of software – one that breaks our fixation on email management.

Design Rules for New Software

How can a software company help users manage time demands? Should they simply replicate the process they use today? Or should they design interfaces and engines that push people to employ unfamiliar best practices?

The time is right for the emergence of software that helps users do their best work, bridging the gap between their current methods and the best practices. This new software would help users manage time demands so that:

1. The capacity of an individual system matches the volume of time demands it must handle.

2. No time demands ever fall through the cracks.

Based on these objectives mentioned before, the ideal system would help a user tap into potential and actual time demands from all sources, such as email messages, tweets, Facebook messages, instant messages, texts and more. It would tap into time demands in all locations, even paper: Livescribe is one such alternative. Also, it would be flexible enough to add in new, future sources of time demands.

Furthermore, there would be a way to filter these sources in intelligent ways, helping users focus on their most important time demands.

Additionally, the system would understand that several time demands could arrive in a single message and that each one has to be managed on its own merits.

Design Rule Number 1 would therefore be to center the system around time demands, not messages.

In this context, an email message is like a wrapper for a present. It's just a carrier for potential time demands. So are physical letters, tweets sent as DM's, text messages, Instagram updates, Facebook messages, Instant Messages, Skype video voicemails, etc. Like little kids, we don't care about the wrapper.

We just want the present inside: the time demand. The particular format in which a potential time demand arrives is irrelevant. Surprisingly, the volume of messages doesn't seem to matter either. An article by the University of Toronto's Bernie Hogan and Microsoft's Danyel Fisher on email overload quotes a study that "found that users' perceptions of overload correspond to the number of unresolved tasks in the users' inbox (and not the volume of messages incoming)."

The ideal interface would not only help us separate the electronic message from the time demand, it would also be flexible enough to accommodate users' different styles. In this book, we've differentiated between professionals who prefer to use a single to-do list, multiple lists or a single schedule. All users should be able to customize the interface so that each morning they are only presented with the features they will actually be using.

For example, someone who uses a single schedule should be able to drag a text message that includes five time demands into five different time slots. **Design Rule Number 2** is therefore that the interface should fit people's way of managing time demands.

Right now, people do the best they can with the software that exists. They use email-centric programs like Outlook, Lotus Notes and Gmail for another purpose: time demand management. Many of these programs (especially Outlook) are filled with amazing features, but they are presented in a way that doesn't give the user easy access: they assume that the user's main goal is email management.

A better design would follow a user's preferred sequence and encourage him/her to start the day by setting up a schedule and lists before checking for new email. It would be the equivalent of those programs that block Facebook – before you look for new time demands via email, you'd be required to check your schedule and to-do lists, putting together a plan for the day.

This is **Design Rule Number 3** – the software encourages the user to follow a more productive process rather than chucking all the features at him/her at all once.

Also, a new kind of program would allow a user to track time demands through to completion. It would alert him/her when time demands are about to go stale and also produce metrics related to how well they are being managed. Further, time demands could be tagged using a number of user-defined attributes. This new way of measuring and tagging time demands would comprise **Design Rule Number 4**.

Here, then, are the **Four Design Rules**, in summary.
1. Design the system around time demands rather than electronic messages.
2. At any moment in time, the interface should offer access

only to preferred features.

3. The program should be designed to be "smart" and help the user follow productive processes.

4. The program should provide a way to tag time demands so that they can be tracked and measured.

These rules are hardly exhaustive. Perhaps an entire book should be written on how to design time-based productivity software so that it helps, rather than hinders professionals. I'm not an expert in design, but I do recognize the challenge developers have in converting an understanding of what people do (and should do) into useful products. Hardware design is no different.

Hardware Improvements: Where's my Capture Button?

As I mentioned before, during the course of writing this book, I made a switch from a Blackberry (BB) to an Android device. On my old BB, physical, programmable buttons on either side of the device could be linked to any program. Mine was set up to launch a text editor whenever I pressed the button on the left side, a motion that initiated my Capturing. It would launch the app even when the device was off.

Now, either due to my ignorance of how my new device works (which is likely) or because of a design choice, I can't do that with my new smartphone. Instead, I have to open an app using software icons only.

Plus, I'm still struggling with the transition from the BB's physical keyboard and its solid, secure feel to the Android's virtual keyboard and its slippery guessing game of try-to-press-the-right-key. It seemed impossible at first, but I'm getting better.

I'm guessing that the makers of my new phone don't know that users need to Capture quickly, with the press of a button. Perhaps if they did, they would have designed the device differently.

Being pessimistic, I don't think that a phone call to them would help.

Needed: A Philosophy

"What you guys must understand is that you won't get far without a working philosophy!" I was pacing around, the phone to my ear, the CEO of a well-known Gmail app development company on the other end of the line..

We spoke for a few hours in total, during which I shared a brief analysis I had done of 1000+ Gmail user comments on an open question on the company's website: "How can we improve Google Calendar?" Fortunately for nosy people like me, the company had left the list of users' recommendations open to the public, giving a rich insight into what people were lacking in the current setup.

This call wasn't with Google. On the phone, I advised the CEO that his company needed a working philosophy around productivity. People didn't care about email messages, I argued, they cared about time demands. I underlined the point: "Without a philosophy of your own, you're just adding nice features. But a lack of features is not the source of the problem users have today."

A few months later, I read Steve Jobs' biography. I particularly enjoyed the breakthrough thinking he brought to products like iTunes. Working with his colleagues at Apple, Jobs introduced a new philosophy: sell people the singles they want rather than the albums they don't want. (Now, a few years later, it seems ludicrous that this was even a point of debate). It was just the kind of breakthrough thinking I had been talking about in that conversation with the CEO.

He also needed a different way of thinking more closely aligned with his users' needs. An email-centric philosophy would produce Outlook-like copycat products that could easily be duplicated, but one that centered around time demands (and therefore people's most cherished commitments) would be different.

Developing a fresh philosophy is not easy – it's "the road less travelled." But if users' needs are going to be met, it's the only road. An excellent book to read on this topic is *The Four Steps to the Epiphany* by Steve Blank.

In a late-breaking development, during the final edits of this book, Google announced a new product: Google Inbox. It appears to be a direct response to the data they shared from the survey. For the first time (to my knowledge), the software appears to recognize that inboxes are being used as a place to manage tasks.

The Problem of Existing Habits

A close colleague of mine, Scott Hilton-Clarke, is a Harvard MBA with a difference. He has a sharp mind for gaps in user experience that can be translated into new products. One of his ideas has been turned into a commercial app called After the Meeting, which was released back in 2011. It's a specific application based on an earlier program he developed for tracking the promises made between working professionals. This particular app focuses only on promises made in meetings.

The reason you don't know his name, or his app, is that people have powerful habits they are unwilling to break. Tracking promises using a website makes sense to people, but they have a hard time converting that piece of common sense into everyday behavior. Having a great idea isn't enough.

Earlier, I mentioned the book by Nir Eyal, *Hooked: How to Build Habit-Forming Products*. He tackles this problem head on, but if you think that he provides any easy answers, you're wrong. This intersection of psychology and technology is new, and in the area of time-based productivity, few keep abreast of the changes that are happening in devices, apps and gadgets.

If your company develops time-based productivity software or hardware, then you must craft your own solutions based on the habits, practices and rituals your market currently uses. Charles Duhigg outlines ways to marry old features with new ones in *The Power of Habit*. It's one way to give users the comfort of familiar habits, even as they try some new ones.

The Way Forward

The result of a lack of a clear new philosophy is that all email clients look and feel alike, with only minor variations. Products that give us new ways to manage tasks or schedule offer a bit more innovation, but they're separate from email. Also, they too follow conventional thinking, so they all look alike.

The good news is that there's lots of room for a Steve-Jobs-like figure to show up and stand out.

Here at 2Time Labs, we're just starting to play our part, as it seems there is a lot more work to be done to help developers craft a new philosophy as a starting point. For example, we're asking the question, "What would a time demand-based graphical user interface (GUI) look like?" We have started sharing these ideas as they become available with members of a small mailing list – just visit http://www.2time-sys.com/application-designers to join in.

As you can imagine, these ideas, if implemented well in terms of both habits and technology, can impact time-based productivity in companies around the world. However, they aren't enough. Massive corporate obstacles, the subject of our next chapter, stand in the way.

Remember and Share

Who says the software/hardware combination you use to manage time demands doesn't matter? It does!

Professionals who manage their lives through their schedules have a difficult time with software that's not built for their methods.

Developing great software to manage time demands remains a huge challenge!

Time management tools have a long way to go to meet users' needs.

Mona Haraty – People have different needs and preferences when using software tools to manage their daily tasks

Mona Haraty – People's changing needs and desire to improve lead to changed behaviors.

Mona Haraty – Without being given the right time management tools, people will be forced to live a *default life* dictated by their tools.

Mona Haraty – The design of (personalized tools) for accommodating behavioral differences is largely unexplored.

Dezhi Wu – Most people select their time management method through random choice rather than assessing their time management needs.

Dezhi Wu – People adopt the tool or combination of tools to

meet their needs without much judgment.

Productivity tool designers need a clear philosophy before they start developing products.

The format that a time demand arrives in is much less important than its contents.

Chapter 23. Productivity in Your Company

(In which you realize that modern professionals are caught in no-win situations that no one playing a traditional role can solve).

Timothy was elated when he glanced down at the email message: he was now the new Senior Vice President of Marketing of Physiton Technologies. He sighed, letting out a gust of air that he had probably been holding in for too long. It had finally happened: he was no longer the "Acting VP of Marketing." He slid over to his text-messaging app and started tapping, eyes focused on the small screen in his lap.

"Wendy, I got VP!"

He stopped typing, fingers twitching, waiting. *Where was she?* He looked up and glanced around the room.

His colleague, Barbara, was still up at the screen presenting her new idea to the nine members of the marketing team. As usual, only three or four were actually looking at her, while everyone else had their heads down, checking email, reading texts, updating their social feeds… whatever.

After a couple more slides, his smartphone buzzed and he looked back down.

"Congrats, honey. Let's celebrate! ;-)"

That was Wendy, always positive and upbeat – his biggest cheerleader in the entire world. The kids were still too young to know what was going on, but maybe in a few years time they could join in an accomplishment like this one – his version of doing a hand-stand for the first time. *Hmm*, he thought, *handstands... that might be a good marketing message for the XLT product.*

"In conclusion..." - Barbara's voice broke into his thoughts, signaling it was time to wrap things up. She went on for a few more minutes and asked for questions. As a veteran of meetings like this, Timothy jumped in first with his pre-prepared question. So what if he hadn't been paying attention?

She cut him off on mid-question: "As I mentioned in my presentation..."

His lips tightened as he saw her eyes sharpen into a tight glare.

Within a few seconds of her answer, he had already formed his follow-up question, the one that would throw her. It would show them that he really was the smartest person in the room, even if he didn't have a clue what the real point of her presentation was.

"I'm sure we all know that, but what I really want to know is..." he started. The tone of his voice and the detailed content of the question made her redden slightly... she didn't have an answer, and Timothy knew it. It referenced a technology choice made several years ago, which no one else really understood.

He felt a little rush of victory, which crept out in a smirk he tried to suppress. Now that he was about to be named the boss of everyone in the room, he could finally afford to back off a bit, maybe. Not that the others had even noticed. Now, only three people were paying attention. All the others had their heads back down, lost again in cyberspace.

A few months later, however, Timothy was in trouble. In the executive suite, he discovered a dynamic he thought he had understood as a manager but now knew he didn't. His stay-a-step-ahead moves so effectively used on Barbara weren't enough to keep pace with his new colleagues. These people were not only a few steps ahead: they were miles away, over the horizon, where he could barely keep track of their moves.

As he explained to me a few years later via Skype, "The CEO had a habit of sending email at odd hours. About a month after I was named Senior V.P., I decided to ignore the beep on my phone telling me I had received a message. It was 3:30 AM! By the time I checked messages at seven, 25 emails had been passed between executives on the team. When I got to the bottom of the thread, I discovered that my budget for the XLT Launch had been freaking cut by 28 million dollars! When I sent him a private message, he told me that the decision had already been made... tough. 'Next time,' he said, 'be more responsive.'"

Now, he shook his head vigorously. "Unbelievable. But

I learned a lesson – I couldn't let these people out of my sight."

That was just the beginning. Even when he got the flu a few months later, he still had to play hard. Lying down, barely able to see the screen through throbbing eyes, he sent emails at 5 AM to argue for a new strategy that would reverse the decision made only a few weeks before. Wendy thought he was crazy. He tried to explain, but she just shook her head as she watched him give up weekends, late nights and public holidays. As she put it to me later, "He always seemed too distracted to give me his full attention."

It prompted her warning: "Just make sure you're not available to these people when we get to Paris. We'll never be able to take a second honeymoon once this new job grabs all of your attention. I'm just glad we aren't going anywhere in the same time zone!"

Three weeks before he left for Europe, as he sat in his cubicle one morning trying to block out the usual noise of his department, up popped a message from Physiton's CEO. "Timothy, I need your team members to manage your time better than this. They need to respond to my messages – in fact, to all executive team messages – within the hour. Anyone who can't isn't being a good team player."

He stretched in his chair and rested his hands behind his head. *How can I tell them to start responding to executive messages like trained monkeys?* he wondered. They'd kill him. He argued back and forth in his mind before deciding that he had no choice. He'd explain it to them as a sacrifice worth making – "Sometimes y'all just have to take one for the team."

In a marketing team meeting later that day he announced the new email response policy. The reaction was immediate. "But that means that we'll have to check all our messages every hour just to make sure he hasn't sent us something!"

"No, you're wrong," added someone else. "We'd better check them every 45 minutes so that we have time to read and write a response." As this sank in, the team looked at Timothy with thinly veiled contempt. Some were rolling their eyes. He couldn't blame them... at least he'd get away to Paris to escape.

When Wendy and Timothy finally landed at Charles de Gaulle airport, it was an early summer morning, and the city was just waking up for what promised to be a glorious day in a dream destination. Tourists whizzed out of the terminals in taxis, buses and trains, happy to be away from home. Wendy's enthusiasm was infectious, making Timothy smile as he started to relax.

Truth be told, he had been tense inside. The XLT launch was planned for the weekend, and he feared the worst. Not that he'd ignored his job – he hadn't. But so many things could go wrong, especially now that two team members had called in sick without warning, complaining about the crazy pressure their lives were under.

He deliberately ignored his smartphone as they reveled in the new city around them. It looked better than they had imagined, and just being there together was fun. It had been a long time.

At the hotel lobby, before he could enter the elevator, he was handed an envelope. Tearing it open with tense fingers, he read it and his heart sank. Based on this message from the CEO, Wendy was about to become very, very disappointed. In his mind's eye, a short movie played like a YouTube clip – Wendy visiting the Eiffel Tower, the Louvre, and fancy outdoor cafes... alone.

By the time he landed back home, he had made a decision. Her ultimatum, issued in their romantic hotel suite, meant that he was leaving Physiton for good.

***

Timothy's problems are not unique to his company or industry. All over the world, employees are busily engaged in technology-driven behaviors that were unthinkable only a few years ago. However, their intention is pure: to boost their time-based productivity. Under stress, they are trying to do better, typically by picking up the following five habits:

1. Multitasking

In hindsight, texting while driving is obviously a bad idea. A driver who texts has the reaction time of a drunk one and is 23 times more likely to get into an accident. As dangerous as it is, many companies actively encourage the underlying impulse: keep up, save time and become more productive by sharing your attention between the task at hand and your smartphone.

In most firms, this habit started with executives. They were the first recipients of these devices at a time when they were still quite expensive and seen as a perk. They developed the practice of checking email, sending texts and answering calls in the middle of conversations, meetings, sales lunches and teleconferences. It wasn't long before they learned to do the same while taxiing on runways, sitting on subways and, of course, driving. Their unwitting choice to multitask prevented them from entering the flow state. It also demonstrated and encouraged a new standard of behavior for all employees. Perhaps you have also been in your share of meetings like ones at Physiton, in which half the team members are focused on a small screen in their hands rather than the discussion... and no one objects.

2. Constant Checking

In one of my training workshops, a participant mentioned that a top executive in his firm made the point of insisting that employees return his email messages within the hour (like the CEO of Physiton). This seemingly innocuous request probably went to a few people at first, and they spread the directive around the company like a virus. In short order, every employee was infected.

In a company of 500, it meant they all struggled to avoid his wrath by checking email every 45 minutes, as Timothy's direct report correctly calculated. Therefore, in the typical working day, they'd check email at least 7 times.

Most knew that the executive hardly ever sent email messages outside his small circle of immediate colleagues. Even among this small group, they'd receive an urgent message only once or twice per month. Given a total email volume of 60 messages per day per employee, his messages would amount to only one in every 300: less than one percent.

Before this "directive," let's imagine that employees were checking email three times per day. The executive's demand, uttered in frustration at a few tardy replies, caused employees to check their email an additional total of 2000 times per day. If each check-in took five minutes, that would amount to 10,000 minutes per day.

Getting employees to stop what they are doing, exit the flow state and check email every 45 minutes is a remarkably effective way to damage corporate productivity. To me, it's breathtaking that this could happen without executives even realizing the damage done.

When I present these facts to participants in my classes, I often get stunned silence, followed by annoyed insistence that their executives take the workshop. Employees instinctively realize how a little fear plus a thoughtless remark can reduce productivity dramatically.

If shown the total impact of this seemingly small request, I'm sure many executives would backpedal. However, the fact that the interplay between technology and productivity isn't well understood means that the threat remains.

3. Intruding into Personal Time

It's not hard to see that the most "productive" way to spend time at home on weekends is to enter the flow state, even when relaxing with friends or family. Kids, in particular, crave the total attention from adults that flow prescribes: deep focus, challenge, engagement and immersion that lead to losing track of time.

However, it's impossible to enter the flow state for long while working for a firm that unwittingly requires employees to be "on call" 24 hours per day. I use the word "unwittingly" because, with the exception of emergency services, few companies have written policies governing smartphone availability outside of working hours. (Volkswagen and Puma are two notable exceptions.) Instead, in many companies, employees have an unstated expectation to be available on weekends, early mornings, late at night, on vacation days, during public holidays, on sick days, etc.

A new policy about availability on weekends is never announced. Instead, the expectation changes slowly, and decision-makers don't notice it. Because no one speaks up, employees inevitably lose, never knowing if they should be available to work or not. They learn to place themselves on permanent alert, willing to drop whatever they are doing to respond immediately to the most trivial work-related request. The recession convinced them that this is what they must do to keep their jobs and stay ahead of others. That muted the normal resistance that would come from new, unwritten policies that have already impacted so many.

This topic is also being examined in a fascinating study at Google. 4000 employees are being surveyed twice a year about their work-life balance and other related factors. Laszlo Bock's article in a 2014 Harvard Business Review blog post reveals that their hope is to find a way to impact wellbeing, leadership, retention and happiness.

Their first round of results reveals two extremes: "Segmentors," who draw a clear line between work and home, and "Integrators," who check email continuously and spend significant personal time working. So far, the split between the two groups at Google is approximately 31% to 69%, as most people fall along a continuum between the most extreme behaviors.

What's troubling is that around half of the Integrators want to be more like the Segmentors: able to draw a bright, clear line between home and work. Experiments like the recent "Dublin Goes Dark" effort are encouraging – people based in the Dublin office reported less stress when they were required to leave their smartphones in their desk drawers before leaving for the night.

4. Losing Track of Strategic Priorities

It's easy for leaders to lose track of long-term priorities in today's frenetic, interruption-driven environment. In the article for the McKinsey Quarterly, Bevins and De Smet report, "almost 50% of executives say [...] that they're not spending enough time on strategic priorities." (This echoes Mark Hortsman's podcast discussed in the chapter on The Problem of Doing Stuff Later). Further, the authors say that the problem has become "more acute in recent years."

Their advice is for leaders to budget their time carefully to include strategic activity, which, as we know from the chapter on Scheduling, isn't easy. It comes only through the use of advanced skills.

5. Getting Distracted by the Office

Many companies have not refreshed their physical

layouts to keep up with the latest research. They still place employees in low-cost, open-office environments with short partitions, making it hard for employees to be productive. In Psychology Today, David Rock wrote, "One study of 42,000 Americans found open-plan offices reduced employee wellbeing 32% and productivity 15%. Those in open offices cited a lack of "sound privacy" and lack of individual workspace as their major pain points. Those with private office were generally more satisfied at work. Another study found that open plan offices help increase levels of stress, conflict, high blood pressure, and high staff turnover."

Employees respond by devoting personal time and attention to work, according to David Rock's article in Fortune magazine online:

"No one is getting much done at the office. One survey of 6,000 workers by the NeuroLeadership Institute found only 10% of people do their best thinking at work. 'I have to go home and work at night to get anything done' is a phrase I hear all too often. Working nights and weekends leads to less time with families and friends and even less sleep, with 30% of Americans not getting the sleep they need today."

A Nagging Problem

Most employees who are under stress and have access to a smartphone are likely to pick up some or all of the five habits listed above. While it's not a guarantee, it's a safe bet that managers make: hand an employee a device as a Christmas gift and watch his/her behavior change once the pressure to perform gets above a certain threshold – usually within days.

Unfortunately, Timothy's story is common – it's a compilation of actual events from the lives of several clients. Powerful forces shape workplace productivity, and nowhere is the pressure felt more acutely than in the executive suite. It's the birthplace of the five habit patterns listed above, and it sets a de facto standard for entire companies.

What's the answer? Was Timothy at fault? His CEO? Human Resources? The shareholders? Employees? Smartphone manufacturers? How can companies react effectively to the changes illustrated in this story? Is anyone to blame?

Without a lot of diagnosis, let's jump to an immediate solution: what Physiton needs is a productivity czar, or a Chief Individual Productivity Officer (CIPO). It might not be a full-time position, but companies need an executive to who is willing to own the issue of corporate productivity by fighting for employees. Here's why.

The McKinsey article mentioned in the chapter on Scheduling goes further than simply giving a prescription for better time management skills. It attempts to raise an alarm – a very loud one. Authors Bevins and De Smet argue that the problem is no longer an individual issue; it's become an organizational concern that requires concerted effort.

According to their survey of 1500 global leaders, almost 50 percent of executives are not spending enough time on strategic priorities. They face increasing time pressure and aren't responding very well, and only a handful (9 percent) report that they are "very satisfied" with the way they use their time. Atypically, those who belong to high-performing organizations "spend at least 50 percent of their time in decision meetings and less than 10 percent of their time in reporting and information meetings."

The problem is partially cultural. Too many organizations make plans, launch initiatives and start projects that simply ignore the fact that their professionals are already stretched thin. According to the authors, they see time as an infinite resource, which it is not. They seem to aim to keep people busy without caring about their effectiveness.

This perversion won't solve itself anytime soon, given our current corporate structures. Instead, someone needs to take ownership of the issue – a CIPO.

Peter Drucker, a management theorist, offers a solution.

He advocates the use of "time diaries" for managers to track their time usage. The McKinsey article reveals that very few executives bother with the practice, experiencing an unpleasant surprise when confronted with real data about their activities. While most can reel off the details about the financial budget, few think in terms of a time budget that needs to be managed just as closely.

Bevins and De Smet reveal that there are companies that set time budgets and also minimal standards of time expected to be spent in different key activities. These companies don't leave executives alone and unassisted to hit these targets – a full 85% of the best time managers report that "they received strong (administrative) support in scheduling and allocating time. Only 7% of ineffective time allocators said the same." It's a strong argument for hiring a great assistant.

Solving the Problem

While I've primarily discussed individual skills, in this chapter, I want to show that professionals face intractable, widespread obstacles to being productive. In spite of their inability to clearly distinguish the source of the problem, they all abhor the symptoms they see every day. After all, no one wants to call and chair a meeting in which participants are distracted. Wasting time has a cost, and it starts with irritation and anger.

Executives must take the lead. From the McKinsey article: "[...] since senior executives' behavior set the tone for the organization, they have a duty to set a better example. The widespread availability of powerful communications technologies means employees now share many of the time- and attention-management challenges of their leaders. The whole organization's productivity can now be affected by information overload, and no single person or group can address it in isolation. Resetting the culture to healthier norms is a critical new responsibility for 21st-century executives."

As I mentioned, an executive team that's serious about his problem could appoint a Chief Individual Productivity Officer (CIPO) who acts as the single point of contact for all productivity-related decisions. A CIPO would be single-minded about boosting employee productivity, but would need more than just a clear purpose. He or she would need expertise.

Decisions regarding issues as different as smartphone use and office layouts don't fall neatly into a single function. A CIPO would need a background in Information

Technology, Human Resources and Business Process Management (at the very least) in order to shape policies and interventions that address the company's needs. With this knowledge, the pace at which new technology is introduced into the company could be carefully managed in order to maximize overall productivity. Employee training would be an indispensable tool to help mitigate the mal-effects of habits like texting while driving.

Fortunately, around the world, there are companies emerging that might not have a Productivity Czar but are implementing policies that a person in that position would champion.

For example, Ford Motor Company has banned smartphones from executive meetings. I don't think they have a CIPO, but they have made a decision that's right in line with what you'd expect from one. Also, Volkswagen and Puma have also made their own improvements by turning off email on weekends and at nights.

Paradoxically, at the time of this writing, there's a lot of fuss about granting employees the power to "Bring Your Own Device" (BYOD). However, the thrust of the concerns center around data security and software compatibility. Few are concerned with the rise of the distracted workforce that these policies encourage – a fact that a CIPO would be concerned with.

As you read Timothy's story, you probably thought of all the commonsense ways that his failure could have been avoided. At the moment, most companies have lots of people from the very top to the bottom who see the problem the same way and even agree on workable solutions, such as barring the use of certain technologies from meetings. However, it's just not enough. Even CEOs and Chairs who might have the power to do something often surrender in the face of bad habits, sometimes being the worst offenders. A CIPO would have to do what other executives don't know how to do.

Unfortunately, your company isn't likely to hire a CIPO anytime soon, so you must take matters into your own hands.

Your Obligation

Pharmacists have a professional duty to control the dispensation of drugs. If a storeowner asks a licensed pharmacist to slip him some of his favorite drugs under the counter, she will refuse – it's her obligation to manage powerful and potentially harmful substances responsibly.

From my point of view, all working professionals have a similar obligation with regard to their time. It's a scarce resource that they must dispense carefully.

When the obligation to dispense time carefully is not rigorously honored, employees fall into a trap of saying "yes" to everything. They treat their managers as the only decision makers, becoming no different from pharmacists who abandon their professional responsibility. In the short term, this might please higher-ups, but it doesn't take long for a perception of weakness to set in.

For their part, managers become anxious when they sense this weakness in their direct reports. Some respond by being heavy-handed. They attempt to make all the employee's decisions with increasing force. When they decide to take this route, one of two outcomes occurs:

Outcome 1: A manager, who has relatively little information, overrules an employee, who has all the pertinent information. As a result, everyone ends up shaking their heads in disbelief at the nonsensical result. The topic becomes a subject of ridicule.

Outcome 2: The best, most creative employees find themselves unable to function productively because the boss is overly intrusive. In order to enter the flow state at work, they have to avoid his/her attention in increasingly creative but evasive ways. When they run out of tactics to get away and work, they either surrender to a condition of terminal mediocrity or start looking for employment elsewhere.

These outcomes occur in workplaces around the world where professionals have abandoned their duty. Time is a scare resource for most, but few are taught how to make wise decisions or face the obligation to do so. When companies enter this state, productivity is damaged, especially for knowledge workers.

With or without a CIPO, professionals need to treat

their time as a precious corporate resource to be expended in a conscious, mature manner to help meet company goals. As they do, they will herald a new era of time-based productivity.

Remember and Share

To kill productivity, require that employees respond to email within the hour. It's a great way to turn them into morons.

Many companies need a Chief Individual Productivity Officer – a CIPO – to help protect employees from unproductive influences.

In most companies, individual productivity is no one's concern, which means that everyday decisions adversely affect it

Tracking your time use is a great way to improve your productivity.

A great administrative assistant helps make 85% of the best time managers most effective.

Employees have a professional obligation to make wise time choices.

Give an employee a smartphone and smartwatch… will he or she develop unproductive habits?

Summary

(In which you summarize your progress and new knowledge, while remaining open to new developments.)

Near the beginning of Time-Based Productivity, I asked you to identify yourself as someone like Julie (with an immediate problem to solve) or like Michael (someone with deep curiosity.)

If you have realized you are a bit like Julie, your journey through this book has brought you to a well-defined destination. In front of you lies a plan for slow but gradual improvement built on the fundamentals of time-based productivity. Its purpose is to transport you safely from your current set of habits, practices and rituals to brand-new target behaviors. It promises expanded Peace of Mind at the end, but also at every step along the way.

Now, you fully understand the route we just travelled: you know you can't ignore the unique system for time-based productivity developed in your teens and practiced over the years. You must continue to use it until the individual changes you want to make take hold, and turn into habits.

Some people need huge behavior changes to reach their ultimate goal. Others might be more modest. Wherever you find yourself, you now appreciate your unique gaps and how you can fill them.

Perhaps, if you are like Michael, you reached this point without filling out a single form. Driven by the research I've shared, you have confirmed a few concepts you already use. Maybe you also discovered a few things you want to work on, or new books, articles, blogs and podcasts you want to explore. It might leave you feeling a little overwhelmed.

My advice is: *Take it easy!* Recognize that you don't need to understand or agree with everything in *Perfect Time-Based Productivity* all at once.

However, I do recommend that if you haven't completed the forms in Part 2: do them. The best understanding does not come from the faraway abstract, but from direct engagement. When you evaluate your own skills you'll see the internal struggle we face as we confront our individual success formulae and attempt to improve them. To make sense of this challenge you must experience it directly.

Don't ignore it by focusing only on concepts. You will be excluding some important data.

With that, I encourage you to tackle any of the ideas in greater depth. Write blog posts, publish podcasts, use social media, comment on research… whatever you want to do. Visit my website and join my mailing lists, or visit the forums - you may find others with similar interests.

As you dive in, remember that *Perfect Time-Based Productivity* needs to be replaced with better books with new research and clearer examples. The more you share, engage and push the envelope on the ideas shared in this book, the sooner it will happen. We'll all be stronger as a result.

Whether you are like Michael or Julie, it's a good idea to consider this experience to be a beginning, or a milestone, and hardly the end of the journey. If you think of yourself a novice in the art of upgrading your system, I'd like you to know that this is just a start. According to the Dreyfus model, when we learn something for the first time, our best approach is to follow the instructions exactly as they are initially laid out. Even then, we often struggle – but it's a sign of progress.

However, as we gain more experience, the model predicts that we make our own pathways for personal development. So don't be afraid to upgrade, change and let go of the process I have detailed in prior chapters. Keep innovating, especially with new technology, to provide new, improved avenues for self-teaching. It's one way to get better results in a shorter time-frame.

In the next few pages, I'll share a few ways in which you can continue your journey whether it involves delving into available research, finding others of like mind, discovering further learning opportunities or getting some direct help.

As a professional, you are in charge of your development. Whichever path you take, I honor your choice as one that, for you, is perfect.

Francis Wade
November, 2014

P.S. To find an update on everything that's happened since the publication of this book, see the first link on the following page.

Appendices

Your Next Steps

Thank you for investing in this book. I'd love to hear from you now that you have completed it!

To see my personal note with updates on what's happened since I wrote the Summary in November 2014, click on this link or paste it in your browser: http://perfect.mytimedesign.com/LiveSummary

If you appreciated this book, please take a moment to leave a review on Amazon at www.amazon.com/gp/product/B00PY5X52Q You can also leave a review on Goodreads - https://www.goodreads.com/book/show/23600431-perfect-time-based-productivity

Where else can you go from here? There's no way I can say for sure, but here are some ideas.

Perhaps the most important way to stay in touch is to sign up to receive updates on the book's website, located at http://perfect.mytimedesign.com. I'll let you know about new information, research findings and programs.

To interact with other readers: visit the discussion forums on my book's website (http://perfect.mytimedesign.com.) on the site you can also find links to Facebook and Linkedin groups. I welcome any suggestions on how this book can be improved, including any errors in facts, spelling or grammar.

To receive personalized, direct assistance: I have trained a small number of time advisers who use the contents of this book to with clients. For more information use my contact page http://ReplytoFrancis.info

To get assistance building a corporate intervention or executive coaching: contact me via http://ReplytoFrancis.info

Research

To ask me questions about a concept from this book: use the forums on my book's website, or interact with me on Facebook or Twitter. My contact page is http://ReplytoFrancis.info

To delve into the research used in this book: pick a concept that interests you and use the References to source some of the articles listed. My library of time management papers on my lab's website may also be helpful - http://bit.ly/WLy6EYTo hear about recent research as soon as it breaks, visit http://2time-sys.com (the official 2Time Labs website) and download my Special Report. You'll be added to my mailing list of those who are particularly interested in raw, new ideas in time-based productivity.

To join my private group of time-based productivity researchers, apply to join the InnerLab at http://bit.ly/12Darst

Time Advising (as a Coach, Trainer, Consultant or Professional Organizer)

To be trained as a time adviser: start with my special report, The 8 Fatal Assumptions Time Advisers Make – coaches, consultants, trainers and professional organizers http://mytimedesign.com

To use these materials as a time adviser with your clients or trainees: consider licensing the materials in this book for immediate use at http://wp.me/P3hu7x-lY

To design a multi-faceted corporate intervention: read my article for Training Administrators at http://wp.me/P3hu7x-mg

Content Creation

To receive these and other cutting-edge ideas for your blog, video or podcast: join my group of content creators in the area of time-based productivity at http://wp.me/PeenO-H0

To download the complete list of Remember and Share quotes provided after each chapter, visit http://wp.me/P3hu5l-ax

Learning

To read a fable of the ups and downs of a man's discovery of this book's ideas, purchase a Kindle or paperback copy of my prior book, *Bill's Im-Perfect Time Management Adventure*: http://amzn.to/Xnauu6

To continue learning: consider taking MyTimeDesign Plus+, a self-paced twelve-lesson exploration of the concepts in this book. http://plus.mytimedesign.com

To download an electronic copy of the important forms in this book, visit: http://goo.gl/Ohe9ju. (No registration is required).

Content Channels

Some people prefer to receive their content through channels they already frequent. Here are a few that I use. Maybe we'll run into each other.

2Time Labs - http://2time-sys.com

Perfect Time-Based Productivity book - http://perfect.mytimedesign.com

MyTimeDesign - http://mytimedesign.com

Videos - http://www.youtube.com/fwadeyou

Audio Podcasts - http://podcasts.fwconsulting.com

Pinterest - http://www.pinterest.com/fwade99/

Linkedin - http://jm.linkedin.com/in/franciswade/

Facebook - https://www.facebook.com/Perfect.Time.Based.Productivity

Google+ - https://plus.google.com/+FrancisWade

Twitter - @fwade

Resource Pages by Special Interest

Time   Advisers   /   Training   Administrators   - http://www.mytimedesign.com/wordpress/a-new-special-report/

Project Managers - http://perfect.mytimedesign.com/calling-all-project-managers/

Academic Researchers - http://linkd.in/1d18iO0

Content Creators - http://wp.me/PeenO-H0

Application and Tool Designers - http://goo.gl/S4gLbf

Acknowledgements

This book is the result of a community effort.

My wife, Dale, has been by my side from the very beginning, when we moved to Jamaica and began trying to fill the productivity gaps we were both experiencing. She was the first person to hear every new distinction, concept and idea in this book. Her unconditional support, even when things got boring or challenging, make this book hers as well as mine.

My parents have been a consistent source of support. My mother, Merle Wade, and her expert adviser, Kerry-Ann Green, spent hours carefully crafting the References from the jumbled set of notes I handed over to her. Thanks to them for persevering.

This book benefited directly from a number of people who gave feedback at different stages. In particular, I received core-changing, big-picture input from Andrew Yee, Dale (my wife), Doug Toft and Joaquín Peña.

Andrew Staroscik's gifts in visual design and data interpretation took the book to a dimension I never envisioned at the start, giving readers one-of-a-kind view of their profile and its comparison against others.

This book, which I thought would be ready in May, didn't get done until November, and a number of editors and proofreaders were there as I stumbled my way from one draft to another. Crowdsourcing is powerful stuff, and I am a firm believer in it. Thanks to those who stood in the crowd and helped make the book better than even I was willing to have it be.

These stalwarts are Audrey Ingerson, Barbara Chauvin, Bianca Welds, Bill Hall, Camille Robertson, Carol Williams, Danielle Allum, Dennis Owen Williamson, Eugene Fucetola, Georgia Donaldson, Glen E. Sharp, Jo-Ann Richards, Jay Carter, Joyce Kristjansson, Lee Lukehart, Marcia Oxley, Marva Gordon, Melanie Wilson, Pat Shako-Parris, Peter Anthony Gales, John Stamp, Keith Ford, L. Aynn Daniels, Peter Gadsby, Sauna Maragh, Susan Johnson, Tammy Emam and Tom Jansen.

I also thank Andrea Sharb, Brijitte Claessens, B.J. Fogg, Dezhi Wu, Janice Russell, Julie Dirksen, Kudith Kolberg, Maura Thomas, Mona Haraty, Raj Venugopal and Tony

Murphy, who all communicated with me, providing clarity to important ideas that were included in this book.

Also, the researchers who did the ground-work described in hundreds of papers from different fields leave me in awe – this book is, in some ways, a tapestry of their findings, woven together for the first time. Helping them meet each other for a common cause in these pages has been my deep privilege.

My professional editor, Ellen Fishbein, did a wonderful job by, once again, shaping my tangle of ideas into materials that could help other people as much as words on a page can. She does more than work hard – she works deeply – which helps learners get all they can get from a book based mostly on abstract ideas.

The work at 2Time Labs has benefited tremendously from the contributions of visitors to the site, members of the InnerLab, participants in workshops, online training and webinars, friends and followers on social media, and others. Their input over the years has been invaluable.

To the members of audiences in a number of countries who heard these ideas in workshops or speeches and helped me craft them into building blocks: your feedback made the difference between boring theory and useful application.

A book of this scope would never have been completed without the powerful resources at the virtual library of the University of Phoenix. The institution has been consistently upgrading itself over the years, giving part-time faculty members like me instant access to world-class search capabilities. It made all the difference in the world.

Biography

Francis Wade was born in Massachusetts, moved to Kingston, Jamaica, spent a year in Tampa, grew up in Kingston, and split the next 21 years between college in upstate New York and work in New Jersey and Fort Lauderdale. Nine years ago, he moved back to Kingston.

He's an alumnus of AT&T Bell Labs and has been an entrepreneur for 21 years, many of which he has spent comparing a U.S. culture that ranks among the top 3 in the world in terms of its productivity with a Jamaican culture that ranks #86. Inspired by the gap, he's authored Bill's Im-Perfect Time Management Adventure and Perfect Time-Based Productivity. Along with the training he's developed, both books help him fulfill his aspiration to make time-based productivity easy to learn and teach in every corner of the world.

Francis completed his Bachelors and Masters degrees at Cornell University in 4 1/2 years in the fields of Operations Research and Industrial Engineering. As a member of the teaching faculty of the University of Phoenix, he enjoys full access to their state-of-the-art research libraries.

Francis is a newspaper columnist, recovering triathlete, avid reader and lover of all kinds of personal improvement. He's always at airports with his wife, Dale, but he has done most of his recent writing from the hills overlooking Kingston.

Also Available

Bill's Im-Perfect Time Management Adventure is the tale of an engineer and project manager and his struggle to avoid being laid off due to poor time management skills. He first tries to save himself by purchasing the latest smartphone and when that fails, he attempts to follow a strict regimen of skills outlined in a popular time management book. After once again falling short, he discovers the wisdom of developing his own system. With the help others he shows the members of his failing team how to do the same, even in the face of hostile opposition they must overcome to give the company the breakthrough it needs.

I published this novel in 2013 to work out many of the ideas that were eventually included in Perfect Time-Based Productivity. It's a work of fiction, but it shows how anyone can arrive at the conclusions presented in my work through rigorous thinking and a bit of help from others. The challenge Bill faces in this book is how to keep asking tough questions even when simplistic answers are being readily supplied by the conventional wisdom.

Available on Amazon.com - http://amzn.to/Xnauu6

References

CHAPTER 1. The Big Picture

Career Builder Survey- Carrier Management, (2014, September 21). Most Workers Don't Want to Lead: Retrieved September 25, 2014, from http://www.carriermanagement.com/news/2014/09/21/129351.htm

Cepeda, N. J., Sana, F., & Weston, T. (2013). Laptop multitasking hinders classroom learning for both users and nearby peers. Computers & Education, 62, 24-31.

Claessens, B. J.C, Eerde, W. V., Rutte, C. G., Roe, R. A. (2007). A review of the time management literature. Personnel Review, 36(2),

Claessens, B.J.C., Roe, R.A. & Rutte, C.G. (2009). Time management: logic, effectiveness and challenges. In: Roe, R.A., Waller, M.J. & Clegg, S. (Eds.) Time in Organizational Research. London, UK: Routledge; pp. 23-41.

Dawson-Cook, S. (2010). Total Immersion Swimming. *American Fitness, 28*(4), 20-20.

Drucker, P. (1999). Knowledge-Worker Productivity: The Biggest Challenge. *California Management Review, 41*(2), 79-94.

Hellsten, L. (2012, March 23). What do we Know About Time Management? A review of the literature and a psychometric critique of instruments assessing time management, from http://www.intechopen.com/books/how-to-link/time-management

Hodson, T., Schwartz, J., Van Berkel, A., & Otten, I. (2014, March 7,) The overwhelmed employee: Simplify the work environment. Retrieved September 17, 2014 from Deloitte University Press.

International Workplace Productivity Survey White Collar Highlights October 2010 LexisNexis http://www.multivu.com/players/English/46619-

LexisNexis-International-Workplace-Productivity-Survey/flexSwf/impAsset/document/34ef84f1-beaa-4a48-98c5-0ea93ceae0cb.pdf

Jeffrey, C., & Bauerlein, M. (2011, July 1). All Work and No Pay: The Great Speedup. Retrieved September 2, 2014, from http://www.motherjones.com/politics/2011/06/speed-up-american-workers-long-hours

Kolberg, J. (2013). The Age of Endless. Decatur:Squall Press

Macan, T. (1989). An examination of time control. Unpublished doctoral dissertation, Rice University. Houston, United States.

Macan, T. H. (1994). Time management: Test of a process model. Journal of Applied Psychology, 79(3), 381-391.

Parker, K., & Wang, W. (2013, March 14). Modern Parenthood. Retrieved September 17 2014, from http://www.pewsocialtrends.org/2013/03/14/modern-parenthood-roles-of-moms-and-dads-converge-as-they-balance-work-and-family/

Quirk, T.J. (1989). The art of time management. Training, January. p.59-61

Rosen, L.., Carrier, L., & Cheever, N. (2013). Facebook and texting made me do it: Media-induced task-switching while studying. Computers in Human Behavior, 29(3), 948–958.

Skuturna, J. (2006). Understaffed and Overwhelmed. Retrieved September 17 2014 from ,H.R. Solutions Inc. website http://www.hr.com/en/communities/understaffed-and-overwhelmed_en078fgl.html

Stoilov, T. (Ed.). (2012). Time Management. Rijeka: InTech.

Superjobs: Why You Work More, Enjoy It Less -

http://online.wsj.com/news/articles/SB10001424052748703859304576309533100131932?mg=reno64-wsj&url=http%3A%2F%2Fonline.wsj.com%2Farticle%2FSB10001424052748703859304576309533100131932.html

Stressed Out by Work? You're Not Alone. (2014, October 30). Retrieved November 16, 2014, from http://knowledge.wharton.upenn.edu/article/stressed-work-youre-alone/

The Forum at Harvard School of Public Health. The Health Burden of Stress - What We Can Do About It. (2014, January 1). Retrieved September 17, 2014, from http://theforum.sph.harvard.edu/events/the-health-burden-of-stress/

Tribolet-Hardy, F, Elfering, A., & Grebner, S.(2013)The long arm of time pressure at work: Cognitive failure and commuting near-accidents. European Journal of Work and Organizational Psychology,22, 737-749.

Virtanen, M., Heikkila, K., Jokela, M., Ferrie, J., Batty, G., Vahtera, J., & Kivimaki, M. (n.d.). Long Working Hours and Coronary Heart Disease: A Systematic Review and Meta-Analysis. American Journal of Epidemiology, 586-596.

Wallace, J., & Chen, G. (2005.). Development and validation of a work-specific measure of cognitive failure: Implications for occupational safety. Journal of Occupational and Organizational Psychology, 78 615-632.

CHAPTER 2. Who Do You Think You Are?

Action learning. (2014, March 11). Retrieved November 7, 2014, from http://en.wikipedia.org/wiki/Action_learning

Ames, L. B. (1946). The Development of the Sense of Time in the Young Child. The Pedagogical Seminary and Journal of Genetic Psychology, 68(1), 97-125.

Bartholomew, C. P. (2013). Time: An Empirical Analysis of Law Student Time Management Deficiencies. University of Cincinnati Law Review, 81(3), 898-952.

Brandstätter,V. Heimbeck,D;,Malzacher,J.,Frese,M.(2003) Goals need implementation intentions.The model of action phases tested in the applied setting of continuing education. European Journal of Work and Organizational Psychology, Vol 12(1),37-59

Foerster,L.M.(1968).The development of time sense and chronology of culturally disadvantaged children. University of

Arizona.

Fourez, M. (2011). Impoverished students' perspectives of time. S.l.: ProQuest, Umi Dissertation Publishing

Heskett, J. (2013), Who should manage our time. Retrieved from Working Knowledge Magazine. Harvard Business School. website http://hbswk.hbs.edu/item/7146.html

Kvavilashvili,L.,(1987) Remembering intention as a distinct form of memory , British Journal of Psychology, 78(4) 507-518

Liu, O. L., Rijmen, F., Maccann, C., & Roberts, R. (2009). The assessment of time management in middle-school students. Personality and Individual Differences, 47(3), 174-179

Macan, T Shahani, C., Dipboye, R., & Phillips, A., (1990). College students' time management: Correlations with academic performance and stress. Journal of Educational Psychology, 82(4), 760-768.

Mantyla, T., Sgaramella,T, (1997) Interrupting intentions: Zeigarnik-like effects in prospective memory. Psychological Research 60(3) 192-199.

Pew Internet Research Project - Cell Phone Activities 2012 - http://www.pewinternet.org/2012/11/25/cell-phone-activities-2012/

Srestha, K., Suvedi, M.,& Foster, E. (2011) Use of Time in the College of Agriculture and Natural Resources at Michigan State University. NACTA Journal, 45-52.

Trueman, M., Hartley, J.(1995) Measuring Time Management Skills: Cross-Cultural Observations on Britton and Tesser's Time Management Scale –University of Keele, UK

Volder,M.L.,Lens, W.(1982). Academic achievement and future time perspective as a cognitive-motivational concept.Journal of Personality and Social Psychology, 42(3), 566-571.

CHAPTER 3. How to Set New Improvement Milestones

Bull, B. (2013, April 23). A Primer on Three "gogies" #pedagogy #heutagogy #andragogy. Retrieved October 13, 2014, from http://etale.org/main/2013/04/23/a-primer-on-three-gogies-pedagogy-heutagogy-andragogy/

Field, S., Martin, J., Miller, R., Ward, M.. Wehmeyer, M. (1998). Self-Determination for Persons With Disabilities: A Position Statement of me Division on Career Development and Transition. Career Development for Exceptional Individuals, 21(2), 113-128.

Hase, S., & Kenyon, C. (2001, January 1). From Andragogy to Heutagogy. Retrieved October 13, 2014, from http://www.psy.gla.ac.uk/~steve/pr/Heutagogy.html

Locke, E., Latham, G.(2006) New Directions in Goal-Setting Theory. Current Directions in Psychological Science, 15(5), 265-268.

Markowitz, D.l The Folly of Stretch Goals Harvard Business Review. http://blogs.hbr.org/2012/04/the-folly-of-stretch-goals/

Martin, J. Marshall, L.(1995) ChoiceMaker: A Comprehensive Self-Determination Transition Program. Intervention in School and Clinic, University of Colorado 30(3), 147-156.

Weick, K.(1984) Small wins: Redefining the scale of social problems. American Psychologist, 39(1), 40-49

Wikipedia- Andragogy. In Wikipedia. Retrieved October 10, 2014 from http://en.wikipedia.org/wiki/Andragogy

CHAPTER 4. What's Happening Behind the Scenes?

Baurlein, Mark http://www.pbs.org/wgbh/pages/frontline/digitalnation/view/ - 14:30 of Video Interview w/ Professor Mark Bauerlein of Emory University, Chapter 2: What's It Doing to Their Brains?

Bergstra, J., & Burgess, M. (2014). *Promise Theory: Principles and Applications* (Vol. 1). Createspace - Amazon.com.

Burrus,J.,Jackson,T.,

Holtzman,S.,Roberts,R.,Mandigo,T.(2013) Examining the Efficacy of a Time Management Intervention for High School Students, Princeton , New Jersey 13-25

Claessens, B.,Roe,R.,& Rutte, C.(2009).Time management: logic,effectiveness and challenges In:Roe, R.,Waller,M.& Clegg,S.(Eds.) Time in Organizational Research.London,UK:Routledge;pp.23-41.

Danziger, K. (1993). Psychological Objects, Practice, and History. Annals of Theoretical Psychology (8). Springer US.

Dismukes, R. (n.d.). Prospective Memory in Workplace and Everyday Situations. Current Directions in Psychological Science, 215-220.

Drucker, P. F. (1967). The effective executive. New York: Harper & Row.

Einstein, G., Mcdaniel, M., Williford, C., Pagan, J.&, & Dismukes, R. K. (2003,) Forgetting of intentions in demanding situations is rapid. Journal of Experimental Psychology: Applied, 9(3), 147-162.

Gerber, M. E. (1995). The E-myth revisited: why most small businesses don't work and what to do about it. New York: CollinsBusiness.

Gilbert, D. (2006). Stumbling on happiness. New York: A.A. Knopf.

Gollwitzer, P. M. (1999). Implementation intentions: Strong effects of simple plans. American Psychologist, 54(7), 493-503.

Haynes, J., & Momennejad, I.(2013) Encoding of Prospective Tasks in the Human Prefrontal Cortex under Varying Task Loads. Journal of Neuroscience, 17342-17349

Holbrook, J., & Dismukes, K. (October 2009). Prospective Memory in Everyday Tasks. Human Factors and Ergonomics Society Annual Meeting Proceedings, 53(10), 590-594..

Kelly,A., Hertzog,C.,Hayes, M.,Smith, A..(Jan. 2013) .The effects of age and focality on delay-execute prospective memory..Aging, Neuropsychology, and Cognition 20.1 101-

124.

Lakein, A. (1973). How to get control of your time and your life. New York: Peter H. Wyden.

McDaniel, M. A., & Einstein, G. O. (2007). Cognitive Psychology Program: Prospective memory: An overview and synthesis of an emerging field. Thousand Oaks, CA: SAGE Publications, Inc

Neal, D.,Wood, W., & Quinn, J. (2006). Habits - A Repeat Performance. Current Directions in Psychological Science, 15(4), 198-202.

Ouellette, J., & Wood, W. (1998). Habits and Intention in Everyday Life: The Multiple Processes by Which Past Behavior Predicts Future Behavior. *Psychological Bulletin, 124*(1), 54-74.

Sellen, A., Louie, G., Harris, J., & Wilkins, A. (1997, 12). What Brings Intentions to Mind? An In

Situ Study of Prospective Memory. Memory, 5(4), 483-507.

Wood, W., Quinn, J., & Kashy, D. (2002). Habits In Everyday Life: Thought, Emotion, And Action. *Journal of Personality and Social Psychology, 83*(6), 1281-1297.

CHAPTER 5. Introducing: 11 Fundamentals and 3 Definitions

Academic World. Retrieved October 13, 2014, from http://chronicle.com/blogs/profhacker/building-an-interdisciplinary-identity-in-a-mostly-non-interdisciplinary-academic-world/23080

Brandstätter, V., Heimbeck, D., Malzacher, J., & Frese, M. (n.d.). Goals need implementation intentions: The model of action phases tested in the applied setting of continuing education. European Journal of Work and Organizational Psychology, 37-59.

Claessens, B., (November, 2004). Perceived Control of Time: Time Management and Personal Effectiveness at Work. PhD Dissertation, Eindhoven University of Technology, Eindhoven, the Netherlands.

Hellsten, L. M. (2012). <u>What do we know about time management? A review of the literature and a psychometric critique of instruments assessing time management</u>. In T. Stoilov (Ed.), Time Management (pp. 3-28). Croatia: InTech, Available from: http://www.intechopen.com/books/timemanagement/

Life Cycle of Human Tasks - IBM - http://pic.dhe.ibm.com/infocenter/dmndhelp/v7r0mx/index.jsp?topic=%2Fcom.ibm.websphere.bpc.doc%2Fdoc%2Fbpc%2Fctasklifecycle.html

Macan , T.,(June 1994).Test of a Process Model. Journal of Applied Psychology .79(3), 381

Stoilov, T.(Ed) (2012) Psychometric Critique of Instruments Assessing Time Management, Time Management, (Ed.), ISBN: 978-953-51-0335-6,

Watrall, E. (2010, April 1). Building an Interdisciplinary Identity in a (Mostly) Non-Interdisciplinary

CHAPTER 6. Capturing - Securing Time Demands for Later Use

Branson, Richard, http://www.virgin.com/richard-branson/always-write-down-your-ideas

Caprara, G. Fida, R.; Vecchione, M.; Del Bove, G.; Vecchio, G.; Barabaranelli, C.; Bandura, A. (2008). "Longitudinal analysis of the role of perceived self-efficacy for self-regulatory learning in academic continuance an achievement". Journal Of Educational Psychology **100** (3): 525–534.

Cowan, N. (2005). Working memory capacity. New York, N.Y: Psychology Press.

Daniels, A. (2009), Oops! 13 Management Practices That Waste Time And Money, (and what to do instead) Atlanta, GA ,Performance Management Publications

Hellsten, L. M. (2012). <u>What do we know about time management? A review of the literature and a Psychometric critique of instruments assessing time management</u>. In T.

Stoilov (Ed.), Time Management (pp. 3-28). Croatia: InTech. http://www.intechopen.com/books/timemanagement/

Maheswaran,R.,Chang,Y.,Su,J.,Kwok,S.,Levy,T.,Wexler,A.,Hollingsworth,N.,(2014).Three Dimensions of Rebounding. Second Spectrum, Inc. Los Angeles, CA

Miller, G. (1956). The magical number seven, plus or minus two: Some limits on our capacity for processing information. Psychological Review, 343-352.

Rapa,L., The Development and Effects of Academic Self-efficacy in School-Aged Youth: A Literature Review. Michigan State University

Rock, D. (2009). Your Brain At Work: Strategies For Overcoming Distraction, Regaining Focus, And Working Smarter All Day Long. New York: Harper Business.

Schiffman, N., & Greist-Bousquet, S. (1992). The effect of task interruption and closure on perceived duration. Bulletin of the Psychonomic Society, 9-11.

The Maritz Institute White paper May 2010. The Neuroscience of Learning: A New Paradigm for Corporate Education http://www.themaritzinstitute.com/Perspectives/~/media/Files/MaritzInstitute/White-Papers/The-Neuroscience-of-Learning-The-Maritz-Institute.pdf

Wikipedia - Self Efficacy. In Wikipedia, Retrieved October 10, 2014, from http://en.wikipedia.org/wiki/Self-efficacy

Williams,R., Why Stretch Goals are a Waste of Time http://business.financialpost.com/2010/08/26/why-stretch-goals-are-a-waste-of-time/ and http://www.psychologytoday.com/blog/wired-success/201104/why-goal-setting-doesnt-work

Zimmermann, T., & Meier, B. (n.d.). The rise and decline of prospective memory performance across the lifespan. The Quarterly Journal of Experimental Psychology, 2040-2046.

CHAPTER 7. How to Complete a Self-Diagnosis

Daniels, A. (2009). Oops!: 13 management practices that

waste time and money (and what to do instead). Atlanta, Ga.: Performance Management Publications.

Goldilocks principle. (2014, November 16). Retrieved November 19, 2014, from http://en.wikipedia.org/wiki/Goldilocks_principle

Rock, D. (2009). Your brain at work: Strategies for overcoming distraction, regaining focus, and working smarter all day long. New York: Harper Business

Williams, R. (2010, August 26). Why 'stretch' goals are a waste of time. Retrieved November 19, 2014, from http://business.financialpost.com/2010/08/26/why-stretch-goals-are-a-waste-of-time/

Williams, R. (2011, April 11). Why goal setting doesn't work. Retrieved November 19, 2014, from http://www.psychologytoday.com/blog/wired-success/201104/why-goal-setting-doesnt-work

CHAPTER 8. Emptying - The Most Difficult Skill of All

Allen, D. (2001). Getting things done: The art of stress-free productivity. New York: Viking.

boyd, danah. Interview with Dana Boyd. http://www.theverge.com/2014/3/13/5488558/danah-boyd-interview-the-era-of-facebook-is-an-anomaly

Britton, B., Tesser, A. (1991, 12). Effects of time-management practices on college grades. Journal of Educational Psychology, 83(3), 405-410.

Cadence Group, National Email Week! http://cadence-group.com/national-email-week/#.UyF38vldV8G

Claessens, B. J., Eerde, W. V., Rutte, C. G., & Roe, R. A. (2010, 12). Things to Do Today   Journal of American Science 7(12) 720-726.

Classens, B.,(2010) A Daily Diary Study on Task Completion at Work. Applied Psychology, 59(2), 273-295.

Cowan, N. (2005). Working memory capacity. New York:

(N.Y.) Psychology Press.

Cowan, N. (2010). The Magical Mystery Four: How Is Working Memory Capacity Limited, and Why? Current Directions in Psychological Science, 19(1), 51-57.

Demarest, L. (2001). Out of time: How the sixteen types manage their time and work. Gainesville, FL: Center for Applications of Psychological Type.

Dismukes, R. K. (2012,).Prospective Memory in Workplace and Everyday Situations. Current Directions in Psychological Science, 21(4), 215-220.

Greist-Bousquet, S., Schiffman, N. (1992). The effect of Task interruption and closure on perceived duration. Bulletin of the Psychonomic Society, 30(1), 9-11.

Heussner, K. (2010, July 20). Tech Stress: How Many Emails Can You Handle a Day? Retrieved October 13, 2014, from http://abcnews.go.com/Technology/tech-stress-emails-handle-day/story?id=11201183

Miller, G. A. (1956). The magical number seven, plus or minus two: Some limits on our capacity for processing information. Psychological Review, 63, 81–97.

Radicati Group, http://www.radicati.com/wp/wp-content/uploads/2013/04/Email-Statistics-Report-2013-2017-Executive-Summary.pdf

Rock, D. (2009), Your Brain at Work New York, HarperBusiness.

Smith, A. (2011, September 19). Americans and Text Messaging. Retrieved October 13, 2014, from http://www.pewinternet.org/2011/09/19/americans-and-text-messaging/

Sutton, R., Rao.,H., (2014). Scaling up excellence: getting to more without settling for less. New York: Crown Business

Tarasewich, P., Campbell, C., Xia, T., & Dideles, M. (2003). Evaluation of Visual Notification Cues for Ubiquitous Computing. UbiComp 2003: Ubiquitous Computing Lecture Notes in Computer Science, Volume 2864, Pp 349-366.

The Myers & Briggs Foundation - How Frequent Is My Type. (n.d.). Retrieved October 13, 2014, from http://www.myersbriggs.org/my-mbti-personality-type/my-mbti-results/how-frequent-is-my-type.asp

The Time Intelligence Report, http://www.timeintelligence.co.uk

Whittaker, S. (2005). Supporting collaborative task management in e-mail. *Human-Computer Interaction, 20*(1), 49-88. L. Erlbaum Associates Inc. Retrieved from http://portal.acm.org/citation.cfm?id=1466573

Zeigarnik Effect. Psychiwiki.com, Retrieved October 10, 2014 from http://www.psychwiki.com/wiki/Zeigarnik_Effect

Zimbardo, P. & Boyd, J.(1999,). Putting time in perspective: A valid, reliable individual-differences metric. Journal of Personality and Social Psychology, 77(6), 1271-1288.

CHAPTER 9. Tossing - Lightening Your Load

Brain Scans of Hoarders Reveal Why They Never De-Clutter

http://blogs.scientificamerican.com/observations/2012/08/06/scans-of-hoarders-brains-reveal-why-they-never-de-clutter/

http://www.thecenterforemotionalhealth.com *Compulsive-Hoarding*

Kolberg, J.(1999), Conquering Chronic Disorganization Squall Press.

Kolberg, J.(2013), Getting Organized in the Era of Endless. Squall Press

CHAPTER 10. Acting Now - Gaining Immediate Relief While Avoiding a Dangerous Detour

Science Daily.(2013) Dopamine regulates the motivation to act, study shows. http://www.sciencedaily.com/releases/2013/01/1301100944 15.htm

CHAPTER 12. How to Solve the Problem of Doing Stuff "Later"

Association for Psychological Science. (2012, July 31). When we forget to remember: Failures in prospective memory range from annoying to lethal. ScienceDaily. Retrieved October 13, 2014 from www.sciencedaily.com/releases/2012/07/120731151745.htm

Claessens, B. ,Rhoe, R., Rutte, C.(2009) Time management : Logic Effectivness and Challenges. In *Time In Organizational Research.* London, U.K. Routledge. 23-41

Dismukes, R..,(2012). Prospective Memory in Workplace and Everyday Situations. *Current Directions in Psychological Science, 21*(4), 215-220. http://www.sciencedaily.com/releases/2012/07/1207311517 45.htm

Liu, O., Rijmen, F., Maccann, C., & Roberts, R. (2009). The assessment of time management in middle-school students. *Personality and Individual Differences, 47*(3), 174-179.i: 10.1016/j.paid.2009.02.018

Van Bentham, K., Herdman, C, Le Fevre, J. Prospective Memory Tasks in Aviation: Effects of Age and Working Memory. *Institute of Cognitive Science*, Carleton University, Ottawa, Ontario, http://mindmodeling.org/cogsci2011/papers/0556/paper05 56.pdf

Wikipedia. Knowledge Management. Retrieved on October 10, 2010 http://en.wikipedia.org/wiki/Knowledge_management

CHAPTER 13. Listing - A Powerful Technique for All Professionals

Anttila, T., Oinas, T., & Nätti, J. (2009). Predictors of time famine among Finnish employees - Work, family or leisure? *Electronic International Journal of Time Use Research,* 73-91.

Bartholomew, C. P. (2013). Time: An Empirical Analysis of Law Student Time Management Deficiencies. *University of*

Cincinnati Law Review, 81(3), 898-952.

Bellotti, V., Dalal, B., Good, N., Flynn, P Bobrow, D.(2004)- What a to-do: studies of task management towards the design of a personal task list manager. Proceedings of the SIGCHI conference on Human Factors in Computing Systems.

Civan, A., Jones, W., Klasnja, P., & Bruce, H. (2008). Better to organize personal information by folders or by tags?: The devil is in the details.Proceedings of the American Society for Information Science and Technology,45(1), 1-13.

Forster, M. (2006). Do it tomorrow and other secrets of time management. London: Hodder & Stoughton.

Holbrook, J., & Dismukes, K. (2009). Prospective Memory in Everyday Tasks. *Human Factors and Ergonomics Society Annual Meeting Proceedings, 53*(10), 590-594.

I Left My Baby in a Hot Car: One Mom Shares Her Tragic Story. http://thestir.cafemom.com/baby/174554/i_left_my_baby_i n_a Hot Car: One Mom shares her tragic story.

Kvavilashvili, L. (1987). Remembering intention as a distinct form of memory. *British Journal of Psychology,* 507-518.

Perlow, L. (1999). The Time Famine: Toward a Sociology of Work Time. *Administrative Science Quarterly, 44*(1), 57.

Waller, M., Conte, J.,Gibson, C.,& Carpenter, M.(2001). The Effect of Individual Perceptions of Deadlines on Team Performance. *The Academy of Management Review, 26*(4), 586.

Whittaker,S., Matthews,T., Cerutti, J.,Badeness,H., Tang,J (2011) Am I wasting my time organizing email? A study of email refinding. Proceedings of SIGCHI Conference on Human Factors in Computing Systems. 3449-3458

CHAPTER 14. Scheduling - Mastering a Complex Skill with Awesome Benefits

2Time Labs Library - http://2time-sys.com/library - A library of the best time management articles we have been able to find at 2Time Labs.

Ariely, D., & Wertenbroch, K. (2002, 12). Procrastination, Deadlines, and Performance: Self-Control by Precommitment. Psychological Science, 13(3), 219-224.

Bandiera, Oriana and Prat, Andrea and Sadun, Raffaella,(December 2013). Managing the Family Firm: Evidence from CEOs at Work.. Harvard Business School Strategy Unit Working Paper No. 14-044. Available at SSRN: http://ssrn.com/abstract=2363528 or http://dx.doi.org/10.2139/ssrn.2363528

Barker, E. How to Stop Being Lazy, http://www.bakadesuyo.com/2014/08/how-to-stop-being-lazy/ Barking up the Wrong Tree

Bartholomew, C. P. (2013). Time: An Empirical Analysis of Law Student Time Management Deficiencies. University of Cincinnati Law Review, 81(3), 898-952.

Bevins, F. & De Smet, A (2013, January). Making time management the organization's priority. McKinsey Quarterly. Retrieved from https://www.mckinseyquarterly.com/PDFDownload.aspx?ar=3048

Bond M.& Feather N.(1988), Some Correlates of Structure & Purpose in the Use of Time, 55 J. PERSONALITY & SOCIAL PSYCHOL. 321, 322–23

Boaz Keysar, Sayuri L. Hayakawa and Sun Gyu An (August 2014), "The Foreign-Language Effect : Thinking in a Foreign Tongue Reduces Decision Biases," *University of Chicago – Psychology*. http://pss.sagepub.com/content/23/6/661

Buehler, R., Griffin, D., & Ross, M. (1994, 12). Exploring the "planning fallacy": Why people underestimate their task completion times. Journal of Personality and Social Psychology, 67(3), 366-381.

Claessens, B. J. (2004). Perceived control of time: Time management and personal effectiveness at work. Eindhoven: Technische Universiteit Eindhoven, The Netherlands.

Claessens, B. J., Eerde, W. V., Rutte, C. G., & Roe, R. A. (2004, 12). Planning behavior and perceived control of time at work. Journal of Organizational Behavior, 25(8), 937-950.

Dean, D. and Webb, C. "Recovering from Information Overload." McKinsey Quarterly January (2011): 3-10. Print.

Dewitte, S., Verguts, T., & Lens, W. (2003, 12). Implementation intentions do not enhance all types of goals: The moderating role of goal difficulty. Current Psychology, 22(1), 73-89.

Drucker, P. F. (1967). The effective executive. New York: Harper & Row.

Fiore, N. A. (2007). The now habit: A strategic program for overcoming procrastination and enjoying guilt-free play. New York: Jeremy P.Tarcher

Keysar,B., Hayakawa, S., and Sun Gyu An, The Foreign-Language Effect : Thinking in a Foreign Tongue Reduces Decision Biases

Kruger, J., Evans, M. (September 2004) If you don't want to be late, enumerate: Unpacking reduces the planning fallacy. Journal of Experimental Social Psychology, Vol 40(5), 586-598.

Locke, E. A., & Latham, G. P. (n.d.). New developments in goal setting and task performance.

Neal, D. T., Wood, W., & Quinn, J. M. (2006, 12). Habits? A Repeat Performance. Current Directions in Psychological Science, 15(4), 198-202.

Rock, D. (2009). Your brain at work: Strategies for overcoming distraction, regaining focus, and working smarter all day long. New York: Harper Business

Roney, C. J., & Lehman, D. R. (2008,). Self-Regulation in Goal Striving: Individual Differences and Situational Moderators of the Goal-Framing/Performance Link. Journal of Applied Social Psychology, 38(11), 2691-2709.

Standing, L., Conezio, J., & Haber, R. N. (1970,). Perception and memory for pictures: Single-trial learning of 2500 visual stimuli. Psychonomic Science, 19(2), 73-74.

Tu, Yanping and Dilip Soman (2014), "The Categorization of

Time and Its Impact on Task Initiation," Journal of Consumer Research, 41(3), 810-22.

University of Chicago Press Journals.(August 2014) "Getting things done: How does changing the way you think about deadlines help you reach your goals?." ScienceDaily. ScienceDaily, http://www.sciencedaily.com/releases/2014/08/1408261210 54.htm

Wang, W., Kao, C., Huan, T., & Wu, C. (2010). Free Time Management Contributes to Better Quality of Life: A Study of Undergraduate Students in Taiwan. Journal of Happiness Studies, 561-573.

Welds, K. (2014, January 1). Time of Day Affects Problem Solving Abilities. Retrieved October 13, 2014, from http://kathrynwelds.com/2014/03/02/time-of-day-affects-problem-solving-abilities/

Wieber, F., Odenthal, G., & Gollwitzer, P. (2010,). Self-efficacy Feelings Moderate Implementation Intention Effects. Self and Identity, 9(2), 177-194.

Wu, D. (2010). Temporal structures in individual time management: Practices to enhance calendar tool design. Hershey, PA: Business Science Reference.

CHAPTER 15. Putting Your Master Plan Together

Dunning–Kruger effect. (2014, December 11). Retrieved November 13, 2014, from http://en.wikipedia.org/wiki/Dunning–Kruger_effect

ObamaCare Website: An Example of How Not to Manage Innovation. (2013, October 24). Retrieved October 13, 2014, from http://newproductvisions.com/blog/?p=353

CHAPTER 16. Flowing - the Art and Science of High Performance Moments

Csikszentmihalyi, M. (1990). Flow: The psychology of optimal experience. New York: Harper & Row.

Dismukes, K. (2006). Concurrent Task Management and Prospective Memory: Pilot Error as a Model for the Vulnerability of Experts. Proceedings of the Human Factors and Ergonomics Society Annual Meeting, 50(9), 909-913.

Gladwell, M. (2008). Outliers: The story of success. New York: Little, Brown and.Company.

Masicampo, E., & Baumeister, R.. (2011). Consider it done! Plan making can eliminate the cognitive effects of unfulfilled goals. Journal of Personality and Social Psychology, 101(4), 667-683.

Stone, L. (n.d.). Continuous Partial Attention. Retrieved October 13, 2014, from http://lindastone.net/qa/continuous-partial-attention/

CHAPTER 17. Interrupting and Switching - Executing the Next Task

Behavioral Buzz, July 2013. (2013, July 1). Retrieved October 13, 2014, from http://www.mdrc.org/behavioral-buzz-july-2013#_edn2

Cirillo, F. (2009). The pomodoro technique. S.l.: Lulu.

Dismukes, K. (2006). Concurrent Task Management and Prospective Memory: Pilot Error as a Model for the Vulnerability of Experts. Proceedings of the Human Factors and Ergonomics Society Annual Meeting, 50(9), 909-913.

Francis-Smythe, J. and Robertson, I (1999), On the relationship between time management and time estimation. British Journal of Psychology, 90: 333–347.

Gawande, A. (2010). *The checklist manifesto: How to get things right*. New York: Metropolitan Books.

Grundgeiger, T., Liu, D., Sanderson, P. M., Jenkins, S., & Leane, T. (2008, 12). Effects of Interruptions on Prospective Memory Performance in Anesthesiology. Proceedings of the Human Factors and Ergonomics Society Annual Meeting, 52(12), 808-812.

Mäntylä, T., Carelli, M. G., & Forman, H. (2007, 12). Time monitoring and executive functioning in children and adults.

Journal of Experimental Child Psychology, 96(1), 1-19.

Richtel, M. (2012, January 3). Multitasking Doctor Imperils Patient, Case Study Says. Retrieved October 13, 2014, from http://bits.blogs.nytimes.com/2012/01/03/multitasking-doctor-imperils-patient-case-study-says/

Svoboda, E., Richards, B., Leach, L., & Mertens, V. (2012). PDA and smartphone use by individuals with moderate-to-severe memory impairment: Application of a theory-driven training programme. Neuropsychological Rehabilitation, 1-20.

Svoboda, E., Rowe, G., & Murphy, K. (2012, August 28). From Science to Smartphones: Boosting Memory Function One Press at a Time. Retrieved October 13, 2014, from http://www.healthplexus.net/article/science-smartphones-boosting-memory-function-one-press-time

Wikipedia, Time-Based Prospective Memory. Retrieved October 10, 2014, from https://en.wikipedia.org/wiki/Time-Based_Prospective_Memory

CHAPTER 18. Reviewing and Warning - Taking Care of Your System

Eyal, N., & Hoover, R. (n.d.). Hooked: How to build habit-forming products.

Wikipedia. Mobile Phone Subscribers per 100 Inhabitants. http://en.wikipedia.org/wiki/File:Mobile_phone_subscribers_per_100_inhabitants_1997-2007_ITU.png

Wu, D. (2010). Temporal structures in individual time management: Practices to enhance calendar tool design. Hershey, PA: Business Science Reference., New York

CHAPTER 19. Habiting - A Way to Increase Your Odds of Success

Barker, E. (2014, November 2). How To Get In Shape Using Psychology: 6 New Tricks From Research. Retrieved November 3, 2014, from http://www.bakadesuyo.com/2014/11/how-to-get-in-shape/

Barnes, C.,Lanaj, J., Johnson (2014) Research: Using a Smartphone After 9 pm Leaves Workers Disengaged, from http://blogs.hbr.org/2014/01/research-using-a-smartphone-after-9-pm-leaves-workers-disengaged/

Bouton, M. (2004)."Context and Behavioral Processes in Extinction." Learning & Memory 11. : 485-94. Print.

Clear, J. (n.d.). Habit Stacking: How to Build New Habits by Taking Advantage of Old Ones. Retrieved September 17, 2014, from http://jamesclear.com/habit-stacking

Clear, J. (n.d.). How Long Does it Actually Take to Form a New Habit? (Backed by Science). Retrieved October 13, 2014.

Clear, J. (n.d.). This Coach Improved Every Tiny Thing by 1 Percent and Here's What Happened. Retrieved October 13, 2014, from http://jamesclear.com/marginal-gains

Duhigg, C. (2012). The power of habit: why we do what we do in life and business. New York: Random House.

Emailmonday - The ultimate mobile statistics overview. http://www.emailmonday.com/mobile-email-usage-statistics

Gardner, B, Abrahams,C. Lally, P., and De Bruijn, G.(2012). "Towards Parsimony in Habit Measurement: Testing the Convergent and Predictive Validity of an Automaticity Subscale of the Self-Report Index." International Journal of Behavioral Nutrition and Physical Activity 9.1 , 102. Print.t.

Lally, P, Van Jaarsveld, C., Potts,.H., and Wardle, J..(2010) "How Are Habits Formed: Modelling Habit Formation in the Real World." European Journal of Social Psychology 40.6 , 998-1009. Print.

Newport, C. (2012, December 27). Want That Promotion? Practice Your Job. Retrieved October 13, 2014, from http://blogs.wsj.com/atwork/2012/12/27/want-that-promotion-practice-your-job/

Ouellette, J., & Wood, W. (1998). Habits and Intention in Everyday Life: The Multiple Processes by Which Past Behavior Predicts Future Behavior. *Psychological Bulletin, 124*(1), 54-74.

Pavlok - The Habit Changing Device That Shocks You. (2014, September 30). Retrieved November 12, 2014, from https://www.indiegogo.com/projects/pavlok-the-habit-changing-device-that-shocks-you

Sood, Benjamin. The Human Behavior Research Centre at the University of Central London. http://www.slideshare.net/thereflectuk/bgs-newcastle-habit-measurement-talk-23-04-12

The What the Hell Effect, http://www.spring.org.uk/2011/03/the-what-the-hell-effect.php

Want that Promotion? Practice Your Job. Cal Newport http://blogs.wsj.com/atwork/2012/12/27/want-that-promotion-practice-your-job/

CHAPTER 20. What's the Best Way to React to New Technology and Fresh Thinking?

50 Emails a Day is Manageable Says US Small Business Workers. (2010, July 21). Retrieved October 11, 2014, from http://www.intermedia.net/about-us/news/press/2010/50-emails-a-day-is-manageable-says-us-small-business-workers

Bahadur, N. (2013, February 21). De-Stressing At Work: What Women Want. Retrieved October 11, 2014, from http://www.huffingtonpost.com/2013/02/21/de-stressing-at-work-what-women-want-destressing_n_2733558.html?ncid=edlinkusaolp00000003

Barnes, C., Lanaj, K., & Johnson, R. (2014, January 15). Research: Using a Smartphone After 9 pm Leaves Workers Disengaged. Retrieved October 13, 2014, from http://blogs.hbr.org/2014/01/research-using-a-smartphone-after-9-pm-leaves-workers-disengaged/

Connolly, L. (2011, January 1). View from the Digital Inbox 2011. Retrieved October 11, 2014. http://www.jonrognerud.com/docs/Merkle_Digital_Inbox_2011.pdf

Fogg, B. (n.d.). BJ Fogg, PhD. Retrieved October 11, 2014,

from http://www.bjfogg.com/

Hamilton, B., Arnold, L., & Tefft, B. (2012, January 1). Distracted and Risk-Prone Drivers - Select Findings from the 2012 Traffic Safety Culture Index. Retrieved October 10, 2014, from https://www.aaafoundation.org/sites/default/files/Distracted and Risk Prone Drivers FINAL.pdf

Song, S. (2011, October 17). Study: 1 in 6 Cell Phones Contaminated With Fecal Matter | TIME.com. Retrieved November 7, 2014, from http://healthland.time.com/2011/10/17/study-1-in-6-cell-phones-contaminated-with-fecal-matter

Weinschenk, S. (2012, September 11). Why We're All Addicted to Texts, Twitter and Google. Retrieved October 13, 2014, from http://www.psychologytoday.com/blog/brain-wise/201209/why-were-all-addicted-texts-twitter-and-google

CHAPTER 21. Creating Your Own Ladders of Improvement

Wikipedia. Issue Tree. Retrieved on October 10, 2014 from http://en.wikipedia.org/wiki/Issue_trees

Wikipedia, Mind Mapping. In Wikipedia. Retrieved October 10, 2014 from http://en.wikipedia.org/wiki/Mind_map

CHAPTER 22. The New Tools We All Need

Bellotti, V., Ducheneaut, N., Howard, M., & Smith, I. (2003). Taking email to task: the design and evaluation of a task management centered email tool. In Proceedings of the Conference on Human Factors in Computing System CHI'2003, New York, NY: ACM Press. 345-352.

Blank, S. (2013). The four steps to the epiphany: Successful strategies for products that win. Pescadero, Calif.: K&S Ranch Press.

Crenshaw, K. (n.d.). Interactive GTD Software Comparison Table by Priacta. Retrieved November 5, 2014, from http://www.priacta.com/Articles/Comparison_of_GTD_So ftware.php

Dean, D. and Webb, C.. "Recovering from Information Overload." McKinsey Quarterly January (2011): 3-10. Print.

Haraty, M., (1929–1932) Supporting behavioral differences and changes in personal task management. CHI Extended Abstracts 2013:

Haraty, M., Tam, D., Hadad, S., McGrenere, J., Tang, C., Individual Differences in Personal Task Management: A Field Study in an Academic Setting. Proc. 38th Graphics Interface conference, GI2012.

Hase, S., & Kenyon, C. (2001, January 1). From Andragogy to Heutagogy. Retrieved October 13, 2014, from http://www.psy.gla.ac.uk/~steve/pr/Heutagogy.html

Hogan, B., & Fisher, D. (2006). A scale for measuring email overload. Microsoft Research, 7-9. Retrieved from http://scholar.google.com/scholar?hl=en&btnG=Search&q =intitle:A+Scale+for+Measuring+Email+Overload#0

Rosin, H. (2014, March 24). You're Not As Busy As You Say You Are. Retrieved October 13, 2014, from http://www.slate.com/articles/double_x/doublex/2014/03/ brigid_schulte_s_overwhelmed_and_our_epidemic_of_busyn ess.html#ixzz2xAbAGGvM

Schulte, B., (2014) Overwhelmed: Work, Love, and Play When No One Has the Time. Sarah Crichton Books. http://www.slate.com/articles/double_x/doublex/2014/03/ brigid_schulte_s_overwhelmed_and_our_epidemic_of_busyn ess.html#ixzz2xAbAGGvM

Venolia, G., Gupta, A., Cadiz, J.J., and Dabbish, L. (2001). Supporting Email Workflow. Microsoft Technical Report. MSR-TR-2001-88.

Whittaker, S. (2005). Supporting collaborative task management in e-mail. *Human-Computer Interaction, 20*(1), 49-88. L. Erlbaum Associates Inc. Retrieved from http://portal.acm.org/citation.cfm?id=1466573

Wu, D. (2010). Temporal structures in individual time

management: Practices to enhance calendar tool design. Hershey, PA: Business Science Reference

CHAPTER 23. Productivity in Your Company

Bock, L. (2014, March 27). Google's Scientific Approach to Work-Life Balance (and Much More). Retrieved October 13, 2014, from http://blogs.hbr.org/2014/03/googles-scientific-approach-to-work-life-balance-and-much-more/

Dean, D. and Webb, C.. "Recovering from Information Overload." *McKinsey Quarterly* January (2011): 3-10. Print.

Hamilton, B., Arnold, L., & Tefft, B. (2012, January 1). Distracted and Risk-Prone Drivers - Select Findings from the 2012 Traffic Safety Culture Index. Retrieved October 10, 2014, from https://www.aaafoundation.org/sites/default/files/Distracted and Risk Prone Drivers FINAL.pdf

Horstman, M. Podcast 40 - Interview with Mark Horstman by Francis Wade on the 2Time Labs Podcast - http://fwconsulting.podomatic.com/entry/2014-03-12T15_53_25-07_00

Rock, D. (2010, July 25). Misunderstanding the brain is bad for business. Retrieved October 13, 2014, from http://www.psychologytoday.com/blog/your-brain-work/201007/misunderstanding-the-brain-is-bad-business

Rock, D. (2013, December 30). 5 Big Discoveries About Personal Effectiveness in 2013. Retrieved October 13, 2014, from http://www.psychologytoday.com/blog/your-brain-work/201312/5-big-discoveries-about-personal-effectiveness-in-2013

Rock, D. (2013, February 20). How to heal our smartphone-addled, overworked brains. Retrieved October 13, 2014, from http://fortune.com/2013/02/20/how-to-heal-our-smartphone-addled-overworked-brains/

Wade, F. (2012, June 10). How executives unwittingly turn employees into morons. Retrieved October 13, 2014, from http://jamaica-gleaner.com/gleaner/20120610/business/business91.html

Wikipedia. Mobile Phone and Driving Safety. Retreived October 10, 2014.
http://en.wikipedia.org/wiki/Mobile_phones_and_driving_safety

Summary

Wikipedia, Dreyfus Model of Skill Acquisition. In Wikipedia. Retrieved October 10, 2014, from
http://en.wikipedia.org/wiki/Dreyfus_model_of_skill_acquisition

Index

<u>Lab Notes</u>

[1] The paper entitled "The long arm of time pressure at work: Cognitive failure and commuting near accidents" was published in 2012 by Achim Elfering, Simone Grebner & Fanny de Tribolet Hardy. They showed that six mistakes in everyday tasks (known as cognitive errors) are caused by time pressure at work.

Safety goals are subordinated to other task goals, leading to an increase in near-accidents. This study focused on commuting and the fact that completing the commute becomes more important than maintaining safety goals.
- Urgent tasks are completed before other tasks, regardless of importance.
- More errors are made when completing tasks.
- Interruptions increase as pressure increases the need to switch from one task to another, more urgent task.
- There is an increase in multitasking, which reduces task performance.
- Professionals think about work while commuting, which impairs cognitive function and leads to mistakes.

Furthermore, Wallace and Chen (2005) hypothesized that "simply having too much work to do in the time available" would increase the risk of cognitive failure. Their research confirmed this notion. (A cognitive failure is a mistake in everyday tasks that a person is normally capable of completing without error).

[2] Thinking that academic research should yield more precise answers, I was surprised to discover (after a lengthy search) that this was not the case. Instead, I was forced to look at studies of freshmen in tertiary institutions.

College students are probably the most studied population in time management research. Their ready availability to on-campus researchers and the high-stakes game they play of attending classes, taking exams, completing papers and hitting deadlines make them an ideal group to poll, survey and examine in depth.

However, high-school students are hard to study as a group. It might be that they resist answering abstract questions about their productivity and time choices. For researchers, who face formidable regulation of research performed in public high schools, it's a lot easier to wait until they enter college.

At the same time, children as a group are the subject of numerous studies; however, very few researchers have focused on their ability to manage time, by any definition. I reasoned that, in the face of the paucity of research, it should be easier to start by determining when children first learn the concept of time itself. But even then, the answers are less than concrete.

One of the first studies to address this question was conducted in 1946 by Louise Ames, who showed that children develop a sense of time by the age of 8. Other studies by Leona Foerster Mitchell and Molly Fourez show that children develop different perspectives about time by the fifth grade, and children from disadvantaged backgrounds demonstrate much weaker skills.

Lydia Liu from the Educational Testing Service (known to teenagers as the SAT company) led a study in which middle-school students assessed their time management skills. By that age, they had largely developed two distinct skills: "Meeting Deadlines and Being Organized" and "Planning and Using Aids to Manage Time." Similar studies of college students showed that they had developed at least four distinct skills, leading the authors to note, "As the task complexity increases and goals become more diversified, more dimensions of time management become appropriate."

In other words, they learn these two additional

skills during the high school years. Another way of framing this finding is to say that students who successfully matriculate in tertiary education discover a way to teach themselves these four skills, while those who don't, fail at doing so. My belief is that they do so without being taught.

In terms of gender differences, Liu's study showed that female students reported higher scores in both factors. When the differences are cultural, Mark Trueman and James Hartley discovered some other interesting changes in the U.K. after they replicated a U.S. study. They showed that the GPAs of UK students four years after original measurement were much less influenced by short-term planning and their attitudes towards time compared to their counterparts in the U.S. (The grades of both groups could be predicted by long-term planning). They did, however, replicate the higher scores achieved by females.

Also, a number of studies track incoming freshman entering college as they demonstrate a wide range of time management behaviors. A study led by Krishna Srestha showed that, on average, freshmen spend more time on class-related activities than students in any other year, implying that their skills continue to improve over the years.

Another, more comprehensive study by Bruce Britton and Abraham Tesser showed that time management skills have a greater effect on college grades than SAT scores.

This is an important discovery, even if it was restricted to students. To what degree are time management skills a predictor of success in other areas, such as corporate careers, entrepreneurship and academia?

These studies show that freshmen are entering college with time management skills; in other words, they are already creating and processing time demands before their college years.

However, it's interesting to note that not all researchers understand time management skills in this way. The abstract from a paper written by Therese Macan and Comila Shahani entitled "College Students' Time Management: Correlations With Academic Performance and Stress" puts it well: "Many college students may find the academic experience very stressful.... One potential coping strategy frequently offered by university counseling services is time management."

Rather than a skill students already possess, Macan and Shahani see time management as a strategy they need to develop, presumably from scratch. The fact that this paper was written in 1989 gives us an idea of how many new ideas have emerged recently.

[3] This is more than self-directed learning (as part of andragogy) as Knowles (1970) defined it in that it recognizes the value of everyday, unorganized experiences and the process of reflection. Capable people are more likely to be able to deal effectively with the turbulent environment in which they live by possessing an 'all round' capacity centered on self-efficacy, knowing how to learn, creativity, the ability to use competencies in novel, as well as familiar, situations and working with others.

[4] Dr. James Martin refers to this capacity as "self determination," which he defines as "the skills, knowledge and beliefs needed to engage in goal-directed behaviors based on an understanding of one's strengths, limitations and self." In another article, he states that "Self-determination consists of self-awareness, self-advocacy, decision-making, independent performance,

self-evaluation, and adjustment skills that facilitate goal setting and goal attainment." This detailed explanation comes from his work as an expert who helps disabled individuals make the transition to working environments. As you can see, he's looked at this challenge closely.

[5] According to Gilles Einstein, a top expert from Furman University, almost no one studied the topic of prospective memory before 1990. However, by 2008, he notes that almost 160 papers on the subject were published. While this growth is a good thing, it reflects the fact that there is much that is not understood about this particular kind of memory.

Perhaps the fact that it's becoming a hot field is driven by the challenge of information overload accelerated by mobile technology. As Einstein says, "If you think about it even minimally, our lives are replete with prospective memory demands." In the same talk, entitled "Remembering to Perform Actions in the Future," he goes on to list a number of everyday items ranging from taking his vitamins in the morning to remembering to meet his wife "at an agreed upon time and location" – simple actions that many find challenging, especially when there is lots of stuff competing for attention.

He highlights the importance of this research: "Prospective memory failures can also have very serious consequences," he says, giving the example of older adults who sometimes have a problem remembering to take three, four or five different medications daily.

"So far, this is sounding a lot like a time demand!" I thought to myself.

It's no surprise that his work and that of many other psychologists, focuses on the ways in which people remember. He has worked with other researchers, including Mark McDaniel, to define ways that we can set up automatic cues or reminders to prompt ourselves to take actions in the future.

For example, my smartphone is set to ring at 3:15 AM each morning (while I'm drafting this book). All I need do is keep it charged in order to be automatically reminded to get up to write with a loud sound and a buzz. This, of course, is the kind of cue we all set for ourselves.

So, we all know that prospective memory exists, and that cues can make a difference, but further research by popular psychologist Peter Gollwitzer of NYU goes a step further. He's known for coining the term "implementation intention," which has been featured in *Psychology Today* and *Harvard Business Review* as well as books on entrepreneurship and marketing.

To understand its full meaning, however, we need to start with another term that psychologists use: a "goal intention." It's just as it sounds. When we create a goal, it's a high-level intention to accomplish a particular result. Gollwitzer went into more detail, defining an implementation intention as a conditional statement that describes the when, what and where related to a particular action that is linked to a goal. It is usually constructed with a conditional component: if _____ then _____. For example, you could form an implementation intention, "if my mother calls me today, then I'll thank her for the mangoes she sent me yesterday."

Another implementation intention might be: "If my alarm goes off at 3:15 AM, then I'll get up and write another chapter of the book in my office."

Gollwitzer's major contribution has been to show that implementation intentions that are properly constructed are far more likely to be executed than ordinary intentions. In an oft-cited study, women who specified when and where they'd perform a breast self-examination were more likely to fulfill their intention than those who did not: 100% of the first group did it, compared to 53% of the second. His work has been celebrated, with good reason. We'll return to it several times in this book from a number of different perspectives.

At this point in my journey, I began to think that maybe I should use either the term "implementation intention" or "prospective memory" in my training and writing, replacing the term "time demand" with something more scholarly. This didn't happen, as I'll show in later chapters: there is much more to creating time demands than I originally envisioned, and these two terms already define concepts that don't encompass enough.

That's not to say that these terms aren't useful. After I settled on "time demands," further research helped me understand how we create them. For example, some UK scientists have gone a step further by defining two kinds of implementation intentions. A Cambridge-based team led by Abigail Sellen devised a study that required subjects to wear and press electric buttons at different times in response to a number of triggers. They were able to separate intentions driven by events from intentions that are driven by time.

The example I cited earlier with my mother and the mangoes is event-driven. It's triggered by my picking up the phone to answer her call. On the other hand, a time-driven intention would be stated as: "I'll call my mother today at 4 PM to thank her for the mangoes she sent us yesterday."

The example of my alarm going off at 3:15 AM is

actually event-driven, because I'm not actually watching the clock. Turn off the alarm, and the task of waking up on time becomes an implementation intention driven by time.

You probably have already determined that "one of these things is not like the other." It probably comes as no surprise to learn from Sellen and her team that event-driven implementation intentions are far more likely to be executed than time-driven ones.

In further research, I also discovered a few academics who added some important pieces. Timo Mantyla and Teresa Sgaramella noted that activating an implementation intention for the first time disrupts our inner equilibrium, creating an unsettling feeling that goes away only when the task is complete. Also, Lia Kvavilashvili, in her paper, "Remembering intention as a distinct form of memory," clearly distinguishes remembering the time at which an intention is to be executed from the action to be taken. They each require a "separate form of memory," according to her research.

A team of German researchers led by Veronika Brandstatter used the term "goal intention" to represent that desire expressed as "I intend to reach Z!" whereby "Z" may relate to a certain outcome or behavior to which the individual feels committed. At first glance, this appears to be a suitable candidate to replace the concept of "time demands," but the origins of the term (goal theory) means that it already has a specific, well established meaning that's not directly related to individual productivity and its relatively mundane daily activities.

Cheshire Calhoun, a philosopher, has a few interesting things to say in his 2009 article, included in the journal *Ethics*, entitled "What Good is Commitment?" He examines the agency underlying all commitments, including what look like time demands, which are part of what he calls "substantive commitments." He writes: "All genuine commitments are active in the sense that they are made, not merely discovered as facts about one's psychology, and they persist through being sustained, not through being persistently suffered." He continues: "That is, a commitment is both an intention to engage with something (a person, relationship, goal, activity, identity, etc.) and a preparedness to see to it that that intention to engage persists."

This kind of commitment-based thought helps to clarify the kind of self-conscious awareness that underlies time demands, but it's missing in our everyday conversations about having "stuff to do" or "tasks to finish." While this awareness may be lost, for our purposes, we'll assume that it's always present when a time demand is created.

Late Breaking Update

During the week in which I received this manuscript from my editor, Ellen, I discovered an obscure reference to a psychological object called a "conscious intention." The term showed up in a paper written by Drs. Judith Ouellette and Wendy Wood entitled "Habit and Intention in Everyday Life: The Multiple Processes by Which Past Behavior Predicts Future Behavior." In their paper, they make a clear distinction between habitual behavior and those which require "controlled reasoning processes."

However, the title of the paper indicates that it's focus is on the study of habitual behavior. "Conscious intentions" are defined as a mere opposite. As a result, the construct isn't taken very far in this paper, in their follow-up work or by other scholars in the field. Their attention is clearly on habitual behavior.

This is unfortunate, because a "conscious intention" is the closest construct I could find in the literature to a "time demand" - by definition.

[6] Wikipedia defines a business process as "a collection of related, structured activities or tasks that produce a specific service or product (serve a particular goal) for a particular customer or customers. It often can be visualized with a flowchart as a sequence of activities with interleaving decision points or with a Process Matrix as a sequence of activities with relevance rules based on data in the process." These are the same tools process engineers (like Laura) use to illuminate the current flow of activities. They also happen to be the ones we'll use, as they represent the best way to gain an understanding of how a process works.

On a separate note, here's the "Proposed process model of time management" in the figure below, reproduced from Therese McCann's 1994 journal article entitled 'Time Management: Test of a Process Model."

Figure LN-1

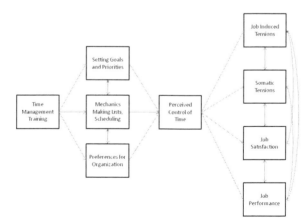

It's been reproduced in many psychology papers

since its publication.

Anyone steeped in process management will notice the discrepancy: Macan's model doesn't follow the conventional description of a process, and by Wikipedia's definition, it falls short. To be more precise, it shows a mix of activities, constructs and outcomes that are connected in some way, but it's clearly not a process model by today's definition.

There's a straightforward explanation for this.

While process modeling has been around since the turn of the century in the field of industrial engineering, the term gained widespread popularity with the sudden rise of reengineering in the early 1990s. The publication of Michael Hammer's 1993 book *Reengineering the Corporation* helped fuel an explosion in process management, popularizing the concept and the term on a grand scale. As an MIT-trained computer scientist turned management consultant, Hammer was named one of Time Magazine's 25 most influential individuals in its first such list, according to Wikipedia. Forbes ranked his book among the "three most important business books of the past 20 years."

Nowadays, process thinking is no longer restricted to industrial engineers, thanks to Michael Hammer. It's a part of mainstream business logic.

With 20 years of hindsight gained from his book, plus the popularization of anything related to "process," it's easy to be critical of Macan's paper, which was published the year after Hammer's book. It claimed to describe a process model, but it's clear that the model is not what we'd call a process today. When Macan published her paper, however, the term "process" was hardly understood in the same way it is after 20 years of industrial usage.

What she has depicted in her "Proposed process model of time management" is much closer to a combination of a cause-and-effect diagram and a correlational diagram. Indeed, that's how she uses the model throughout the paper — she's not confused, even though the modern reader, expecting to find a true process, would be disappointed by the label. Once the confusion is cleared up, her test of a "cause and effect/correlational model" makes perfect sense.

Update: In separate research, Veronika Brnadstätter and her European colleagues offer a process for managing intentions, as described in their article "Goals need implementation intentions: The model of action phases tested in the applied setting of continuing education." They describe a model first espoused by Heckhausen and Gollwitzer that comprises four action phases: pre-decisional, pre-actional, action and post-actional.

[7] In her 2004 dissertation, Claessen noted that "Macan (1994) was the first and to date the only one to suggest a theoretical process model of time management." At first, she appears to be confirming the mistake made by so many academics.

In fact, she uses the paper she wrote to point out the yawning gap between academic research at the time Macan wrote her paper and the programs used by trainers in the real world.

Claessens didn't leave the gap the way she found it. She narrowed it by introducing a process that is much closer to what a modern professional would expect. Interestingly, she doesn't call it a process, but a model, in which elements such as planning behavior, task assessment and time-monitoring would create particular time management behaviors at work, which in turn would produce real-world job-related outcomes, such as job satisfaction and job performance.

The direction of her overall research, however, doesn't add much process knowledge to her model - instead, it focuses on the relationship between variables in each of these elements. These are interesting and useful findings for the academy, where work is done inside a context not intended for immediate application in the workplace.

Claessens appears well aware that academics have ignored the process research needed to provide practical advice, noting, "There has been little research on how people decide which tasks to perform and which tasks to complete during their workdays."

A summary of Claessen's revision of Macan's research can be found in a chapter written by Jan Francis Smythe for the book *Timing the Future: The Case for Prospective Memory*, edited by J. Glicksohn and M. Myslobodsky. It's simply entitled "Time Management" and communicates that Claessens found little support for "perceived control of time" as a strong mediator of time management behavior. Instead, these behaviors have a direct effect, according to Claessens, who states: "engaging in time management behavior may lead to a better temporal fit between personal resources and demands, allowing one to distribute energy and attention more effectively, thereby helping to avoid or reduce delays and overload."

This notion of a fit between one's capacity and the time demands one faces is important in *Perfect Time-Based Productivity*. In fact, it's part of the definition of what it means to be "perfect."

[8] The Brain Science of Training Failure

According to brain scientist Dr. David Rock, author of the bestseller *Your Brain at Work,* we shouldn't be surprised that people fail after they leave time management workshops. It also happens in poker.

Inexperienced players who aren't used to the ups and downs of the game often get lucky, drawing amazing hands. Unfortunately, it's a prelude to a familiar sequence of events in which they become overexcited, make a mistake and fail. Rock teaches us that at that moment, their limbic systems are in a highly aroused state.

Experience tells me that the same happens with learners when they turn the last page of a good productivity book, walk out the door of an inspiring program or click to close the last screen of an interesting eLearning program in productivity. Motivation is at a high, fueled by a dopamine rush, as they jump into the real world, thinking to themselves, "I can't wait to put this stuff into practice – it makes SO much sense!" The rush is, of course, heightened if the training is live and there are lots of others in the same frame of mind. (If you have ever participated in a fire-walk workshop, you may understand this feeling all too well).

While this state of arousal might feel pleasant, there are actually fewer resources available for you to make clear decisions and a sound plan. You can easily miss holes in your plan that you would normally catch. In other words, high expectations can lead you to make a bad plan.

As Rock explains, an expectation is an unusual concept. It represents a possible improvement, versus an actual one, but the same reward circuitry in your brain is activated in both cases. In fact, after you set a goal, you start noticing different things, much in the way that an intention to buy a new car leads to your noticing that particular model everywhere you look. You also start to see what's not there: now, you see what you're expecting, according to Rock and other neuroscientists.

As you read *Perfect Time-Based Productivity*, you may notice your mind sifting the information through your expectations. In particular, if there is anything you don't expect to hear, your mind may discard it entirely, because "the brain is built to avoid threat, (and) people tend to work hard to reinterpret events to meet their expectations," says Rock.

Unfortunately, when you create unrealistic plans for success and they don't materialize, there's also an effect on your brain chemistry, according to researchers cited by Rock at the University of Michigan. Failure to meet an expectation causes a sudden drop in dopamine levels that feels a lot like pain.

It's no wonder, then, that the immediate steps you take after ending a training opportunity are so fraught with failure. High expectations get us into trouble, setting us up for negative feelings, which increase with the size of the unmet expectation.

***

Instead of falling into these traps, we can use an idea used by athletes called the "Goldilocks Principle" to create our plan. They know that it's a mistake to become either over or under-excited as they start a game or prepare to sprint – both the extremes are counterproductive, working against peak performance. Instead, they need be excited at a level that's above normal, but between the extremes: "just right."

This means that, as you carve out plans to improve your skills in Capturing in this chapter, you need to be conservative... and maybe even slightly pessimistic. Plan to go slower than you might expect and put in place more support than you think you'll need. Assume that failure is right around the corner, not to depress yourself, but to implement mitigation steps.

Remember, in that moment when you re-enter the world, your motivation is at a high – maybe at a peak that you will not reach again. Instead of assuming that the high will continue indefinitely, make your plan suitable for the average day at work. This translates into taking small, highly supported steps, rather than big leaps of faith. I'll show you how to space these steps out over time so that you plan to make realistic, steady progress.

This coaching, of course, applies to your analysis of all the fundamentals, not just Capturing. By the time we bring together all your plans for each fundamental into a single Master Plan, you'll have practiced several rounds of realistic planning that have a high probability of success. It's as simple as that – let's jump right in.

[9] Brain scientists tell us that Wally's inability to delay gratification is, in rare cases, linked to the health of his development hippocampus, which controls his ability to imagine future rewards. He just can't wait. More likely, however, it has something to do with how well his prefrontal cortex developed during adolescence, giving it the ability to override a part of the limbic system known as the ventral striatum, which hungers for immediate rewards.

In all cases, however, dopamine is involved, as it actively encourages us to act to gain pleasure or avoid pain. Also, the level of dopamine varies among individuals, giving some people a stronger urge to quit Emptying and start Acting Now.

[10] Is "information overload" a myth? Certainly, stressed professionals experience some very real symptoms, as we outlined in the opening chapters. However, there has been confusion about the source. In

this book, the answer is clear: the source of "information overload" is an inability to manage all the time demands a person has created. Information Overload isn't like the common cold – it's not something you catch from merely walking through a library. However, there are people who avoid libraries because of overwhelm – they can't resist creating new time demands based on the books they see on the shelves.

In earlier chapters, we mentioned the Zeigarnik effect, the psychological pressure created when commitments are established but not fulfilled. Information overload appears to be a modern-day manifestation of this effect, magnified by the efficiency of technology and rising expectations of those around us.

By contrast, if you have ever quit or been fired, you may have experienced the phenomenon of seeing a number of time demands instantly disappear. It can be an amazing moment when the time demands that appeared to be so real in our lives go away, all of a sudden. Any information overload related to the job disappears with them.

[11] In a recent article written for the Psychowith6 blog, I outlined the reasons why top college students and CEOs are so alike in the way they manage their time demands. Both groups tend to push the limits of what their schedules can handle, leaving little or no unassigned time. Their ambitions require time, yet they are limited to the same number of hours we all have. http://www.psychowith6.com/college-students-ceos-manage-time-way

A recent article at the Harvard Magazine website reinforces this finding. It's titled "Nonstop: Today's superhero undergraduates do 3,000 things at 150%.'" http://harvardmagazine.com/2010/03/nonstop

[12] Revealing Research

Psychologists who study high performance have

touched on the behaviors related to time-based productivity. Mary Waller of the University of Illinois was the lead researcher for a paper that described "time urgency" - a sub-component of Type A behavior. "Time-urgent individuals also tend to schedule more activities than comfortably fit into the available time." She distinguished sharply between their performance and that of non time-urgent individuals, who "tend to be less attentive regarding time resources and tend to underestimate the passage of time."

In Chapter 7 on Emptying, we looked at the difference between individuals who have a present time perspective versus a future time perspective. Dr. Waller also studied these differences, showing that someone with a combination of time-urgency and a future time perspective is likely to be the most productive and therefore have a greater need to use a daily schedule.

Also, the University of Michigan's Leslie Perlow spent nine months in the late 1990s embedded with a software engineering team at a Fortune 500 company. As she watched them struggle to complete a major project under short deadlines, she used the term "time famine" to describe the feeling of having too much to do and not enough time to do it in.

At her instigation, the team as a whole made a remarkable switch from indulging in numerous, random interruptions to setting aside "quiet time" in order to allow team members to focus on individual activity. The intervention made a remarkable difference in the team's productivity, demonstrating the power of using scheduling techniques to drive time-based productivity. We'll examine this approach in more detail in the chapter on flowing.

Waller and Perlow conclude that the deadline-driven nature of corporate life has implications for how professionals view time and manage their schedules.

The term "time-famine" has also been used in studies conducted by the American Bar Association. According to Christine Bartholomew, who conducted research in the legal profession on their time management deficits, they noted that a "significant cause of the diminishing quality of lawyer's health and lives is the fact that they 'do not have enough time for themselves and their families — what many have come to call "the time famine."' They note that there was a 33% increase in the number of lawyers suffering time famine between 1984 and 1990.

She also quotes research performed in Finland: Predicators of Time Famine Among Finnish Employees - Work, Family or Leisure?" This study showed that women aged between 25 and 54 years old who were well educated and had children were over-represented in the population of time-starved professionals. Also, in men only, there was a correlation between time famine and occupation status, indicating that "being busy is a symbol of full and valued life, a badge of honor. Those in high-status occupations tend to overestimate their busyness in order to emphasize their status (Gershuny, 2005)."

[13] In the Holbrook and Dismukes study, the researchers lump these techniques (and perhaps others) together, labeling them as cues created by the participant intended to prompt the initiation of the activity being studied.

They discovered that these cues (plus other reminders) had a huge influence on whether tasks were completed. A little under half (12 out of 29) of the successes were prompted by unplanned environmental cues, while 8 out of 29 were initiated by cues created by participants. It led them to conclude that "creating cues can enhance performance." They also showed that spontaneous remembering could also occur when cues had been created.

A few others findings immediately jump out:

1. In terms of relative use, the most popular technique was #2 -- a "mental note" – which was employed by 34.8% of the test population and followed by Technique #3 at 24.6% and Technique #4 at 17.4%. A full 23.2% (#1) didn't create a time demand to begin with.
2. Using Technique #3 was just as effective as using Technique #4, in terms of the success/failure rate.
3. Using memory (the second technique) was ineffective, with more failures than successes. The failure rate was 58.3%.
4. Not forming time demands at all (Technique #1) was the least effective method with a failure rate of 87.5%.

Let us, for the sake of discussion, take some liberty with the work done by these researchers and make the following assumptions.

- Users of to-do lists (either sorted or unsorted) cannot be included in Technique #2.
- Users of calendars can only be users of Technique #4.
- Users of to-do lists are unlikely to report that they used Technique #4 (this is admittedly, debatable)

Taken together, these assumptions would lead us to think that Techniques #1 - #4 correspond (approximately) to the evolution that professionals make when they are confronted with greater numbers of time demands. That is, they learn to make time demands, start putting them in lists, sort these lists using tags like location, and eventually replace these lists with the use of a calendar.

These assumptions cannot be proven using Holbrook and Dismukes' paper. However, if they are true, then we'd conclude the following:
- Most people have the habit of using memory, which is more likely to fail than succeed.
- A few people have migrated to the use of to-do lists or calendars, with equal rates of success.
- Far fewer people use calendars than to-do lists.
- People who are using calendars have already tried to-do lists.

This last conclusion makes sense in the context of this experiment. The users of Technique #3 tagged their tasks with information related to "How" or "Where" it would be completed. By contrast, the users of Technique #4 (calendars) added another tag: "When." It's likely that the members of the latter group were once users of Technique #3 and underwent an upgrade. There's no proof of this conclusion in the paper, but it's one that I draw from observing participants in my workshops.

Based on my assumptions, it's not too hard to infer that Techniques #1 through #4 represent a progression of skills. The report did in fact show that there was an improvement in results from Techniques #1 through #3 and #4. According to the researchers, "The level of planning… was positively correlated with remembering to perform intentions." This finding is supported by a study we'll mention in the next chapter by Dan Ariely about the strong positive influence of setting time-based deadlines.

The Dismukes study involved only a few participants from a single California college, but it's the only data I could find that measures the relative success of different techniques. The researchers are silent about other factors that might interest us, such as the number of time demands each of the group's members were trying to manage. However, they have given us some clues about the skills we human beings use to create and manage time demands.

While their discoveries may seem abstract, their intention is to save lives by helping airline pilots remember what to do. Pilots frequently switch from one task to another, interrupting the original task with an intention to return to it. The techniques they use to remember important tasks determine what gets done and what gets forgotten.

Remembering exact sequences of tasks and continuing to execute interrupted tasks saves lives; in another study, Dismukes discovered that some 20% of major aviation accidents are caused by a failure to "complete delayed intentions." Sometimes, our self-created methods for creating and managing time demands do more than make us forget to pick up the milk.

[14] On Calendar Use

Dezhi Wu is a relatively new Associate Professor at Southern Utah University. She received her PhD in 2005 from the New Jersey Institute of Technology, but she's not in the psychology department, as most of the other experts cited in this book are. She's a computer scientist who, in her seminal book *Temporal Structures in Individual Time Management: Practices to Enhance Calendar Tool Design*, makes it clear that subjects in her study who use calendars and schedules are more productive than those who don't. Her research covered over 700 respondents and noted the following:

"Most (of the subjects in the study)... were using some form of electronic calendar system... (Public events involving other people) were often listed in the calendars while (private activities) were used to guide the allocation of time in the schedule but were maintained in the (person's) head."

She then refers to three groups of people uncovered in her research, naming the first group the "better time managers." She explains:

"(There) were individuals who complained less about the difficulty of managing their time and who also had more time for personal activities and additional achievements... [they] were better able to estimate the amount of time a task required, or to control the amount of time required for a task... they created their own temporal structures to manage their life, that is, they allocated units of time for specific types of repeating activities. These better time managers also recorded more of the (significant events involving other people) in their electronic calendars."

A second group does things differently: "In contrast, another set of respondents who complained about a lack of time for accomplishing anything significant, were much less likely to record and manage their time in a calendar system. (They) worked longer hours than the better time managers and were constantly scurrying to meet deadlines. They indicated that much of their work was overdue. They were much less likely to create (scheduled activities in their calendar) of their own, much less likely to be aware of the (publicly scheduled activities) that impacted their lives."

The third group apparently took a step back in an attempt to limit the number of time demands they had to deal with, as they "managed their time by simplifying the temporal demands (i.e. time demands) on their life. They limited the number of external activities they engaged in... and... spent large units of time away from the work environment they found to be interruptive. However, unless these individuals then created (activities in their calendar) for managing this less demanding time schedule, they were relatively unproductive in contrast to the better time managers, that is, they produced less work product."

Wu's findings were later echoed by Christine Bartholomew in her 2013 paper "Time: An Empirical Analysis of Law Student Time Management Deficiencies." In her study of 219 students, Bartholomew showed that those who developed calendaring skills were more productive. She concluded: "Students should be asked to allocate the 'to-do' items across a calendar... Calendaring should include not only the date a task will be done, but also the time during that day. Students should be reminded that attempting to complete numerous tasks in large chunks of time is not as productive as spacing out the tasks with scheduled breaks..."

Bartholomew also showed that students who use plans and schedules also set up more structured routines to get work done. These have clear benefits, being associated with "less hopelessness, less anomie, less extraversion, lower anxiety, more optimism about the present and future, more Type A behavior, and stronger work ethic." These individuals also report higher self-esteem and less depression.

She also makes the case that having a detailed schedule helps in making future time estimates, an activity so important to professionals in many areas, including law. "Without reflection on how long it took, for example, to brief a case, it would be difficult to estimate how long it will take to complete the next night's homework." Those who rely on the list-centric approach would be hard-pressed to improve their skills at estimating how long work takes.

These two researchers have focused their work on academic environments, with Wu also studying faculty and administrative staff. However, their findings are echoed in 2 studies shared in the McKinsey Quarterly.

In their 2011 article entitled "Recovering from Information Overload," Derek Dean and Caroline Webb speak of the scourges of "information overload and its close cousin, attention fragmentation." They "hit CEOs and their colleagues in the C-suite particularly hard because senior executives so badly need uninterrupted time to synthesize information from many different sources, reflect on its implications for the organization, apply judgment, make trade-offs, and arrive at good decisions." The only way to ensure that they have this time available is to reserve it explicitly, and they quote Peter Drucker to help make their case: "most of the tasks of the executive require, for minimum effectiveness, a fairly large quantum of time." They list his solutions: "reserve large blocks of time on your calendar, don't answer the phone, and return calls in short bursts once or twice a day."

The later 2013 study by Frankki Bevins and Aaron De Smet confirmed these findings with empirical data. In their report, "Making time management the organization's priority," they make note of the fact that some powerful administrative assistants carve out "quiet zones" for their executive teams before major meetings, making sure to give everyone time for preparation. It's like calling a meeting that never actually meets – instead of coming to a conference room, you are expected to spend the allocated time in your office doing all the legwork required for the event.

That's just the beginning: they also found that the best time-managers spend 24% of their time alone, a feat they simply couldn't accomplish without planning that time in their calendars. Also, they get lots of help. 85% of effective time-managers report that "they receive strong help in scheduling and allocating time." Among ineffective ones, only 7% get that kind of support.

If you sense that the organizational forces behind this lack of productivity are larger than the individual, you're right. This is a topic we'll discuss at length in Chapter 22 on Productivity in Your Company.

[15] Recent research highlights the cases of two middle-aged subjects who have suffered from a loss of key memory functions and have learned to operate without full executive function.

Charlie Numbers (a pseudonym for a 66-year-old subject) is a retiree who returned to using a PDA during an experiment. After he mastered the use of reminders, his wife reported that she no longer had to interrupt him to take his medication and attend medical appointments – she knew that if he used the device, tasks would get done. This also impacted his self-confidence, a benefit that both of them reported.

Ruby Reardon (a pseudonym for a real 55-year-old) discovered that she was able to use her smartphone to plan future events, such as appointments and daily tasks. Where, in the past, she had to rely on family to manage these activities, her smartphone helped her achieve a level of independence and capability and recapture some of the social roles she had lost, including being a grandmother.

She needed the help, given the fact that she had suffered a significant impairment to her memory following the removal of a colloid cyst in her brain. While most of us aren't afflicted with Ruby's severe health issue and don't have the memory lapses that Charlie experienced, many of us have the same symptoms.

We too forget to stop what we are doing in order to initiate a task at the right moment. Fortunately, we can copy these individuals' example, as we live in a time when mobile phones have become an essential part of our individual environments. Even the simplest of devices can help play the role of a flawless administrative assistant who never forgets to interrupt.

The same applies to our personal computers, tablets and watches. They can all help create the embedded cues that researchers have found to be so effective.

Why go to such great lengths? One reason is to help us remember to start a task, as in the cases of Ruby and Charlie, documented in an article from *Technology in Medicine* entitled "From Science to Smartphones: Boosting Memory Function One Press At a Time." However, that's not the only benefit.

Printed in Great Britain
by Amazon